fundamental feminism

Contesting the Core Concepts
of Feminist Theory

Judith Grant

Routledge
New York   London

Published in 1993 by

Routledge
29 West 35 Street
New York, NY 10001

Published in Great Britain in 1993 by

Routledge
11 New Fetter Lane
London EC4P 4EE

Library of Congress Cataloging-in-Publication Data

Grant, Judith, 1956–
    Fundamental feminism : contesting the core concepts of feminist
theory / by Judith Grant.
        p.   cm.
    Includes bibliographical references and index.
    ISBN 0-415-90825-6 — ISBN 0-415-90826-4
    1. Feminist theory.   I. Title.
HQ1190.G7   1993
305.42'01—dc20   93-17451
                                                  CIP

British Library Cataloguing-in-Publication Data

Grant, Judith
    Fundamental Feminism: Contesting the Core
    Concepts of Feminist Theory
    I. Title
    305.42

    ISBN 0-415-90825-6
    ISBN 0-415-90826-4

For Danny

Contents

	Acknowledgments	ix
1.	Introduction	1
2.	Inventing Feminist Theory	17
3.	Feminist Strategies: From Core Concepts to Feminist Theory	41
4.	Feminism and Epistemology	89
5.	Feminism and Postmodernism	127
6.	Solutions: A Basic Outline of the Issues and Some Suggestions	153
	Notes	193
	Index	219

Acknowledgments

I want to thank the following people for much needed encouragement, help, and substantive advice on this book. First, Stephen Bronner who has been my mentor, friend, critic, and comrade since my early days in graduate school. Thank you for all you have taught me. Many, many thanks to Mary Hawkesworth, whose unflagging support and intelligent feedback on several versions of the ideas herein have helped enormously in the ultimate completion of this project. Thank you to Lynne Rienner, who has always had faith that I would finish this book, and to Wendy Sarvasy, who reminds me of the importance of political commitment and is one of the smartest people I know of to talk with about politics and theory. Lila Karp and Ti-Grace Atkinson gave me much appreciated counsel during the last stages of this project. In particular, I am thankful for their insights about early radical feminism and the state of feminism today. Various scholars have helped me to think through these ideas in the course of many panels at the American Political Science Association, Northeastern Political Science, New England Political Science Association, Southwestern Social Science, Western Political Science Association, and the National Women's Studies Association meetings. I thank them all for the contributions they have made (willingly or unwillingly) to this project.

Thanks are also due to the institutions where I have worked over the course of my thinking about feminist theory. My colleagues at California State University, Long Beach (CSULB), in political science and women's studies were always more than supportive. Remarkably, the institution provided financial help for this project even given their disgraceful underfunding by the state of California. A comprehensive list of the people who helped me at CSULB would be quite long, but I would like to single out for special thanks Elyse Blankley, Jan Gist, Kathryn McMahon, Susan Rice, Ron and Rosemary Schmidt, and the many fine, motivated, and politically committed students at CSULB for providing a very special community.

Thank you to my many splendid colleagues and staff at University of Southern California (USC) in political science, the Program for the Study of Women and Men in Society (SWMS), and elsewhere in the university, who are increasingly dear to me. I am not sure I could have written this without the institutional environment provided by USC, and the very bright and kind people I have met here.

Many undergraduates and graduate students have passed through my life at Wellesley College, CSULB, and USC, almost all of whom have made me grateful that I am a professor. I have loved teaching them. Among these students have been quite a few teaching and research assistants who have saved me untold amounts of time, and I thank them herein.

Thanks to Cecelia Cancellaro, the anonymous readers, and the staff at Routledge for making publishing this book as painless as possible. They have been a joy to work with.

I am blessed with many personal friends and family members without whom my life and work would be painfully and irreparably diminished. Much love and thanks to all my women friends, but especially to Devra Weber, who has been constant source of encouragement, comfort, and fun. Big hugs, Devra. I cannot let this project end without acknowledging my dog-friend and spirit guide, Ms. Coffee Bean. She has sat patiently under my desk for the last 11 years while I have stared, inexplicably it must have seemed to her, at books and computer screens. I thank her for her tireless love, for all those walks in the snow back east, and for her smiling face. Thanks to my entire extended family, but especially to my parents, Mr. and Mrs. Harold Caplan, whose love and support during some of the toughest times of my life has made this book possible. Thanks also to my brother, Joseph Grant, who is now very far away but always close in my heart. In thanking my family, I also acknowledge the debt I owe to my late grandmother Agnes McNulty Kehoe and my departed friend, Patrick Campbell. Thanks to Chuck Noble, for all that time we spent together in our other life, and for his continued intellectual counsel and much treasured friendship. Howard Gillman has been my confidant and fellow traveler since my first semester at USC. I am not sure that I could possibly convey how grateful I am for his friendship. My many conversations with him about life and theory have enriched this book enormously, and his words are thoughts are sprinkled throughout these pages. I owe him a special debt.

Last and most important, thanks to Dan Aviles for his saintly patience, common sense, and absolute constancy. I have never known a human being with a bigger heart, and I expect I never will. His steadfast confidence has enabled me to persevere through this very long process. Incredibly, he brought me some warmth in L.A. just when it was feeling particularly cold.

1

Introduction

There is a sense in which a particular orthodoxy about feminist theory has been created by the ways in which we have studied it. The orthodoxy goes like this: There is no one feminist theory. Rather, feminist theory is multicentered and undefinable. It is divided according to its attachment to one or another of several male theories whose terms it has attempted to appropriate and whose male-biased assumptions it has tended to mitigate. While this hyphenation model has lead to many interesting discussions of "liberal feminism," "Marxist feminism," "psychoanalytic feminism," "existentialist feminism," and so on, it has left us with a feminist theory that understands itself to be a kind of bandage on the basically misogynist canon of Western political and social philosophy. This way of analyzing feminism is reflected in most of the major, general treatments of feminist theory.

Jean Bethke Elshtain, for example, has divided feminist theory into four categories: radical, liberal, Marxist, and psychoanalytic. Elshtain, in accepting the formulation of feminism as divided, has gone on to comment that all feminist theories are political theories in search of politics, the public, and citizenship.[1]

Likewise, Alison Jaggar has divided feminist theory according to the categories radical, liberal, Marxist, and socialist. The problems with understanding feminism as hyphenated are underscored in Jaggar's account, which attempts to fit all theory into a preassigned grid. For example, Jaggar's discussion of liberal feminist theory concentrates, without comment, almost solely on the first wave.[2] This conspicuous lack of second wave liberal theorists leads one to the intuitively unlikely conclusion that second wave liberals look exactly like their first wave predecessors. So too, Jaggar seems at times unconcerned about the problems of fitting feminists from varied theoretical traditions into a the model she presents. For example, Jaggar places the French feminist Monique Wittig in the same category as American radical feminists,[3] thus obscuring important questions about the influence of existentialism and postmodernism in French theory as opposed to the relative lack thereof in American thought.

In contrast, Josephine Donovan has been careful to explicitly acknowledge differences between the first and second waves, and between American feminists and their European counterparts.[4] She has linked contemporary liberal feminism to the first wave, arguing that both are the intellectual products of Enlightenment thinking. She concludes by arguing in favor of a feminist moral vision based on the idea of female difference.[5] Donovan too follows a hyphenation model and continues to emphasize differences in feminisms over similarities. She divides feminist theory according to cultural, Freudian, existentialist, Marxist, and radical feminisms. Interestingly, her category "cultural feminism" links contemporary radical feminists who speak of female exceptionalism (as she herself does) to a similar first wave tradition including Charlotte Perkins Gilman and Margaret Fuller.[6] Donovan also makes mention of radical feminism's now familiar historical roots in the New Left. Donovan argues: "Much of radical feminist theory was, therefore, forged in reaction against theories, organizational structures and personal styles of the male New Left ... In terms of theory, radical feminists became determined to establish that their own personal 'subjective' issues had an importance and legitimacy equal to those great issues being dealt with by the New Left."[7]

Another popular book, one by Rosemary Tong entitled *Feminist Thought: A Comprehensive Introduction,* divides feminist theory even more than the others.[8] Her formulation includes liberal, Marxist, radical mothering, radical sexuality, psychoanalytic, socialist, essentialist, and postmodern. Interestingly, despite its claim to be comprehensive, there is almost no discussion of texts by women of color. Indeed, this omission exists in all of the texts mentioned above, though an understanding of the roots of feminist theory by women of color is essential to a full understanding of feminist theory.

ALTERNATIVES TO A HYPHENATED FEMINISM

I think it is politically significant that we have not looked at feminist theory as it has developed out of feminism itself, but instead have looked at it in terms of the history of Western thought. It is as though we believed that we had no way of understanding theory except in terms of the canon. Perhaps even more crucial is the fact that the hyphenation approach allows us to miss certain crucial and fundamental points about feminist theory and its history. In reading certain women's studies texts, we might think that (e.g.) liberal feminists thought of liberal feminism after having read Locke. Being extremely dissatisfied with his approach, they decided to come up with a feminist version and called it liberal feminism. Surely, this is not how feminist theory was born.

Curiously, feminist theorists have almost reveled in this fragmented self-perception. Why? I think it is because there is something about "feminism itself" that portends the development of hyphenated feminisms. Indeed, the hyphenation model shows how furiously we have sought to maintain the idea that feminism is a disparate body of thought. This desire is itself an ideological manifestation of something that is precisely a similarity among feminisms—namely, the almost fanatical devotion to the ideas of personal experience and difference. Somehow we have decided that differences among women are and must be reflected in differences among theories, and that if we did not have many different theories we would be somehow authoritarian.

Paradoxically, these kinds of notions have imposed a structure upon feminist theory, a structure that reinforces certain aspects of the theory and ignores others. I think we do not know enough about what makes feminist theory feminist. It is time to do a history of feminist ideas that does at least two things: (1) looks at the development of feminist theory in terms of early feminist writings and practice, and (2) looks at the similarities among the various feminisms about which we have read so much. This is part of what I want to do herein.

Many questions came to mind for me once I began to think about feminist theory this way. How did so many different feminisms come to exist? If there are similarities, how can one account for them? What is this feminism that has been added to traditional Western political thought to yield so many variations? What leads one to recognize "liberal feminism," for example, as "feminist" and not simply "liberal"? In short, is there a "fundamental feminism"?

FUNDAMENTAL FEMINISM

Since we have talked about feminism so long in terms of hyphenation and identified ourselves as members of one or another camp, by now there actually are liberal, radical, and socialist as well as many other feminisms, and I do not dispute this reality. What I do want to suggest is that besides the differences, there is also an underlying *feminism* that has remained undisclosed, undiscussed, and undiscovered. Part of my job then is to disclose, discuss, and discover.

I shall argue that much of the richness of feminist theory as well as a good portion of its problems are directly traceable to what I shall call its core concepts. They are: (1) "Woman," (2) experience, and (3) personal politics. These concepts were developed incrementally by early radical feminists in pamphlets and manifestos written as the Women's Liberation Movement was breaking away from the largely Marxist Left. The ideas that women were an oppressed group, that women's problems were political and not psychological, and that feminism was revolutionary echo these extended discussions between feminism and the Left. I have made a concerted effort to include thinking by women of color; not just for their discussions of race, but for their contributions to the development of feminist theory in general. The very fact that women of color have felt that there has had to be a special feminist theory for women of color says something about the rest of feminist theory. In fact, the combination of Woman and experience has led to a fragmented feminism, not merely in terms of hyphenated feminisms, but in terms of more pernicious kinds of exclusion around race, class, and ethnicity. The structure of feminist theory as built around the core concepts I list above is partly (not entirely) responsible for the ethnocentricism of feminism. In short, referring to one's own experiences as a woman to sustain a commentary on all women can be dangerous if the writer tends to be white.

In no way do I mean to imply that any early feminists were self-consciously creating theory for the reasons I will be describing in the following pages. What I want to show is how the concepts were developed in the course of accommodating certain political problems and commonly held beliefs. I want to argue further that these core concepts developed in political pamphlets became the rudimentary basis for theory. Finally, I contend that these ideas, however powerful as political rhetoric, may not always make the best theories.

It is important to note that the concepts were interpreted, taken up, and used in ways that may diverge completely from the use intended by the original authors or audiences. It is the nature of words, once uttered, to become subject to interpretation by the stream of history and debate. Thus, I am not sympathetic to founding feminists I have met over the years who claim that they were not intending to do this or that by saying thus and so in X or Y pamphlet. For the purposes of this discussion, the intent of the author is irrelevant. What matters is how the ideas have been used by subsequent feminist theorists and how they have evolved to become contemporary feminist theory.

By labeling the ideas I will be discussing as core concepts, I do not mean to say that they constitute an exhaustive list of the core feminist theoretical continuities. Clearly, others can be derived and there is room for much exploration on this topic. I also do not think it is necessary that each and every single feminist adhere to these as "core" for my thesis to be correct. I have in mind to delineate a basic and widespread tendency in feminist theory. In fact, part of my point is that the concepts are often implicit rather than explicit. That is, a thinker can rely on them without really being aware that she is doing so. I am also saying that (postmodern feminisms aside, for the moment) these ideas dominate the current feminist discourse.

Though the core concepts were originally no more than political tools, they soon became more properly theoretical due to the urging of theoretically minded feminists like Shulamith Firestone and Ti-Grace Atkinson. It would be wrong to say, however, that the ideas improved as they became more theoretical. Alas, the earlier, primarily political, conceptualizations were often superior. This is especially the case insofar as many contemporary feminists have built upon the most problematic aspects of the core concepts, the subjectivism of the idea of experience and the essentializing qualities of the category Woman. Often these have led to rather romantic, abstract assertions about the nature of women.

What makes the core concepts fundamental to feminism is that they are used across seemingly divergent feminisms. In fact, some non-radical-feminist theories (socialist feminism, for example) can be conceptualized as feminist theoretical strategies designed to meet problems with the original concepts. Thus, aside from analyzing early and contemporary radical feminist theories, I also intend to examine the precise manifestations of the core concepts in what I think of as revisionist feminist theories. Revisionist strategies such as socialist feminist and so-called mothering theory can be thought of as responses to inadequacies in the radical construction of the core concepts. Some theories by women of color also fall into this revisionist category. Part of my claim is that the concepts recur with a surprising tenacity as do their problems. Many of the criticisms that have been recently leveled against radical feminism can just as easily apply to much of the whole of feminism. My main claim is that the core concepts need to be acknowledged and either substantially revised or abandoned.

METHODOLOGY: THE SOCIAL CONTEXT

One subtext of the history of feminist thought has been the move from Marxism to postmodernism as part of a general paradigm shift in twentieth century social thought. As political acts, theories, and the theories one chooses, are important to divulge. I find, like many feminists, that I have come from a position of basic hostility to postmodern thinking to the view that it is extremely important and useful to feminist and other social and political theories. In this study of feminist theory I have therefore drawn heavily on both Marxist and postmodern theory.

I think Edward Said was right to observe that "there is a reluctance to allow that political, institutional, and ideological constraints act in the same manner on the individual author as they do on general bodies of thought which exist in historical contexts."[9] I think my personal intellectual changes have to do with the social context in which I am unalterably embedded.

Although I do not consciously perceive it as related, I cannot help but notice that my turn to postmodernism and my distance from Marxism, as tentative as both are, coincide with the failure of communism in the Eastern Block. Even though I never believed the Soviet Union was a communist society, never thought Lenin was in the spirit of Marx, and never joined a revolutionary party, I have nonetheless come to believe that the failure of Soviet communism means that Marxist theory cannot go on as it was, and that Michel Foucault was right to move social constructivism and historicism to another level of analysis. I am still struggling with the tension between Marxist and Foucaultian modes of criticism and remain much more Marxist than postmodern.

For example, like many feminists, I am not ready to give up on either the Enlightenment or socialism. There are those of us who look for some neo-Enlightenment position, for some compromise between essentialism and constructionism. In particular, I look for the creation of some space where the insights of radical social constructionism can be combined with what is good about humanism, the rule of law, rights, freedom, equality, and socialism. I think a neo-Enlightenment position would be the Enlightenment without all the caveats about "human nature," "truth," natural rights, and autonomy. I think its reformulation would require the insights of postmodernism and Marxism, and that, to be applied to feminism, this reformulation would have to take place in the context of an active movement.

I am a feminist, and I see myself as part of the tradition that I will be discussing. Still, much of this book is very critical of feminist thought and is even critical of many works from which I have learned tremendously. My purpose is not to demolish or disrespect, but to fully investigate the foundations of feminist theory and to provide a strong case for the acknowledgment and reevaluation of the core concepts. At times I may seem to ignore what is good about a given theory in the course of my critique. That is because I am only concerned with tracing the core concepts in these theories, and much that is good about what given feminists have said is not directly related to my current inquiry.

WHY I WROTE THIS BOOK, OR; SCHOLARLY WORK AS AUTOBIOGRAPHY

If you are the kind of scholar who finds autobiographical interjections tedious, you can disregard this section. Though I think it gives purpose to my argument, the rest of the book does stand on its own.

I have been a feminist and a socialist since I was eighteen years old. Actually, the values attached to my politics were probably present much earlier, but I did not have names to put to my feelings about injustice and inequality until college. The feminism I learned about as an undergraduate in the late 1970s was a feminism that I understood to be about androgyny and making women powerful. We did not shave our underarms. We wore no makeup. We wore no bras. We vowed to keep our "maiden" names when we married if, in fact, we married at all. Feminist politics was a politics with an alternative lifestyle that made me feel radical and empowered because I was not capitulating to sexist female norms.

There were problems, of course; problems that have been written about often and at great length by later feminists. Sometimes I denied what I identified as traditionally feminine feelings because they were not politically correct. And perhaps I judged other nonfeminist women too harshly. Still, I have to admit that, basically, I felt very at home with that old feminism.

In graduate school I studied political theory in a political science department where there were no female theorists, let alone any who taught feminist theory. Though there were many strong feminists at Rutgers, they were in other fields and I did not come to know them until very late in my graduate school education. Mostly, I was interested in studying nineteenth and twentieth century political theory, especially Marxism, and I approached this endeavor with great enthusiasm. I never let go of my feminist politics, but I did leave off reading in the field long enough to learn the canon of Western theory from Plato to Marx.

All of that set the stage for the genesis of this book.

This project really began one summer day in 1984. I had just passed my doctoral exams and was feeling as exhausted and beleaguered as any whiny graduate student has ever felt. I saw a flier on some kiosk advertising that the National Women's Studies Association was meeting on the Douglass College campus at Rutgers and decided to cheer myself with some feminist company. I was also curious about what was happening in feminist scholarship these days and glad for a chance to escape obsessing about my as yet unchosen dissertation topic. Having no program for the meetings, I simply popped into a few rooms to hear what was being said.

I must have spent the whole afternoon at the conference. I could not believe what I was hearing. Androgyny was being criticized. Heavily criticized. They were talking about "feminine values" and "women's ways of knowing." I was very, very surprised—I might have even been appalled. What had happened? Had I changed? Had I become so much a rationalist Marxist that I had lost my feminism? I did not think so. Or had feminism changed and left me out? It was then that I decided to write my dissertation about feminist theory. It has come to pass that I have devoted many years of my life to answering the questions that occurred to me on that day in 1984.

This book is significantly different from the dissertation I eventually wrote, but I have always stuck by a few basic insights that I had that day in New Jersey: there is a set of underlying feminist principles, they are internally contradictory, and they have led many feminists down a path that I did not feel comfortable following. I have at times in the course of this work felt as though the development of the new feminine feminism has left me. I always felt better about the old-style feminism—the pre-different-voice feminism—and I still do. Actually, so do a lot of people.

I have read and understand all of the critiques of early radical feminism. It was racist and exclusionary, to be sure. It tended to be authoritarian. It was naive about liberalism and libertarianism. Its model was to try and fit women into the world as men had made it, and on and on. However, it is my personal observation that a lot of fairly sexist men and some very conservative female students feel pretty comfortable with the new feminine feminism, and I wonder why that is.

My speculation is that feminine feminism grew and became orthodoxy in the feminist movement so quickly because we had become afraid of having alienated all those women who stayed at home and did not want to be "liberated" the way liberation was being defined in the 1960s. As Marilyn Quayle said at the 1992 GOP convention, "Not everyone concluded that American society was so bad that it had to be radically remade by social revolution . . . Not everyone believed that the family was so oppressive that women could only thrive apart from it . . . Not everyone joined the counter-culture." So, in a way, because many women would not come to the counterculture, the counterculture came to them. My feelings about having insulted some women with 1960s style feminist politics is that you can not make an omelette without breaking eggs. Nor can you have a revolution without offending some people.

My opinions aside, and on a more serious and theoretical level, Woman as a universal category created a situation where right-wing women were, indeed, a very big theoretical problem. The notion of male-identification only went so far to explain their feelings. The category Woman created a structure that greatly facilitated the rise of gynocentric feminism, which I think is basically a feminism on the run from the Right. When right-wing women said (as articulated by Marilyn Quayle to the GOP), "most women do not wish to be liberated from their essential natures as women,"[10] feminists seem to have responded by retreating into an essentialist understanding of the female and a revaluation of the feminine. Of course it was important for us to stop defining human as "male," and the revalorization of the feminine was a very important tool in that reconstruction. Still, it is a strategy that must be understood in the context of its rise in the 1980s.

On the other hand, I have to say that many of the most radical women I know are talking about female values. I go back and forth on it myself. In many ways, my feminist practice is completely essentialized. I have gone to more than a few feminist spirituality gatherings and enjoyed them immensely. With very few exceptions, I only read novels by women. I listen almost exclusively to music performed by women. My favorite actors (sic) are women. I do not do this for political effect. It honestly just happens that I mostly prefer what I have no way of describing except as "female" things.

But I don't know if this is really a feminist impulse. My interpretation of those things is feminist, but to like the things themselves does not guarantee a feminist reading. To be sure, feminine feminism feels good, nurturing, caring, and warm. But again, I'm not sure it is really changing anything, or even that it is particularly political. More to the point, for the reasons I outline in this book, I am convinced that notions of women's superiority and difference do not translate into sound theory.

My thinking on the history of feminist theory seems to have led me back to the early radical feminists. Though they talked about female values, they also talked about female power. I was reminded of this again on 13 March 1992, at a small but impressive conference on Women and Reason at USC. I was sitting in the audience watching several well-known feminist theorists sitting in the front of the room having a closing summary panel. All of them were well known as academics in the fields of philosophy, history and literature. The exception was Ti-Grace Atkinson who, though a brilliant mind, was better known for her activism and writings in the early years of the feminist movement. The energy in the room was low during this final hour, since most of the conference participants were exhausted by then, and many had left for home to beat the L.A. traffic. I remember the scene this way:

Ti-Grace hardly says anything. Actually, she has seemed a bit lost during the entire two-day conference. She, one of the major figures in early feminist theory, seems now curiously out of the loop as to its most raging academic controversies. She sits up there looking from one to the other as the three other feminist theorists talk about power. One, reading the text of another's body language, comments good-naturedly, almost as a tossed off remark, that the latter had used male gestures when she spoke of toughness—a deliberate stance, a bent arm with a menacing clenched fist. Ti-Grace speaks. She asks almost the only question she has asked during the entire roundtable: "What about women's political power?" But no one responds.

In that moment it was as if Ti-Grace was deconstructing feminist theory. Her very presence highlighted the new feminism and its current debates. She was juxtaposed against them, and their presence emphasized hers. Her nonunderstanding of academic feminism pointed up our forgetfulness about what early radical feminism had been about. And they seemed not to want to answer a question about female power. I do not think anyone was purposefully ignoring her. It is simply that the discussion was about other things. Things not about that *kind* of female power. I am sure, in fact, that all of the other feminist theorists present cared deeply about empowering women. This story is not about them. It is about what I felt at that moment. I felt that academic feminist theory had gotten very out of touch with activism; that it was out of touch with any concrete sense of female power. And, of course, I include myself as part of that problem.

At that conference, I watched, seeing someone else, seeing Ti-Grace Atkinson have the same reaction I had at NWSA in 1984. But by 1992 I think I had figured out what had changed in feminism and how that change had occurred. That change in feminism is the subject of this book.

This is the end of the autobiographical section (unless you read between the lines).

THE PLAN OF THE BOOK

Chapter 2 begins by locating the core concepts in their origins at the outset of second wave feminist theory and in the political context of the 1960s. The history may be familiar, but the meaning of the documents that came out of that history is not. What we see in going back to those documents is that the groundwork for feminist theory in the 1990s was there in the early 1970s. Concepts were developed in that period that remain central to feminist theory to this day.

I continue in chapter 3 by elaborating the manifestations of those core concepts throughout various revisionist strategies. These strategies include attempts to find a materialist grounding for feminism, attempts to link Woman to some universal experience of mothering or sexuality, and the development of various identity theories based specifically in the experiences of women of color. In this chapter I show the reasons feminist theory evolved in these directions and explain why the concepts have continued to fail.

Standpoint theory is another strategy for theorizing the core concepts, and I discuss it in chapter 4. The attempt to develop a feminist epistemology out of the idea of female experience provides a fascinating window into the centrality of the core concepts and their gross inadequacies. Here I begin to look at the notion of a feminist interpretive lens, and this problem of interpretation becomes central to the rest of the book. In this section (and the one on socialist feminism in chapter 3), I also present a critical explication of the use of Marxism in feminist theory. I am primarily concerned with three issues: (1) can Marxism be adapted to feminist concerns by analogy, (2) which versions of Marxism are used in which feminist theories, and (3) what are the effects of linking the core concepts to Marxist ideas? Finally, I place standpoint theory in the context of the general project of epistemologies to investigate what is assumed in epistemological discourses, and how these assumptions interact with the core concepts of feminism.

In chapter 5 I look at the relationship between postmodernism and feminism. Again, I am particularly interested in the ways postmodern feminism solves or does not solve problems with the core concepts of American feminist thought. However, I also point out some interesting similarities and dissimilarities between the two schools of thought. I ask, What is feminist about postmodern feminism? and, Is there anything postmodern about Anglo-American feminism? My observations lead to a renewed discussion of interpretation, as well as a review of issues the two schools of thought have in common vis-à-vis theory and politics.

In my final chapter, rather too boldly entitled "Solutions," I suggest alternative strategies for feminist theory that are based on my arguments and observations about the history of feminist ideas. I begin to explore a new feminism based on the notion of gender as a relatively autonomous ideological structure that must be criticized and dismantled. My hope is to outline some strategies for a new direction for feminist theory that takes insights from both Anglo-American and postmodern feminist theory in order to foster self-determination for all people.

In the end I reject Woman and experience, but preserve the idea of personal politics. I counsel a shift away from epistemology and the standpoint of women, and toward the development of a feminist interpretive lens, and a feminist subject who is determined in practice. Focusing not on the female experience, but instead on the abolition of the ideological structure "gender," will, I think, help us to escape concerns about essentialism while maintaining some notion of practice and subjectivity.

What may appear as a cost to some feminists is the fact that I see all of this as necessarily a move away from gynocentric feminism and to what I will now loosely term neohumanist or neo-Enlightenment feminism. This would be more like the old-style radical feminism, though transformed to reflect many of the criticisms that have justly been lodged against it. I understand this new feminism to include humanist notions modified by critiques about its class, race, and gender biases. I still retain beliefs in universal connections among people but see those connections as part of an ongoing process rather than as predetermined definitions into which all people must fit. This type of feminism rejects nationalism (including female nationalism), but not multiculturalism. It would advance the idea that, to quote a popular political button, "Feminism is the very radical notion that women are people." This is not mere humanism, as the feminist interpretive lens and the stress on gender as a particular kind of structure should guard against androcentricism.

A revitalized feminist theory must be, in some ways, a theory against feminist theory. There can be democratically determined, universally applicable values, but they must be derived in practice by local struggles in order to avoid setting up abstract notions of humanity that recapitulate problems of exclusion endemic to older humanist models. It must be a feminism that talks about women's freedom and self-determination and that iterates the need for feminists to defend the rights of women to make bad choices. It cannot advocate a priori a "politically correct" standard of sexual or any other behavior. Chapter 6, then, is devoted to exploring this proposed new feminism.

In the end the point of this book is really very simple. It is meant to be a kind of working through of questions about what has happened to feminism, and how it has come to pass that feminist theory has become feminized and overly epistemologized. Given the problems I identify, the book goes on to make some suggestions for new directions for feminist theory. It is important to note that I have wondered and theorized about these things from a particular political—even polemical—perspective. Then again, don't we all?

2

Inventing Feminist Theory

It is well documented that many of the women who were to become second wave radical feminists first came to political consciousness in the New Left and civil rights movements.[1] As the story goes, various gender-based exclusionary practices in those movements fostered a nascent feminist consciousness among some women who went on to form various grass roots radical feminist organizations—WITCH, Redstockings, The Feminists, New York Radical Women, to name but a few.

Indeed, the history of feminist *theory* is tangled up with this well-known narrative. But it is a slightly different history; a history of ideas. The story of the invention of feminist theory begins with different questions: Why were radical feminists so concerned with theory building? How did it happen that we ended up with the feminist theory we have? In short, What did we know and when did we know it? rather than, What did we do and when did we do it? What I want to do is to tell a new story using some familiar events.

Feminist theory was invented in the midst of a struggle on at least two fronts. First, radical women realized that the Left, for whatever reasons, could not incorporate politics relating to problems of sexism.

In the course of this realization, feminists began to write their own new ideas on the subject, in the process detailing how they were different from the Left at large, and speculating about why the Left would not or could not accept them. In part, feminist theory was invented in the course of this conversation between feminism and the Left.

If feminist theory was not standard left-wing fare, neither was it the same as the ideas percolating around as "women's issues" among government activists and those liberals who were to become mainstream feminists. There were many activities on behalf of women already occurring in a liberal form before the advent of radical feminism (e.g., the formation of the National Organization for Women [1966], the Kennedy Commission on the Status of Women [1961], the passage of the Equal Pay Act [1963], the passage of Title VII of the 1964 Civil Rights Act, and the publication of Betty Friedan's *Feminine Mystique* [1963]). Despite this activism, liberal feminism of the 1960s was curiously atheoretical. This is reflected in current hyphenation models of feminist theory, which let pass without comment the fact that there are virtually no second wave liberal feminist theorists.

One reason why radical feminists became the primary·builders of feminist theory is simply that the academic roots and intellectual nature of the New Left meant that the women who came out of that tradition were predisposed to consider theory as essential to politics. It was in this sense quite logical that radical feminists struggled hardest at developing theories that could guide them in their sustained effort to change the situation of women.

In addition to the importance of theory per se, the particular direction of radical feminist theory toward a theory of personal politics was foreshadowed by the cultural radicalism of the sixties, which placed a lot of stock in issues of lifestyle, clothing, language, and so on. Indeed, even the most hard-core left-wing groups of the period (e.g., Maoists, Black Panthers, Weather underground) made a great deal of the congruence between personal life and political commitment.

Finally, the disparity between second wave liberals and radicals on the question of theory building can be explained by the fact that liberals already had a theory. Liberal theory per se could explain the kinds of activism that were centered around government and legal change. The trick for liberal feminists seemed to be simply to get the powerful structures in society to treat women as though they were rational and, therefore, according to the classical liberal definition, human beings. Radicals, on the other hand, were politicized within the context of social movements attuned to the limits of liberalism and committed to a critique of economic and cultural imperialism. Absent the connection to liberal statism, radical feminists were free to make a much broader criticism of the private/public distinction.

Although we may associate feminists who engaged in liberal practices post hoc with "liberal feminist theory," it is much more to the point to say that liberal feminists were liberals in their practice. In fact, *second wave* liberal feminists had no unique theory to begin with. Moreover, the term liberal feminist does little to explain how we recognize what is *feminist* about them. In part, we know they are liberal feminists because they talk about women. And although Jean Bethke Elshtain is somehow correct to characterize liberal feminists as people who ask the question, "Why can't women be more like men,"[2] it is also true that Zillah Eisenstein was right to see its connection to radical feminism.[3]

The connection that is most significant is not the one Eisenstein talks about, however. It is not, as she argues, that liberal feminism has a "radical future" or potential. Rather, something happened to the practice of second wave liberal feminism after the advent of radical feminism that changed the focus of feminism itself. The widespread adoption of the practice of consciousness raising, the discussions of lesbianism (admittedly accomplished with much resistance, but accomplished nonetheless), and the acceptance of a politics of sexuality and a politics of housework are just a few examples of the ways in which radical feminism began to exert a major influence on shaping the feminist agenda. The two practices (radical and liberal) began to converge around an identity that was recognizably "feminist" and that included as its central pillars the category Woman and the notions of experientialism and personal politics. It is no exaggeration to say that the presence of concepts developed by early radical feminists are what enable us to recognize a theory as feminist. The presence of these ideas as employed in liberal feminist politics today enable us to speak of a feminism that is distinct from liberalism.[4]

WOMEN ARE OPPRESSED AS WOMEN

The category Woman has become one of the most foundational if contentious ones in contemporary feminist theory. The category derives from an early radical feminist notion that women are oppressed not by virtue of their class or race, but simply by the fact of their womanhood. That is, women are oppressed *as women*. The notion served an important political purpose both in differentiating feminism from the Left and in developing the very concept of feminism. Early radical feminist defenses of women (and sometimes, of femininity) necessitated the recognition of women as a collectivity.

From the radical women's perspective, the fact that they were treated collectively as an inferior group by the Left justified the emerging view that the connections between them as women—in many cases regardless of politics, race, or class—outweighed all others. The negative left-wing reaction to the idea that women were an oppressed group *as women* only increased the tension between the Women's Liberation Movement and the Left until finally, radical women began to see themselves as the founders of a new and distinct movement.

> In the standard radical view, women's liberation is a part of the Left and women a constituency like the students or GIs. Granted that we suffer our own forms of oppression and that radical men have oppressed us as women, the emphasis is on contributing our special insights to the Left as a whole and using feminist issues as an organizing tool. In return, male radicals are expected to endorse women's liberation and combat their male chauvinism. Many of us now reject this view of our purpose as anti-woman. We have come to see women's liberation as an independent revolutionary movement.[5]

Thus, separating from the Left meant perceiving the connections between women as primary to all others. It seems that initially, the idea of a specific women's oppression functioned to differentiate radical feminist women from the generic Left and enabled feminists to cultivate an independent theory and politics. Feminists no longer were, nor did they want to be, a "part" subordinate to a "larger" New Left. Many radical feminists came to question whether feminism shared interests in common with the Left at all. As Ti-Grace Atkinson explained succinctly, ". . . a communist woman might well be a moderate or even a right wing feminist. Feminism has its own issues."[6]

If feminism had become a truly distinct movement and politics, Atkinson argued, it seemed to need its own theory. Indeed, no other radical theories spoke directly to the concerns of the new feminist movement. The acknowledgment that women constituted a group in and of themselves immediately implied a question: What was the basis for the connection? Thus, from the beginning, Woman put feminists on potentially essentialist terrain and foreshadowed a de facto acceptance of female difference. It was almost foretold by the very term "women's liberation" that the category Woman had to be reinvented by feminism, and that, once invented, it would become a fundamental category of feminist theory. In fact, as I shall argue, its invention also foretold the creation of the other core concepts of feminist theory that form the basis for feminist theory as we know it.

In early radical feminist writings, we can see how radical feminists grappled with the possibility that real women did indeed conform to some of the stereotypes of women (e.g., passive, emotional, "bitchy"), and they sought to explain how these "female" traits were rational reactions to oppression. In a defense of the derogatory valuation of women, Joreen argued in the "Bitch Manifesto" that so called bitches were, in fact, women who had resisted traditional socialization and were persecuted for not being feminine. She neither apologized for bitches nor disputed their existence.

> BITCH does not use this word in the negative sense. A woman should be proud to declare that she is a BITCH because BITCH is beautiful. It should be an affirmation by self and not negation by others . . . Bitches are also uncomfortable around other women because frequently women are less their psychological peers than are men. Bitches don't particularly like passive people. They are always slightly afraid they will crush the fragile things. Women are trained to be passive and have learned to act that way even when they are not.[7]

For Joreen, bitches and nonbitches alike are explainable as two alternative means of coping with male supremacy and compulsory gender roles. Joreen's idea is that some women become bitchy to rebel against the oppression of femininity to which most women have capitulated.

Her claim that "bitches have been oppressed by other women as much if not more than by men and their hatred for them is usually greater,"[8] also raised the uncomfortable possibility that women can be oppressed by other women, an idea that again raised the question of exactly what it is that unites women and even suggested that not all women were, in fact, united under the same banner. The idea that women could oppress women would also have raised important questions about the conceptualization of men and the male.

Early radical feminists argued that women's traits did not necessarily make them inferior. To the contrary, most emphatically defended female ways of being, declaring that women should not simply be like men. Although they explicitly argued for an androgynous society, early radical feminists did not mean by this that women should give up the female (as the term is often misinterpreted today). In arguing for androgyny they claimed that much behavior associated with women was desirable for humans in general. As one radical feminist put it, "If these maternal traits, conditioned into women, are desirable traits, they are desirable for everyone, not just for women."[9] Another proclaimed that

> only the suppressed female culture in all races, in all lands, can be proud of the female principle. For females need not prove their "manhood," as they can never be males or a part of the dominant male world culture. Therefore women will be forced, by the very fact of being female, to defend and raise the banner of the female principle . . . It is only by asserting the long suppressed and ridiculed female principle that a truly human society will come about. For the split between the male and the female will only be bridged and a fully human identity developed—encompassing in each person all human characteristics which were previously split up into male and female—when the female principle and culture is no longer suppressed and male domination is ended forever.[10]

As these passages show, early radical feminists may have been likely to conflate sex and gender in the course of exploring questions about the roots of women's oppression, but they were not rejecting the female in discussions of androgyny. On the other hand, the casual use of "female culture" is the genesis of the problem of essentialism in feminist theory today.[11]

WOMEN ARE OPPRESSED AS WOMEN: THE PROBLEM OF FEMALE NATURE

In asserting the idea that women were oppressed as women and that, therefore, women should band together regardless of class or political persuasion, radical feminists were led into uncomfortable discussions about "female nature." Female nature, they polemicized, was the result of "male supremacy."

The idea of male supremacy implied a correlative male nature that was power hungry and aggressive enough to account for men's continued and universal oppression of women. Male nature was held responsible for the sorry state of the world, while women's innocence was verified by the fact of her victimization.

> The demand for an end to sex roles and male imperialist domination is a real attack on the masculine citadel of war. After all, women don't declare or fight in offensive wars. War is a male institution—as are all other institutions in the society—and war is simply an extension of the colonial policy of the subjection of the female culture and the "weaker" male cultures . . .[12]

Kate Millet wrote that "the image of woman fostered by cultural media, high and low, then and now, is a marginal and demeaning existence, and one outside the human condition—which is defined as the prerogative of man, the male."[13] Another feminist held that "there is no group other than slaves that has been singled out for such systematic and total exploitation and suppression as the class of women."[14]

In satirically characterizing male nature, Betsy Warrior claimed that it makes men an obsolete life form since they are principally responsible for wars and the destruction of the environment. "The qualities of Man make him unfit for life today . . . If females feel some compunctions about eliminating him entirely, Man preserves and zoos might prove a rational alternative."[15] Thus, the analysis of early radicals tended to accept the categories male and female, while simultaneously and problematically asserting that these separate natures were in no way biological.

The tacit acceptance of female and male natures and the attempt to change the value judgments made about those natures accepted the form of these traditional categories while merely attempting to revaluate them. Therefore, at times, early radicals appeared to be able only to explain why women behaved in the ways misogynists described and not to challenge the categories of gender per se. In this reversal the "bad" female traits were now to be considered "good," at least for the purposes of political discussion. Thus, value judgments about female nature were attacked while the categories themselves remained intact. In this way, the gendered patriarchal discourse that had created the oppression remained alive. Radical feminists did not shift the terms of the debate, but only negated existing categories given to them by the oppressive apparatus. The result was that the dominant ideas about women were accepted, but valued differently. Radical feminists disputed judgments made about female behavior, and some disputed the source(s) of female behavior, but all agreed, at least by their written words, that it existed, and that accepting it constituted a fundamental part of feminist politics.

In general, radical feminists have stressed the connectedness of women across time and culture, and while most have not been willing to argue that the female body is a sufficient explanation for women's oppression, all have implied that the female body is a necessary precondition for continued patriarchal oppression. In a sense, to argue that a female body is not a necessary precondition for women's oppression would have left radical feminists with no basis for their original argument that women are oppressed as women. If the body does not unite us as women, what does? Initially, therefore, the word "woman" was understood to include both biological and socially constructed gender traits. The early radical's acceptance of the patriarchal category Woman implicitly conflated sex and gender, and this is why they became so unclear about the role of the body and biology in women's oppression.

Shulamith Firestone was virtually unique among American radicals in attempting to explain the connection between materialism and biology.

> Why postulate a fundamental Hegelian concept of Otherness as the final explanation—and then carefully document the biological and historical circumstances that have pushed the class "women" into such a category—when one has never seriously considered the much simpler and more likely possibility that this fundamental dualism sprang from the sexual division itself?[16]

It was not dualistic thinking in humans that created otherness, she argued against de Beauvoir, but literal, biological dualism. Thus, she reasoned, women's liberation had to be fundamentally linked to physical changes in female reproductive functions. Like Marx who had attempted to historicize the essentialist category "human," Firestone attempted (and failed) to turn Woman into a materialist category.

Firestone's work has been heavily criticized. However, at least it attempted to provide a solution to what was to become one of the major charges against radical feminist theory: ahistoricity. Firestone offered a plausible, if undesirable, justification for the "universal oppression of women" thesis advanced by radical feminism. Firestone's argument was that the problem transcends historical periods because the problem is, in part, ahistorical and biological.

Whereas most radical feminist theory has been particularly poor at explaining why women have been oppressed across time and cultures, Firestone asserted that sex-class "goes back beyond recorded history to the animal kingdom itself"[17] and followed through by offering what she saw as a material (as opposed to idealist) explanation. The presence of the female body, she claimed, was the only explanatory variable that did not change across time and culture. Thus, it was sufficient to explain the pervasiveness of women's oppression. In contrast to Firestone, most radical feminists, even today, have yet to be persuaded of the need to find a historical or material grounding for female oppression.

"Woman" created contradictions within radical feminism from the beginning. On the one hand, radical feminists wished to criticize "female nature" as an oppressive, male concept. On the other hand, since women seemed to behave in "feminine" or "female" ways (they were unclear as to which) and radical feminists wanted to defend women, they found themselves defending female behavior and, by implication, female "nature" because they had found no convincing way to conceptually separate the two. The resulting contradiction was that women's ways of being were simultaneously understood negatively, since they had been foisted upon women as a means to oppress them, and positively, as a set of behaviors that was uniquely female and to which all people might even aspire.

In many ways the category Woman was responsible for the initial formation and subsequent transformation of the other two core concepts in feminist thought: experience and personal politics. The belief in an organic relationship among women that superseded time, space, culture, and class precipitated further incremental changes in radical feminist ideas about politics and subjective experience.

The core concepts have much to do with the hegemony of the white perspective in feminist theory. Hazel Carby has written about how in the nineteenth century discourse on women, both patriarchal and feminist versions, the word *woman* meant *white woman*.[18] The same can be said of early radical feminist literature. A striking example is Gayle Rubin's essay, "Woman as Nigger," in which she asserts that "the major premise of women's liberation is that women are an oppressed class, like black people, but that unlike blacks, they are not marginal to our technocratic society."[19] Because Rubin writes as though all women are white, the implication is that any cross-racial alliance as fellow victims would be between white women and black men.

We know that many of the white women in the early Women's Liberation Movement were active in civil rights struggles. Frankly, it is difficult to understand how they could have made such a costly omission when talking about "women." The omission becomes easier to fathom when considered as structural outcomes of the deployment of the twin ideas of experience and Woman. That is, early feminists repeatedly stressed the need to talk about their own (i.e., "our") experiences as the only reliable methodological tool for defining oppression. Further, it was assumed that one's personal experiences were linked to a universal experience of womanhood. Add to this the fact that most of the women writing were white. Therefore, by drawing on only their experiences and assuming in those experiences a universal womanhood, they were able to ignore many kinds of women simply by following their own methodology. It told them there was no need to look outside of their own experiences; that their experiences were common to all women. Woman and experience in those circumstances created a structure that allowed these rather politically astute women to forget differences among women. It even required that they do so.

On the other hand, I would not lay the blame for the exclusion of African-American women solely at the feet of the Women's Liberation Movement. The male dominance of the Black Power movement contributed as well, by speaking of change in terms of the "Black Man,"[20] it further facilitated this kind of thinking. In a sense, the Women's Liberation Movement and the Black Power movement conspired to create the deplorable idea that (to paraphrase Gloria T. Hull, Patricia Bell Scott, and Barbara Smith) all the women are white and all the blacks are men.

Ironically, feminist women of color continue to use the very core concepts that contributed to their exclusion from the early feminist movement. This is not surprising. For the language of the core concepts became the language of feminism so quickly, that to align with feminism *meant* to use the core concepts. What this has meant in turn, however, is that we find in feminist writings by women of color similar kinds of essentializing theories both about themselves and white women. Although my discussion draws primarily on works by African-American women, I think that the substantive point is applicable to writings by women of color in general.

Once again, we can see the origins of the core concepts by looking at the early pamphlets and writings of the black feminist movement. The 1977 "Combahee River Collective: A Black Feminist Statement" was written as a socialist feminist text and shows the influence of that movement in its attempt to think about systems of oppression other than gender: "The most general statement of our politics at the present time would be that we are actively committed to struggling against racial, sexual, heterosexual and class oppression and see as

our particular task the development of integrated analysis and practice based upon the fact that the major systems of oppression are
interlocking."[21] It also shows quite strikingly and in no uncertain
terms the acceptance of the core concepts of feminism. About experience, the Combahee collective writes, "We have spent a great deal of
energy delving into the cultural and experiential nature of our
oppression," since racial politics itself does not allow "most black
women to look more deeply into our own experiences . . ." The collective also states its support for the notions of "identity politics"
(discussed in white feminism more simplistically as "women's identity") and "personal politics." It is clear that core concepts are not
simply a white feminist phenomenon, though their history seems to
begin in a predominantly white feminist movement.

"EXPERIENCE"

Again the story of feminist theory begins in political history. In short,
early radical feminists responded to Left ambivalence about the
notion of Woman and women's issues by asserting an essential connection among women as women, and by claiming that their personal
and subjective experiences of oppression constituted a valid proof of
the existence of the category. These interrelated ideas developed more
or less simultaneously.

I want to try and explain this development in terms of the conceptual problem that faced early radical feminists. The Left, under the
influence of Marxism, understood politics as a rational discourse that
could make positive judgments about justice, exploitation, oppression, and liberation. Thus, it tended to define exploitation according
to standards that it alleged were objectively determined. For example,
in Marxist theory, workers can be objectively disadvantaged whether
or not they are subjectively aware, or self-conscious, of their oppression. The New Left followed Marxian theory in positing objective
conditions of oppression and exploitation (such as "class") that may
or may not be subjectively felt or realized by the revolutionary agent.
Likewise, the Black Power movement had an objective standard for
oppression, i.e., skin color.

But neither of these objectivist definitions of oppression would do for feminism. The creators of feminist theory, many of whom were neither black nor working class, at first could discern no argument that might enable them to create a compelling testament to their own structural oppression. Firestone thus complained that sex-class was "invisible." Others went on to boldly assert that middle- and upper-class women were not only oppressed, but a type of vanguard: "A few of us have emerged from the masses of women in this country . . . to identify the problem and the enemy . . . many [of us] are well educated and professional. Some are from the ruling class."[22]

For feminist women, the objectivist elements in Marxism were dangerous since they prevented the male Left from acknowledging female oppression especially when it existed among ruling class women: ". . . after all women were leaving the Left in increasing numbers—and the men began to play guilt games. 'So what makes you think you're oppressed, you white middle-class chick?' . . . That tactic made some women even madder but it began to cut deep into many women."[23] Yet it was a logical and political necessity that feminism come up with some way to define all women as oppressed if the claims regarding women as an oppressed class were to be sustained.

The problem was that women were present in every oppressed *and oppressing* group. Indeed, many women, such as those who were white and middle class, would not have been considered oppressed by any existing measure save the newly emerging feminist one. To the contrary, by most gauges many women seemed more free than many men; ruling class women were more free than working class men, and even black women seemed to be more accepted in white society than black men.

Yet, it seemed to early radical feminists that the category Woman had to include all women or risk dissolution. As one early radical feminist defending the idea that upper class women were oppressed put it, "One tends to forget that they are *women* that they belong to their husbands or fathers (owners) and that they are used by their owners in the same or equally degrading ways as other women."[24] Thus, that ruling class women *were not allowed to work* and were "put on a pedestal"[25] was defined as oppressive according to radical feminist analysis, whereas any other existing radical theory would have labeled this pedestal a privilege.

The category "women" necessarily included women of racial and economic privilege who would not have been considered oppressed according to existing progressive theories. This again raised the thorny question implicit in Joreen's "Bitch Manifesto": Can women oppress women? But the question was avoided by arguing that middle-class and ruling-class women were actually suffering if we measured suffering in terms of their *female experience*. At least one feminist saw fit to meet these attacks on the bourgeois nature of feminism with an equally passionate defense of the powerlessness of ruling class women. "The threat of the bourgeois woman is in part purely and simply a reflection of masculine ideology, of sexism. This produces, and is manifest by, among other things, the displacement of hatred of the oppressor—the capitalist—on to his servants and possessions. The 'bourgeois woman' is the favorite target of 'male revolutionaries.' She is hated much more than the real oppressor, the bourgeois man."[26]

To argue persuasively that oppression was common to all women, feminists had to define oppression differently. And this new definition had to accommodate middle- and upper-class women. However, early feminists could point to no theory that proved that women as women were in an *objectively* oppressed situation. For that matter, there was virtually no political theory that referred to women at all except in derogatory terms.[27] Although radical feminists perceived a need to design a concept that might provide some irrefutable grounding for the idea that women per se were oppressed, the task at hand presented an extreme difficulty.

The solution that prevailed was to define "oppression" subjectively. Oppression included anything that women *experienced* as oppressive. It is important to note that as with the concept Woman, the subjectivism of nascent feminist theory was developed as an exact inversion, an opposition to, the allegedly objective view of oppression outlined above. Once again, the prevailing patriarchal categories were not altered, but merely reversed. The radical feminists' solution worked against what they perceived as objective theories of oppression by asserting the validity of a subjective one. This counter-formulation also warded off those who claimed that sexual problems were invalid because subjective and personal. "Experience" became the byword of the new feminism.

We regard our personal experiences and our feelings about that experience as the basis for an analysis of our common situation. We cannot rely on existing ideologies as they are all products of male supremacist culture. We question every generalization and accept none that are not confirmed by our experience.[28]

The Redstockings manifesto (quoted above) invokes the inability to trust the "male supremacist culture" as justification for the use of experience. In fact, the use of "male" and "female" and the implicit acceptance of the patriarchal alignments of "male" with "objective" make it easy to understand why "female" was eventually linked with "subjective" and "experience" as complements to the category Woman.

In a sense, feminist theory was becoming captured by the patriarchal ideas it sought to oppose. So far, it had created a stereotypical Woman, a monolithic, abstract being defined only by her source of oppression. It then reunited "her" with a notion of subjective experience, which is where "she" had been all along under patriarchy.

The problem of using an experiential standard was reflected in the Redstockings "pro-woman line," an explicit, political position that basically held that, in the name of sisterhood, women should not criticize each other.[29] The idea of experience was necessary because of the need for some kind of evidence that women were oppressed. That is, it was necessary to prove that the category Woman existed because if women did not have something in common, the full analytic value of the major foundational category of feminist theory would disappear. The idea behind experience was that it would unite women through what it was assumed would be their common feelings about oppression.

FALSE CONSCIOUSNESS

But experience had its own problems. First, white, middle-class women generalized from their own particular experiences to arrive at the experiences of women in general. This problem has been explored by many feminist scholars at length.[30] Just now I am more concerned with the second problem, namely, the conceptual appeal to experience made it theoretically difficult if not impossible to discount the opinions and/or actions of any given woman. It should be noted that these are the same problems that arose in the original formulation of the category Woman, problems that had only been deferred by transferring them onto experience. The original problem was with men's reactions to the idea of women's oppression. The new problem reflected women's reactions to it. The problem was this: Real women often had different, even contradictory, interests based on class, race, or individual politics.

A related problem was that many women either did not feel oppressed or, if feeling it, did not admit it. But by now, the ideas of Woman and experience reinforced each other such that the movement seems to have had a lot at stake in maintaining them as a unit. Still, the contradiction between (what turned out to be a hypothesis about) women's common experience and the reactions of real women to feminism did not go unnoticed in radical feminist circles.

Clearly, some way had to be found to discount or at least to criticize the ideas of women who rejected feminist liberation. The predicament had to be handled delicately since the coherence of the original category Woman depended on universal inclusion. It followed that women who did not feel oppressed suffered from some form of "false consciousness." Early radical feminists concluded that some women were "male identified" as they were unable to subjectively differentiate their interests as women from those of men. Male identification became the feminist version of false consciousness and was viewed with appropriate suspicion by many early radical feminists, some of whom mistakenly attributed it to an authoritarian Marxist influence. In fact it stemmed from feminism itself, following easily from experience.

The idea of male identification was not without its difficulties. False consciousness arguments necessarily presuppose some notion of objective truth according to which one can judge a thing to be false. But feminists had spent a good amount of time debunking arguments based on objectivity and many had come to mistrust them as "male." Since feminism had made subjective experience so important to its own theory, it really had no working notion of truth apart from experience. Nonetheless, an objective, but never explicitly stated, definition of "the objective truth of female oppression" was employed every time someone dismissed the experiences of "male-identified" women. Truly, if women were allowed to define their own ideas of oppression, there was no theoretical basis upon which radical feminists could claim that women's perceptions of those experiences were false. The fact is, a feminist false consciousness argument was utterly insupportable if feminists were to base their analyses upon women's experiences.

Anyway, feminists had yet to define what was meant by male and female and thus had no way, really, to differentiate male identification from female or feminist identification. Without knowing what was meant by Woman, feminism could not recognize her experiences. Thus, at that early stage in feminist theory, it had already come full circle and returned to the problem of defining Woman.

Experience was to have profound ramifications for feminist theories of knowledge. Gradually, feminists began to see objectivity as an exclusionary device.[31] This was, after all, what the short history of feminism's association with the Left showed. Given this equation of objectivity and maleness, feminists reasoned, it followed that every theory and institution based upon so-called objective truth embodied a male bias. Furthermore, if the very idea of objectivity could not be trusted to be "objective" (in this case meaning gender neutral) what could? And so it was that the appeal to experience was also a nascent claim about epistemology. In short, female "knowledge" subjectively determined was the only knowledge women could trust. All of this became attached to a new notion of politics. "Personal politics," once a contradiction in terms, became the third core concept of feminist theory.

THE PERSONAL IS POLITICAL

"The personal is political" was a slogan used in feminism to combat the charge that women's problems were merely personal complaints. Just as the ideas of Woman and experience were the result of debates with the Left, so too "the personal is political" was an appropriation of Left ideas and an opposition to its criticisms. Part of the justification New Left men used to exclude women from their political analysis was that female problems were "personal" while the problems addressed by them were "political." The implication was that political was always more important than personal, the latter being whining and womanly. Radical feminists responded by dubbing the personal political. As theory, the new feminist formulation included three postulates: first, that there was a system of gender domination; second, that that system was political; and, third, that the personal was political in a direct and immediate sense. Personal politics carried with it expansive notions of political oppression, issues, and institutions. Personal politics was the third ingredient in the three-pronged system of radical feminist concepts which was the harbinger of feminist theory.

This time the problem of objectivity emerged in the form of a lack of empirically observable institutions of domination. Indeed, the controversial issues raised by the women's liberation movement were defined as political despite the fact that they lacked the presence of what were traditionally taken to be coercive institutions such as capitalism or the state. Radical feminists set about to define "political" so that it could accommodate the new notions of domination and oppression. One defined a political institution simply as any structured activity that perpetuated male domination,[32] thus assuming a new and as yet unnamed political system in which men were the ruling class.

Kate Millet summarized her definition of politics as follows:

> When one group rules another, the relationship between the two is political. When such an arrangement is carried over a long period of time it develops an ideology (feudalism, racism, etc.). All historical civilizations are patriarchies: their ideology is male supremacy.[33]

Politics, she said, involves a power relationship regardless of whether or not that power has to do with the public sphere.

Other radical feminist groups and theorists made the same claim that politics was essentially power, though some set about to uncover the political institutions that supported this power. Atkinson defended her notion of sexual intercourse as a political institution by invoking the philosophy of John Rawls. In quoting him she defined institutions as "any form of activity specified by a system of rules which defines offices, roles, moves, penalties, defenses, and so on, and which gives the activity its structure."[34]

Atkinson used Rawls's definition by giving a very broad and construction to his use of the term "rules." Moreover, she did not
attempt to enumerate those rules. It would have been helpful, for
example, to know the nature of the rule that maintains sexual intercourse as an institution. In Atkinson's formulation, rules are not
legal, and may not even be explicit. In fact, in the case of gender relations, they are *usually* completely invisible ideological constructs that
are internalized as the norm within female consciousness (the point
about the invisibility of the system of gender was also employed by
Firestone). Atkinson discusses the institution of sexual intercourse
and the rules that maintain it as being part of a system of institutions
and rules that consistently keep men in power and women oppressed.
Thus, she argued, social convention is in reality the ideology of male
domination. It followed easily from this that radical feminists should
critically investigate every male-dominated "institution" and "rule."

There is evidence that this new conceptualization of political rules
was also explored with regard to sexuality. For example, Anne Koedt
used it in her essay on the "Myth of the Vaginal Orgasm."[35] In providing a feminist analysis to the work of sex researchers Masters and
Johnson, Koedt reiterated that it was the clitoris and not the vagina
that was the source of female sexual arousal. If vaginal orgasms were
a myth, the origins of that myth could be traced to the fact that male
sexual pleasure was induced by intercourse. It was therefore logical in
patriarchal terms that society assumed female behavior to be physically analogous to the male and that deviation would be viewed by
the dominant culture as "incorrect." Therefore, it came as no surprise
to Koedt that women who did not have orgasms from intercourse
were labeled "frigid." Koedt argued that they could be sexually
aroused in ways that may not automatically stimulate men and that,
therefore, the label "frigid" constituted a type of coercion, or in
Atkinson's terms, a rule.

Atkinson expounded upon sexuality further in addressing the
problem of how feminists were to deal with the fact that some
women claimed they had vaginal orgasms. To the contrary, Atkinson
argued that the function of vaginal orgasm (as well as childbearing)
was to oppress women,[36] and that the presence of vaginal orgasmic
capabilities in some women was, in fact, a mass hysterical survival

response, no different in physical form than a "facial tic." That which seemed to disprove the theory was only oppression in disguise, or male-identified experience.

> Vaginal orgasm is an excellent illustration of the way men oppress and exploit women. It's ironic that you insist men and women respond the same in the one place no one can deny men and women are different—in their genitals . . . Male orgasm is analogous to clitoral orgasm. Where, then, does the vaginal orgasm come from? People say its learned. And by God you'd better learn it, lady, especially if you're with a liberal man; you'd better learn to shuffle nigger . . .

As Atkinson theorized it, orgasms were a feminist political issue and sexual intercourse itself was a major political institution.[37] But, she argued, vaginal orgasms should be a central concern of feminism only insofar as the myth explained the continued acceptance by women of the oppressive institution of marriage.

> The construct of vaginal orgasm is most in vogue whenever and wherever the institution of sexual intercourse is threatened. As women become freer, more independent, more self sufficient, their interests in (i.e., their need for) men decreases.[38]

Atkinson was taking this idea to its logical conclusion when she said that "feminism is the theory and lesbianism the practice."[39] That is, women's continued participation in institutions of male domination served to buttress and legitimate those institutions and in doing so it seriously damaged feminist attempts to liberate women.

One of the most controversial analyses made by radical feminists was one that explained love as an institutional weapon of the oppressor. Once again Atkinson emerged as a fabulous rhetorician and theoretical talent: "The most common female escape is the psychopathological condition of love . . . in which the victim transforms her oppressor into her redeemer."[40] In a manifesto of The Feminists, one of the feminist groups to which Atkinson belonged, love, sex, and the family are pointed to as the clearest examples of institutions "designed on the assumption and reinforcement of the male and female role system." As such, these institutions had to be "annihilated."[41] Similarly, Shulamith Firestone called love "the pivot of women's oppression today," reasoning that "men were thinking, writing, and creating, because women were pouring their energy into those men; women are not creating culture because they are preoccupied with love."[42]

The new definition of personal politics carried with it vastly expanded notions of institutions, oppression, coercion, and rules. Politics was defined as a system of male domination in which women were complicitous out of love (manipulation), male identification, and fear. Indeed fear was sometimes the result of "terrorism." Indeed, it was this political language of terrorism that formed a theoretical basis for the early feminist analysis of rape.

> To see rape within the system of female oppression is to understand its non-accidental and non-arbitrary nature and to gain insight into its special purpose for the class of men . . . Rape supports the male class by projecting its power and aggressiveness on the world. For the individual male, the possibility of rape remains a prerogative of his in-group; its perpetration rekindles his faith in maleness and his own personal worth.[43]

Once one assumed that women were oppressed as women and that women's experiences were the proof of their oppression, it followed that female political oppression had to be charted where women experienced it: in their daily lives. Therefore, "the personal is political" combined with the categories "men" and "women" to facilitate the idea that a system of domination was entrenched at the level of every woman's most intimate relation with every man and that those relationships were, moreover, political.

This formulation too began as a strategy to oppose New Left criticisms of feminist practice as "not political." For example, in a defense of consciousness-raising groups, which the nonfeminist Left derided as therapy, Carol Hanish persuasively argued that consciousness raising was itself a political act and that so-called personal problems could only be solved collectively.

> One of the first things we discover in these [CR] groups is that personal problems are political problems. There are no personal solutions at this time. There is only collective action for a collective

> solution . . . I am getting a gut understanding of everything as opposed to the esoteric, intellectual understandings and noblesse oblige feelings I had in "other peoples" struggles.[44]

Hanish seems to be suggesting in the above that there was an inherent link between collective and political solutions to problems. Of course, it is not at all clear that collective action is always political action. Sadly, many such enormously provocative ideas from early radical feminist manifestos and pamphlets remain to this day undefined and untheorized.

The presence of political problems suggests the presence of a political system of domination. By describing every problem in political terms, radical feminists found themselves in the methodologically tenuous position of positing an almost mystical, invisible, transhistorical, cross-cultural political system. Hanish's statement about consciousness raising (above) reflects this new definition of politics, which can be summarized as follows: Politics was (1) that which involved power and (2) that which must be dealt with collectively. In fact, positing a transhistorical, cross-cultural political system, the purpose of which was to oppress women, left the theorist in the position of viewing every relationship between men and women as a relation of power (i.e., political) and of finding it difficult to ever conceive of any such relationship in any other terms.

The politicization of personal experience meant that politics did not always include visible coercive institutions such as the state and the workplace. Since it had been established that all relations involving power were political, and that men oppressed women, it only remained to explain exactly what form that political oppression took in specific cases. Moreover, female oppression was not always apparent because it seemed to be part of the "natural" order of things. If true, it was possible that it could *only* be detected subjectively and that previous theories about domination and oppression were based on a misunderstanding of power. What is more, what had been understood as symbolic or psychological oppression could now be termed the result of a newly discovered political system. Now, e.g., the verbal harassment an upper-class woman might suffer from male construction workers was not merely symbolic of women's place in society, but actually was political oppression in and of itself since it was an expression of a political relationship between men and women. In short, the idea of personal politics allowed the now familiar feminist political analysis of personal life.

Radical feminists subsequently labeled the oppressive political system of male domination "patriarchy." Patriarchal institutions were those which had developed in the context of and adopted the style, form, or effects of male domination. Since male domination was present across time and cultures, very few institutions could be conceptualized as having escaped patriarchy. And since patriarchal male-domination existed in every sphere, virtually anything could be defined as political. The new political analysis strongly implied that women shared a reality apart from men. Male domination, the early radical feminists argued, excluded women from history, theory, and politics, and from all prevailing explanations of reality.

But to whom radical feminists were referring when they spoke of "women," what was implied in the term "experience," and what was included in "personal politics" all had yet to be explained. Along with its enormous insights and tremendously powerful prose, this triage of questions remains the albatross around the neck of feminist theory. The task of answering these questions has proved endless. It is, unfortunately, one of the major legacies of early radical feminism.

3

Feminist Strategies: From Core Concepts to Feminist Theory

The core concepts, especially the ideas of Woman and experience, have become foundational to feminist theory. Likewise, the idea of personal politics effectively forms the backdrop for what is considered political by feminists. The tendency to see the world as gendered, and to buttress the category Woman with some notion of experience was evident even in early radical feminist texts in which it was taken for granted that, in the words of Shulamith Firestone, "there exists a wholly different reality for men and women."[1]

By now, this early idea that male and female experiences differ, and that those differences have important implications, in particular for theories of knowledge, is nearly the orthodoxy in academic feminism. Knowledge, it is held, is apprehended directly through gendered experiences, and all knowledge that we have heretofore viewed as "truth" is really something more like male opinion. That is, "objectivity" is really the misnomer given to the world when it is viewed and experienced from the "male perspective." As Alice Jardin has written, "Feminism, while infinite in its variations, is finally rooted in the belief that women's truth-in-experience-and-reality is and always has been different from men's and that it as well as its artifacts and productions have consequently been devalued and always already delegitimized in patriarchal culture."[2]

The claim about gendered experience and knowledge has led to a very involved search for a feminist epistemology. Presumably, this would be an epistemology that would account for the gendered differences in knowledge implicit in the idea of gendered experiences. The search for a feminist epistemology has also sought a foundational grounding in "truth." At least initially, feminists wanted to develop a metaphysic that would "prove," if you will, the authenticity of both the category Woman and of her experiences. The implication was further that this theory was necessary to provide a foundation to feminist notions about personal politics. The claim that politics is not just about government and in fact exists everywhere was justified by the idea that experiences matter and the belief that women inhabit a different reality than men.

The search for an epistemological foundation has been fraught with problems. For one, the move toward an experiential epistemology has necessarily created problems with regard to the category Woman. That is, the notion of gendered experience and knowledge suggests a universal female experience. If knowledge is not gendered, there seems to be little use in developing or making any point about the need for a feminist epistemology. Furthermore, the very idea of epistemology assumes a subject and an object—a knower and a known—both of which must be described and named.[3] Therefore, it became incumbent upon feminists to define and describe who women are (and what Woman is) in order to say exactly what it is that she knows, how this knowledge differs from "male" knowledge, and why female knowledge is important for feminism. Finally, in epistemological discussions all of this defining and describing takes place a priori. The question of "what women know" becomes a very abstract one.

For a movement that tries to be conscious of the myriad natures of women, the problem of defining women's knowledge is especially nettlesome. It does not take much familiarity with feminism to know that real women are divided by the cross-cutting experiences of other oppressed peoples (African Americans, Latinas, lesbians, etc.). Further, the very nature of experientialism suggests that all of these groups have equal claims to defining their own realities.[4] Thus, it has proved hard to argue that the perspective of *women* should be privileged in an experiential knowledge system. Yet, if no one is privileged, the fear is that we will be led down a spiral to a completely relativistic, pluralistic, ever-expanding additive model of theories of knowledge. The experiences of black women, Jewish lesbians, Jewish lesbian mothers, etc., etc., etc., would all have to be included as unique "perspectives" on reality. The more marginal the perspective, the closer it would mirror reality. This notion, then, constructs unity as problematic.

It is also not clear how to define what counts as a group. An experiential standard seems to suggest that groups would self-select. But sometimes groups *feel* beleaguered when they clearly are not (I am thinking here of so-called "White Power" groups, or the young white men in my undergraduate women's studies classes). On the other hand, why should only victims get to define reality? Why not any group at all which claims specialized knowledge? Even if we accede that victims' knowledges count more, what about competing claims by various victims? This is especially a problem if none of the classes are distinct (e.g., the category *women* includes African Americans and vice versa). Related to all of this is the question of why the experiences of a given group need to be included to make the human view of the world "whole." Once again, when all is said and done, it is unclear why the experiences of "women" would count more heavily than those of any other group as being "true" measures of reality. But if the experiences of women do not count more heavily than those of others, have we not transmuted feminism into a type of humanism? Is it acceptable for feminism to drift into a type of humanism?

Many feminists have grappled with these formidable concerns, some with more success than others. One way to avoid devolving into a completely pluralistic theory of knowledge would be to conceptualize "women" as the primary category of oppression from which all others follow. This strategy is exemplified in the early work of Adrienne Rich[5] and has been followed by other radical feminists, such as Gerda Lerner.[6] Rich's later work, however, obliquely wonders about the epistemological problems posed by identity, the category Woman, and the idea of a female experience.

Iris Marion Young has ventured to solve the problems of feminist epistemology by coming up with a plan in which experiences of oppression are determined in practice rather than in theory. Rather than beginning with epistemology, Young argues, we must begin from a commitment to justice defined as an aversion to oppression and domination.[7] A society based on such a concept of justice would, moreover, have to be based on some notion of group oppression rather than a merely individualist one. A social group, writes Young, "is a collective of persons differentiated from at least one other group by cultural forms, practices or way of life. Members of a group have a specific affinity with one another because of their similar experience or way of life . . . a group exists only in relation to at least one other group." Thus, a group would be defined in practice and its experiences would count definitively as knowledge only insofar as it is oppressed or dominated by another group. This privileging would be justified by the initial premise that the main goal of the society is to promote a particular definition of justice as being against group domination. Moreover, groups would exist within groups to deal with the problem of multiple oppression. Thus, the group "African Americans" would include within it the group "gay African Americans" and the group "gay" would include a group "gay African Americans," etc. This justice-oriented scheme allows Young to talk about experience and insure diversity while avoiding the usual epistemological morass.

Innovative questions and solutions like those suggested by Young and some works by Rich have been a long time coming. What I do in this chapter is follow the development of three strains of feminist theory. I look at these as three potentially corrective strategies for problems with the core concepts and discuss the successes and failures of each in regard to that project. As I talk about the evolution of the core concepts in this way, I have in mind to show two things: (1) the problems usually restricted to critiques of radical feminism are far more widespread than is usually admitted and (2) the problems stem almost entirely from the attempt to use the core concepts as a foundation for feminist thought. Most of the problems I pointed to at the beginning of this chapter are usually leveled as criticisms against radical feminism or one or another given feminist theorist. In fact, the problems that have been associated with radical feminism persist throughout contemporary feminist theory. Feminism as a whole has actually been remarkably responsible at attempting to rectify problems like the exclusion of women of color, the bias toward middle-class women, and the problem of defining women's experiences. But overall, the problems persist. I think the core concepts are part of the reason why.

One strategy for dealing with the concepts has been socialist feminism. It is a particularly interesting case. Socialist feminism was developed explicitly in contradistinction to early radical feminist ideas, which were viewed as insensitive to differences among women and overly essentialist. The solution suggested by socialist feminism was to talk about women in their myriad existences and to search for a material grounding for the notion of male domination. This grounding would enable us to historicize and deessentialize the concepts of male and female while still tracking women's experiences. The failure of socialist feminism to accomplish this is one of the most compelling proofs of the impossibility of grounding feminism in the core concepts as presently constructed.

While socialist feminists sought solutions to the essentialism and abstraction of the category Woman in Marxist historicism, other feminists sought instead to ground feminism in one or another universal female experience. Mothering and female sexuality have been two popular suggestions in this regard. I will analyze the use of each here.

In both instances, feminist theorists have argued that these common experiences are universal, but socially produced (again in order to avoid the charge of essentialism). But the important point is that the notion of a universal female experience was necessary in order to ground feminism. Yet, the need to prove this at all, and moreover to prove it in terms of experience, is itself merely a relic of early radical feminist rhetoric. The more I review the way these concepts have grown out of early radical feminism, the more I am convinced that this rhetoric has grown into high theory far beyond the expectations of the original radical feminists. This has occurred without sufficient feminist critical self-reflection.

THE CORE CONCEPTS IN SOCIALIST FEMINISM

In general, socialist feminists since Juliet Mitchell have accepted the core concepts, but not without debate. They have also tried to improve them by subjecting them to historical material analysis in order to concretize the abstract category Woman.[8] Like Marxists, socialist feminists have connected politics to economics. In so doing socialist feminists have expanded the core concept "the personal is political" into one that includes economic relationships by noting that the power of gender is also related to class and economic interests.[9]

Early socialist feminists had two audiences. Besides grappling with issues raised by radical feminist formulations, socialist feminists were "trying to be good marxists . . . [and] trying to create a theoretical language that paralleled marxism," one that was "more likely to be heard by marxists" than was radical feminist theory.[10] Unfortunately, since the response of most Marxists has been to ignore both socialist and Marxist feminist analyses, Marxism has remained decidedly untouched by feminism.[11] That this has been so thoroughly ignored is itself an example of why feminism is necessary.

In fact, socialist feminism was never able to explain why women have been systematically oppressed across cultures and time, nor exactly how this oppression can be materially grounded so that one can comprehend the universal construction of genders in a nonessentialist way.[12] The aim of the following analysis is emphatically not condemnation. The point is, rather, to show that most of the criticisms currently lodged against radical feminists and their categories *remain present in subsequent feminist theories, including socialist feminism.* This is true even when, as is the case with socialist feminism, the core concepts are discussed and attacked head on. It is important to understand why this is so.

Despite many attempts, socialist feminists have thus far been unable to put forth a convincing feminist-materialist analysis, let alone one that is able to explain the intersections of race, class, and gender. Still, it must be said, as Barbara Ehrenreich has observed in defending socialist feminism, "No longer do people who meet, as many of us did, intensely and repeatedly, with an agenda of discovering the connections between *everything*—sex and class, housework and factory work, the family and the state, race and gender, sexuality and profits. If 'capitalism plus patriarchy' was too easy an answer, at least we [the socialist feminists of the 1970s] asked the right questions."[13]

Socialist feminist endeavors to synthesize Marxist and feminist categories somehow missed the important fact that the core concepts were developed in opposition to the Left and were, almost by definition, antithetical to Marxism, or at least to a particular version of it.[14] Moreover, as Seyla Benhabib and Drucilla Cornell have pointed out, the call to unite Marxism and feminism relied on a particular interpretation of Marxism, namely, orthodox Marxist-Leninism. They remind us that "the concept of production, which is based on the model of an active subject transforming, making and shaping an object given to it" may not be "adequate for comprehending activities like childbearing and rearing, care of the sick and elderly," which are "intersubjective" activities.[15] Charting the genesis and evolution of this attempt are, however, instructive in terms of the history of feminist theory.

The clearest example of the problematic nature of this synthesis of Marxism and feminism is illustrated by the socialist feminist use of the idea of experience. Since it is a subjective notion developed as a way to combat the Marxist claim that one's oppression could be determined objectively by one's class position,[16] there has always been an epistemological contradiction between it and Marxism. From the perspective of Marxism, theories based on experience fall into the irrationalist tradition Marx criticized.[17] Because of contradictions like that one, Marxism has not proven useful to feminist analyses that rely on the core concepts. Therefore, many of the original problems with the core concepts have only resurfaced in a different form in socialist feminism.

Socialist feminists tried to improve feminist theory by addressing the abstract nature of the category Woman. As originally constituted, this category derived from the idea that all women were oppressed as women, which exacerbated the difficulty of addressing issues such as the class differences among women. By the same token, the feeling was growing that the feminist notion of experience only described the experiences of the middle-class women who published in journals and wrote manifestos. In her 1972 assessment of the class issue, Charlotte

Bunch wrote with some bitterness that "recently, the primary reaction has been to retreat from the issue [of class] and label it divisive to a feminist movement."[18] Class could only be divisive to a nascent theory that had much at stake in the notion that what was common to all women was far more crucial than anything that was different.

It was not only the category Woman that had become problematic. Rita Mae Brown expressed concern over the feminist use of "feelings" (i.e., experience as feminism understood the term at that point), which she connected to a lack of class analysis.

> Many middle class women, fearing that intellect will be mistaken for middle class behavior and remembering *their* college experience, bury their brains in a morass of "vibes," "gut feeling," and outright hysteria. This is dogmatically declared "true woman" behavior since men don't express their feelings . . . Such an idea spells death to real political change if people cling to it.[19]

In anticipation of socialist feminism, Brown suggested a revision of Marx that would define class more broadly to include how "you think, feel and act."

Eventually, socialist feminists found the idea of experience problematic (in ways that Brown did not predict) because it assumed that all women had similar experiences of womanhood and of oppression; that is, it did not account for differences among women. Furthermore, socialist feminists contended, it contained no sense of history, culture, or class. Similarly, the notion that patriarchy was the operative system in the oppression of all women everywhere could not account for variations in oppression such as the exploitation all people experience under capitalism. An extraordinary element of the story of socialist feminism is precisely the extent to which the usefulness of the core concepts was discussed and debated before the concepts were accepted as fundamental aspects of socialist feminism.

During the mid-1970s some feminists began to explore the idea that existing socialist and feminist theories were equally inadequate to understanding oppression. Yet, at the same time there was an intuitive conviction that the two theories were politically compatible and that each could complement the goals of the other. As Ehrenreich wrote, "We know that there is a political consistency to socialist feminism."[20]

What was under contention was exactly how much socialism and how much feminism should be included in the new socialist feminist analysis. For example, criticisms leveled against the 1975 Antioch conference on socialist feminism show that the core radical feminist assumptions were, at this stage, coming under close scrutiny. Nancy Hartsock complained of the conference that many of the participants believed that beginning with personal experience was wrong,[21] and that very few of the speakers had any concept of patriarchy at all. Thus, for Hartsock, there was very little feminism and too much socialism.[22] Hartsock, in contradistinction to those she criticized, accepted the core concepts of radical feminism and sought to a way to transfer them in toto to the new socialist feminist discourse.

Clearly, then, one aspect of the debate in early socialist feminism was a questioning of the extent to which the core concepts should be maintained in materialist feminism. The view that eventually prevailed claimed to seek a true integration of feminism and socialism, but argued that Marxism (and presumably other materialist theories) had to be adapted to feminist categories and goals. That is, the new theory had to center around women's oppression as such.[23] Since the Left did not emphasize gender as a major category, it appeared that the new socialist feminism would have to be relatively autonomous from it.[24]

Importantly, the position of keeping the core concepts and fashioning materialist theories around them was only adopted after considerable debate. The concepts themselves were discussed as being central to feminism, and many of the problems with them were also considered at some length. For example, in a sympathetic critique of Juliet Mitchell's work, Lise Vogel argued that it was a mistake to build a theory around the category Woman.[25] Relying heavily on Marx to stress the importance of categories, she urged instead that socialist women analyze "the family" in its relation to the dominant mode of production.[26] Marxism, Vogel was pointing out, began with a historicized category (class), and feminism should do the same. Vogel used Marxist categories to reason that women were but one aspect of a larger oppression that permeated both the spheres of production and reproduction. Other feminists insisted that socialist feminists, "while agreeing that there is something timeless and universal about women's oppression, have insisted that it takes different forms in different settings, and that the *differences* are of vital importance."[27]

Indeed, the early 1970s were marked by various similar critiques of feminist goals made from the perspective of a socialism sympathetic to feminism. In a 1973 critique, Eli Zaretsky urged feminists to make use of Marxism. However, Zaretsky was also wary of socialists in that they had mistakenly restricted "the meaning of the economy to the sphere of surplus value." In so doing they "lost the sense of capitalism as an integrated social system."[28] On the other hand he said, radical feminists "assumed the view of the family and personal life as a separate sphere ruled by its own laws." Zaretsky claimed that radical feminists had made a methodological error in failing to conceive of the family as historically specific.[29] In being ahistorical they were led to accept such stereotypes as the "moral superiority" of women and the "idea of woman's culture," which grew out of the desire to praise women's experiences but which did not take into account the social construction of those experiences. Ultimately, Zaretsky suggested that women's liberation could not be achieved unless the family became less private.

Juliet Mitchell made the first comprehensive attempt to synthesize Marxism and feminism into the mode that we now recognize as socialist feminist.[30] Speaking to a dual audience of socialists and feminists, Mitchell urged feminists to see women's problems as (only) one of the possible major oppressions in presocialist societies.[31] To socialists she explained that an analysis of women was important since women were the most international of any group and experienced their oppression in the most immediate way, in the home.[32] Thus women, unlike any other group, were oppressed in all realms. Ultimately, Marxism without feminism was only an abstract (because ungendered) socialism,[33] while feminism without Marxism tended to overemphasize the primacy of woman's oppression.

Mitchell proposed to combine Marxian economic analysis with the feminist idea that women were oppressed as women. Mitchell also included the relatively new feminist ideas about experience and personal politics. Succinctly explaining her understanding of the role of experience she said,

> The politics of experience is the term now loosely used to suggest an
> analysis of society from the perspective of one's self. The experience
> of personal alienation is the means of testing the total social alien-
> ation which is the product of our decaying capitalist society.[34]

Cautiously accepting the radical feminist use of experience, Mitchell
pointed out that even though it played into the stereotypes of
women,[35] it was useful in combating what she perceived to be a male
style. One should not "only analyze the so-called 'objective' situation" because this "normally means, quite simply, somebody else's
problems somewhere else."[36] According to Mitchell, a socialist feminism would expand upon the radicals' uses of experience, personal
politics, and Woman by concentrating upon the structures that reproduced female experience.[37] For Mitchell it was in this study of
structures that Marxism could prove useful. Mitchell suggested that
further study be devoted to four areas that she claimed led to the
"structural domination of women." Those areas were: (1) production,
(2) reproduction, (3) sexuality, and (4) the socialization of children.[38]

This idea articulated so clearly by Mitchell, that there were material structure(s) that oppressed women, had a profound effect on
feminism. In the same way that Shulamith Firestone's book had
raised many of the questions that feminists would debate for the
decade to follow, Mitchell's list of areas where women were "structurally dominated" in society became, in effect, the agenda for
socialist feminist scholarship, far surpassing other socialist feminist
work of the period in its impact. It is also important to note that her
work contributed heavily to the transference of the core concepts to
the new socialist feminism.

Ultimately, socialist feminism has devoted much time to studying
the structure and historical nature of "patriarchy." Therefore, it is
worth differentiating the socialist feminist understanding of that term
from the radical feminist one in relation to the core concepts. The
main difference is that the socialist feminist notion of patriarchy conceptualizes patriarchy as a *structure* with a material basis, while
radical feminists tend to think of it as the *idea* or the day-to-day lived
reality that men universally oppress women.[39] Both, however, are
linked to the core concepts in maintaining that all women (are)
oppressed, albeit by a gender-based system of domination that may

vary according to the mode of production.[40] The socialist feminist analysis is historical to the extent that it accepts variation among women across time and cultures, and it is economic in that it attempts to link women's oppression to the modes of production and reproduction.

Socialist feminists have also used the idea of experience in their work on "modes of reproduction"[41] and "domestic labor."[42] As Zillah Eisenstein has explained the connection, "Our daily lives are the materialization at a personal level of the features of the social formation as a whole."[43] The idea of using Marx to understand issues of personal politics proposes generalizing from the particular experiences of women to know the general experience of Woman. Significantly, this formulation exactly reverses the Marxist dialectic, which was to begin with the universal in analyzing the particular and, from the perspective of Marxism, it is a methodological error.

Nancy Hartsock has emphasized the importance of the idea of experience, and alluded to the contradictions feminist experientialism posed between feminists and the rest of the left: "We cannot work . . . with people who will not use their own experience as a fundamental basis for knowledge . . . The only condition for coalition with other groups is that those groups share our method."[44] Indeed, Hartsock's position, that experience qua experience is actually an epistemological category, makes good sense when one considers the perennial feminist problem. Namely, if one does not accept experience as the basis for knowledge, the category Woman becomes conceptually problematic insofar as it is confronted with other critical theories that claim that some women are not in fact oppressed. Socialist feminists insist that there are at least two characteristics determinant of oppression and exploitation. These two, class and gender,[45] are often compounded by others such as race, ethnicity, and sexual preference. This formulation of oppression attempts to expand upon the Marxist view that class is the primary oppression.

Socialist feminists have employed the Marxist method to address the problem of women's oppression by assuming that "one can do this because marxist analysis provides the tools for understanding all power relations; there is nothing about the dialectical and historical method that limits it to understanding class relations."[46] Unfortunately, this is not true. The Marxian method relies on the idea that class conflict is the fundamental driving force of history. All power relations can be understood by using Marxism, it is true, but when using Marxism all power will be understood as related somehow to capitalism and class domination. The attempt to adapt Marxism to feminism has resulted in a metaphorical use of Marxist terms such as "production" and "reproduction."

This calls to mind Zaretsky's early critique of socialist feminist's failure to remember that, for Marx, capitalism is an integrated social system. In contrast, socialist feminists tend to think of production and reproduction as absolutely separate, not unlike the liberal public/private dichotomy.

> Of special interest to feminists is the fact that childbearing and childbearing practices are taken to be part of the non-economic or "superstructural" realm. Socialist feminists propose a much broader interpretation of these categories . . . Not only are the means to satisfy the needs for children and for sexual and emotional satisfaction produced through human labor; humans can also distribute and exchange the means of fulfilling these needs . . . Because these sorts of transactions are possible, the system of producing and distributing the means to satisfy needs for children, for sexual satisfaction and for emotional nurturance is in fact an economic system . . .[47]

The socialist feminist formulation conceptualizes production and reproduction as separate and then claims that the separation is male biased. This fundamentally misunderstands Marx. Marx did not want to show an absolute separation between production and reproduction, but, on the contrary, discussed the necessary relationship between the two as one of the defining characteristics of capitalism. Marxism, socialist feminists contend, wrongly puts women in the realm of reproduction and thereby claims that women's labor is not productive. However, Marx uses the word "unproductive" not as a value-laden pejorative, but as a way to indicate that no commodity is being directly produced. Marx is well aware that production cannot exist without reproduction and that each is a moment of the other.

What Marx meant by reproduction was much more than "that which occurs in the home." It included many activities outside the home such as education and the circulation of capital (e.g., teaching is, technically speaking, unproductive labor).[48] Expanding the category "production" to include reproductive activities invites one to question whether the system being described by socialist feminists can still be called capitalistic in Marx's sense. Marx set up the original categories and analyzed them separately precisely to stress that surplus value is extracted in a wage labor system that separates production from reproduction. Marx's concepts of "class" and "exploitation" depend on this separation.

Obviously, one does not stop being a worker upon leaving the factory, but one is not always a worker in precisely the same way. Thus, one cannot speak of "workers" or "classes" in the sphere of reproduction[49] in the same sense that one can speak of them in the productive realm. Women in working-class families are members of the proletariat because their objective class interests are the same as workers laboring outside the home, but, at least in Marxism, they cannot be considered a class in and of themselves any more than unemployed men whose roots are working class can be. In short, any usage that speaks of classes in the realm of reproduction as though the latter were an unmediated part of the production process is a merely metaphorical one and uses Marxist categories analogously rather than analytically.

Marx claims neither that production and consumption are completely separate aspects of the production process, nor that they are one and the same. Indeed, his point is that questions that inquire *only* into their relationship are irrelevant and abstract. In this regard he soundly criticized bourgeois economists who focused only upon production and consumption, exposing their error as the result of a tendency "to regard society as one subject . . . With a single subject, production and consumption appear as moments of a single act . . . in which production is the real point of departure and hence also the predominant moment."[50] Socialist feminists make the same error in focusing on reproduction as a way to analyze all women.

The point is similar in regard to production and consumption. Marx claims that neither can be understood apart from distribution, or, in effect, apart from class. The key to the production/consumption relationship, Marx claimed, was distribution. Thus, class is the most important factor in understanding the realms of production and consumption.

> In society . . . the producer's relation to the product, once the latter is finished, is an external one, and its return to the subject depends on his relations to other individuals . . .
>
> *Distribution* steps between the producers and the products, hence between production and consumption, to determine in accordance with social laws what the producers share will be in the world of products.

That is, the problem is not that capitalism produces too well, but that it distributes too poorly and unevenly. Moreover, in a market economy, demand is defined not by need, but by ability to pay. Thus, a rational capitalist will be more likely to produce what is demanded by the rich who are able to pay than what is needed by the poor who are not. The system of distribution, therefore, determines what is produced.[51]

> Production creates the objects which correspond to the given needs; distribution divides them up according to social laws; exchange further parcels out the already divided shares in accord with individual needs; and finally, in consumption, the product steps outside this social movement and becomes a direct object and servant of individual need, and satisfies it in being consumed . . . Thus production, distribution, exchange and consumption form a regular syllogism; production is the generality, distribution and exchange the particularity, and consumption the singularity in which the whole is joined together.

In linking feminism to historical materialism, socialist feminists have rejected in principle the a priori, naturalistic quality associated with the radical feminist construction of the category Woman. Likewise, many socialist feminists have been actively critical of the romanticization of female nature that is connected to the organicization of the category Woman.[52] However, none of this means that socialist feminists have been successful in developing a materialist feminist theory. The category Woman remains a transhistorical one in socialist feminist work. For the most part, socialist feminists begin from the assumption that all women everywhere are oppressed and use materialist analysis as a way to prove this on a case-by-case basis. However, the analysis assumes what it seeks to prove in that it begins from the premise of universal female oppression. Gayle Rubin suggested very early on that to find valid results one cannot begin from this assumption. Thus, her "sex-gender system" was an attempt at a non-Marxist materialist theory that does not imply the inevitability of female oppression in every instance.[53]

Despite Rubin's suggestion, socialist feminists have tended to use a double bind theory to claim that although some women are dominated by both men and capitalism, all women are dominated by men.

> We must not just reexamine the way women have been fit into class categories. We must redefine the categories themselves . . . What does it mean to say that a middle-class woman's life is "easier" than a working class woman's life when her status is significantly different from that of a middle class male?[54]

The case of socialist feminism presents an especially stunning illustration of the problems presented by the core concepts. Here is a group of theorists who debated the merits of the concepts, understood their pitfalls, discussed them at some length in the 1970s, and attempted to design a new feminist theory that would solve these problems. And they still failed. The core concepts have failed to generate a feminist theory that works. The same problems continue to recur and reverberate throughout feminism because of our foundational categories.

Socialist feminism is fixed in the feminist tradition insofar as it accepts that women are oppressed as women; that there is a universal female experience of oppression (albeit one that is differentiated by class, race, sexual preference, etc.); that this experience makes the claim about women's oppression valid; and that the personal is political. In using Marxism to rectify problems in the old radical feminist formulations, the problems of knowledge, experience, and the politics thereof have been dealt with in increasingly sophisticated ways. These contemporary feminist theorists have responded to the abstractness of the category Woman by attempting to formulate a materialist theory of women's experience. But socialist feminism is conceptually flawed in that it fails to acknowledge the fundamental, and I think irresolvable, tension between Marxism and the core concepts. In order to use Marxist theory to understand gender, it distorted Marxist categories so badly that they can no longer understand capitalism. Or gender.

Socialist feminists are in fact aware that it would take a materialist grounding for patriarchy to make the socialist feminist understanding of women's oppression markedly better than the original radical feminist idea. Yet, while socialist feminists have suggested that patriarchy has a material base, they have been unable to show how it can exist across so many different modes of production, and on so many different levels within modes of production, except by resorting to radical feminist assumptions about transhistorical male domination.

Neither has socialist feminism made a marked improvement to the original Marxist understanding of female oppression. As socialist feminist critiques of Marxism originally charged, Marxism can explain why there would be a reserve pool of unemployed persons and that there would be a division of labor in the home, but it cannot explain why that reserve pool of unemployed persons is overwhelmingly female. Marxism may have no explanation for why the division of labor in the home is a gendered one, but socialist feminists have not been able to explain this either. The result has more often than not been a series of assertions regarding the presence of patriarchy and male domination, which are then analyzed *alongside* modes of production rather than as integral to them. At best socialist feminism provides a functional explanation for the existence of the sexual division of labor in the home.

In attempting to explain differing levels of oppression among women living in the same modes of production due to racism or anti-Semitism, socialist feminists have layered oppression in double, triple, and even quadruple bind theories.[55] By the same token, explanations about similarities among women living in societies with different modes of production (e.g., the similar situations of upper-class women across cultures) have also been lacking. In each case, the situations of women are explained by recourse to what is, in effect, a tertiary category—patriarchy. Since there is no materialist explanation for the *universal* existence of patriarchy, it can only be explained materially in each of its *specific* manifestations as it is linked expressly to modes of production. Thus, in its transcultural phase, it is still assumed to exist and posited as an idealist or psychological category. Dierdre English summarily laments,

> The whole capitalism plus patriarchy model was a political and theoretical dead end, and that was the basic political model we came up with. Multinational, post-industrial capitalism turned out to be a lot less paternalistic and a lot harsher than we expected . . . The capitalism plus patriarchy model just misconstrues what happened in history: it completely fails to understand that the men who run this system are the sons who overthrew the patriarchal fathers and not the father themselves. It fails to understand the rise of multinational corporate dominance which doesn't see women as women at all—just as workers, and throw away ones at that.[56]

In a way, the use of patriarchy as an explanatory system of domination masks the fact that what is actually being said does not differ that dramatically from the radical feminist notion of domination. The politics and emphases are very different, however, in that socialist feminists are more bothered by issues of race, class, historicity, and in their connection to the left at large. This is not to say that radical feminists are not bothered by racism and classism. They have simply decided to ignore any questions about our ability to invoke "Woman" unproblematically.

Picking up on the problems with any notion of patriarchy, as both Vogel and Rubin did years before, Barrett concluded that it should be replaced by some notion of the "family household system."[57] This system, she argued, exists simultaneously at the levels of the social structure and of ideology. It was not determined by capitalism alone, but originated in precapitalist ideas of "woman's place," which then created the conditions for a sex-based labor market. Thus, Barrett and others seem to have given up on the quest for a materialist feminism, allowing instead that patriarchy is an ideological structure. Other questions having to do with the nature of female oppression, experience, and the category Woman remain unanswered.

This analysis of socialist feminism is important as a review and reassessment of old issues in a new light. What is feminist about socialist feminism? The core concepts. If we look at the history of socialist feminist debates and theory, we can see that socialist feminists really were trying to solve some of the more esoteric problems raised by the radical feminist constructions of the core concepts. The case of socialist feminism provides an excellent illustration of the resilience and deficiency of these categories.

The debates in socialist feminism also show the extent to which the core concepts have forced us into far too many discussions about things that cannot be decided a priori in theoretical debates. Even with the best intention of fortifying the concepts Woman, experience, and the politics of personal life, and with the best method materialism has to offer (Marxism), the result in socialist feminism was basically the same. That is, many of the problems with the original radical feminist system, which socialist feminists sought to avoid, recurred.

MOTHERING THEORY

"Mothering theory" is relevant to this discussion of the core concepts in feminist theory insofar as it posits a universal female experience through which one can begin to explain the oppression of all women.[58] I mean by mothering theory, theories that claim that women have learned certain values from their practice as mothers that can be used to understand gender, and even to build alternative social theories centered around the "female values," like altruism and care. Unlike the materialist feminist use of Marxism, mothering theory has an advantage in its easy relationship with the core concepts. It accepts as given that women are universally oppressed as women and that women's common experiences confirm that oppression. It goes on to seek an allegedly *socially produced, universalizing experience* that would both substantiate the category Woman and serve as a starting point for further theorizing about women and gender. Mothering is being explored as both a universal experience and a patriarchal institution, which can account for the unique behavior and epistemological perspective of women.

In a sense, mothering theorists have reversed the "personal is political" formulation. In their view, the political realm should be based upon private values. Public-spiritedness can be derived from private values culled from personal experiences like mothering. This construction of experience ignores the reality that one's immediate perception of one's own experiences is inevitably affected and skewed by the hegemonic culture (patriarchy, capitalism, or both). Moreover, the experiences themselves are unlikely to be liberatory by virtue of the fact that they are occurring in this society. In fact, I would say the trend to look to mothering as a universal female experience occurred not accidentally in a generally pronatalist period dominated by the Right.

Mothering theory began with Carol Gilligan's enormously influential revisionist work on psychological theories of gender and morality. Gilligan's familiar argument was lodged against Lawrence Kohlberg's claim that women are morally underdeveloped. She presents an alternative interpretation of moral development theory and claims that women have a "different," even better, moral imperative; "a feminine voice."[59] Whereas girls tend to resolve hypothetical dilemmas by trying to change the rules to save the relationships, the boys depict the relationships as easily replaced.[60]

> The moral imperative that emerges repeatedly in interviews with women is an injunction to care, a responsibility to discern and alleviate the "real and recognizable trouble" of this world. For men, the moral imperative appears rather as an injunction to respect the rights of others and thus to protect from interference the rights to life and self-fulfillment. Women's insistence on care is at first self-critical rather than self-protective, while men initially conceive obligation to others negatively in terms of noninterference. Development for both sexes would therefore seem to entail an integration of rights and responsibilities through the discovery of the complementarity of these disparate views.

Gilligan proceeds by imposing a new conceptual grid upon what she exposed as the rather facile interpretation of female behavior made by the male psychological establishment. However, Gilligan begins by agreeing with her male colleagues about one thing: female difference. This point of agreement between Gilligan and the male theorists she criticizes—already latent in some early radical feminist texts—changed feminist theory in the 1980s. Her willingness to accept the original, what I would argue are, presuppositions of psychologists like Kohlberg and Erik Erikson is disturbing. Gilligan questions the interpretation of male/female difference, not whether there is a difference in the first place.

Gilligan does the same in her use of literature as further support of her finding of difference. She reifies figures from literature, assuming without question their authenticity as examples of female ways of being. She does not comment on the fact that these "females" are creations from the imaginations of male fiction writers, and neither does she question the extent to which the differences between the girls and boys of Kohlberg, et al., are creations of the psychological test.

Gilligan's book begins with a rendering of a scene from Anton Chekhov's *Cherry Orchard,* upon which she comments:

> Conceptions of the human life cycle represent attempts to order and make coherent the unfolding experiences and perceptions, the changing wishes and realities of everyday life. But the nature of such conceptions depends in part on the position of the observer. The brief excerpt from Chekhov's play suggests that when the observer is a woman, the perspective may be of a different sort.

Even if one does not quarrel with the substance of her statement, one must pause at her willingness to take Chekhov's fictional rendering of female behavior, without comment as to its status as fiction or to Chekhov's maleness, and to use the behavior of his fictional women and men as examples of differing "ways of imagining the human condition." Gilligan's book is rife with such examples of the use of literature.[61] In each case, she begins by accepting their nonfeminist interpretations and representations of the female and goes on to valorize the differences. The same method is evident in her rereading of Kohlberg. Stories of difference are taken as true. Gilligan's work, and all mothering theory after hers, is about revaluation of the traditionally feminine.

If it is at least possible that Chekhov, et al. misrepresent women, it seems equally plausible that the differences that Erikson, Kohlberg, and others saw between the men and women they tested were the products of a preconceived grid, which they merely superimposed in the creation of their subjects. This does not appear to occur to Gilligan. Rather, she seems to agree that real women comport with what I would argue are stereotypes of women reproduced by male writers and psychologists.

Judy Auerbach, Linda Blum, Vicki Smith, and Christine Williams point to methodological difficulties with Gilligan's social science in assuming male/female difference. They point out that even where Gilligan is generalizing from her own primary research, that research is predisposed to a finding of difference.

> ... the design of the abortion study predetermines the finding that female and male responses to moral dilemmas are extremely different. Gilligan includes only women in the sample; we have no way to compare how men might approach such a decision. Moreover, the fact that abortion is something only women can experience physically adds to this difficulty. Gilligan set out to discern differences in the moral perspectives of women and men, yet she chooses to analyze an event that distinguishes us biologically. How is it possible to dispute the claim that women and men have different attitudes about abortion given that only women can have abortions?[62]

Auerbach, et al., argue that Gilligan "valorizes the different developmental experiences and moral sensibilities of females." This, they say, accounts for the popularity of her book among feminist scholars. The thesis plays into traditional images of women in a particularly pernicious way, and they conclude that the problem "is not that its politics are bad, but that it lacks a politics altogether . . . This lack of politics and any notion of conflicting interests makes Gilligan's a highly palatable work for both nonfeminists and antifeminists . . ."[63]

In a project that has often been connected with Gilligan's, Nancy Chodorow has developed a theory of the way mothering is reproduced. In Chodorow's more socialist feminist view, the culprit is gender-based child care in which women are virtually always mothering. Girls (inexplicably) identify with this maternal role. Boys, on the other hand, develop their identities in contradistinction to their mothers. Thus, mothers reproduce in their daughters the different ways of being that predispose them to be mothers.[64] Chodorow, like Gilligan, suggests that female ways of being can provide a model for society superior to the traditional male one.

Both Chodorow and Gilligan seek to explain differences among women and men that they take as given.[65] For them, women have weak ego boundaries, separation anxieties, and are more empathetic, while men have trouble with intimacy and tend to be more aggressive and competitive. For Chodorow, Gilligan, and mothering theory in general, female traits are more positive human qualities. Although it is insightful to consider these traits in a positive light, it is undesirable to inextricably link them to a particular sex, or to let go unacknowledged the fact that these are only half of human traits, and they are only the ones that have flourished in the context of these social relations. It is dubious to imply, as Chodorow[66] and Gilligan strongly do,[67] that these are the characteristics of all women everywhere. In short, it is not clear to me why an argument that women are different and better than men is any more sound than one that claims that women are different and inferior.

Dorothy Dinnerstein takes a different tact in subjecting the female-as-mother *stereotype* itself to psychoanalytic scrutiny. Her idea is not simply that men and women are different, but that humans have a psychological need to believe in their differences. This is a crucial variation on the Gilligan/Chodorow position, as it makes an argument about mothering theory that does not treat female stereotypes as real, but analyzes them as real social constructs. Indeed, Dinnerstein claims that mother imagery is a neurotic myth. Just as Freud used psychoanalysis in *Future of an Illusion* to understand the presence of a mythic Father personified in religion, Dinnerstein's neo-Freudian approach attempts to persuade us as to the presence of a mythic Mother. Indeed, Dinnerstein's mothering theory can be used to reflect upon some of the methodological/psychological misconceptions in other mothering theorists.

For example, in assessing radical feminist preoccupations with matriarchal cultures, Dinnerstein points out that myths of matriarchal cultures are not history, but interesting fables from a psychoanalytic perspective[68] in that they invent and pay tribute to a magical woman who is not real. Perhaps we can use Dinnerstein to understand Gilligan and Chodorow. For Dinnerstein, the myth of mother is simply the other side of misogyny in that it expresses ambivalence about human creativity.[69] Womanhood, symbolic of the body, disqualifies women (even in their own eyes) from taking part in the defilement of bodily things that is the world of creation.[70] In return, women are offered immunity from the risks of history-making and are protected from the male malady, which is to wonder at the value of what they are doing.[71] To maintain the myth, both men and women have a pathological need to express that there is something trivial and sad about what men do. Female exclusion performs this neurotic function.[72]

In this psychodrama of human malaise, women, "who introduced us to the human condition" through her exclusive mothering function, "carries for all of us a pre-rational onus of ultimately culpable responsibility forever after."[73] Thus, women as archetypal, tolerant, and caring beings are the scapegoats for human resentment of the human condition. Dinnerstein's point is not to stress that mothers are evil, but only that humans have a collective need to see her that way. If Dinnerstein is right, the assumptions of mothering theorists like Ruddick, Rich, Chodorow, etc. are merely reproducing a patriarchal assumption.

The move back to a universal understanding of the female experience as typified in the figure of the mother is also present in writings by African-American women. The most recent illustration is Alice Walker's collection of essays, *In Search of Our Mothers' Gardens*. In these essays, Walker develops the notion of "womanism."

> **Womanist 1.** From *womanish*. (Opp. of "girlish," i.e., frivolous, irresponsible, not serious.) A black feminist or feminist of color. From the black folk expression of mothers to female children, "You act womanish," i.e., like a woman. Usually referring to outrageous, audacious, courageous or *willful* behavior. Wanting to know more and in greater depth than is considered "good" for one. Interested in grown-up doings. Acting grown up. Being grown up. Interchangeable with another black folk expression: "You are trying to be grown." Responsible. In charge. *Serious.*
>
> 2. *Also*: A Woman who loves other women, sexually and/or nonsexually. Appreciates and prefers women's culture, women's emotional flexibility (values tears as natural counterbalance of laughter), and women's strength. Sometimes loves individual men, sexually and/or nonsexually. Committed to survival and wholeness of entire people, male *and* female. Not a separatist, except periodically, for health. Traditionally universalist, as in: "Mama, why are we brown, pink,

and yellow, and our cousins are white, beige and black?" Ans.:
"Well, you know the colored race is just like a flower garden, with
every color flower represented." Traditionally capable, as in:
"Mama, I'm walking to Canada and I'm taking you and a bunch of
other slaves with me." Reply: "It wouldn't be the first time."

3. Loves music. Loves dance. Loves the moon. *Loves* the spirit.
Loves love and food and roundness. Loves struggle. *Loves* the Folk.
Loves herself. *Regardless.*

4. Womanist is to feminist as purple is to lavender.[74]

Although Walker wants to link womanism to a specifically black
folk culture, her description of a womanist is virtually identical to
radical feminist and natalist feminist definitions of Woman per se.
Walker advocates a revaluation of the feminine (e.g., of the phrase
"you act womanish") and talks generally about a woman who loves
other women. Yet, she ends by saying that "womanist is to feminist
as purple is to lavender," presumably because, by including women
of color, "womanism" is a fuller definition of a "feminist" woman.
Womanist is not the kind of "feminist" who links woman to white.

Another of Walker's essays complements this understanding of
womanism. She writes with great passion and clarity: "It is, apparently, inconvenient, if not downright mind straining, for white
women scholars to think of black women as *women,* perhaps because
"woman" (like "man" among white males) is a name they are claiming for themselves, and themselves alone. Racism decrees that if *they*
are now women . . . then black women must, perforce, be something
else."[75] Using the rhetorical device of womanism, Walker urges
women of color to *own* womanhood by reasserting their connection
to the female archetype. Like the Black Power movement, which (in
part) urged black men to seek their rightful ruling place in the patriarchy, womanism urges African-American women and women of
color to follow a twofold process that responds at once to racism in
the world and racism in the feminist movement. First, black women
are exhorted to assert that they *are* women and, second, they are
urged to follow the current trend in feminist scholarship—to revalue
that femininity. White women have no need for womanism, as feminism already defines them as women. They can proceed directly to

Walker's step two, as we see is the case in mothering theory. By womanism, Walker clearly intends to develop a strategy to deal with the structural racism of the core concepts by expanding them. Yet, this expansion accepts the basic premises of the core concepts and the construction of Woman given to them, especially in mothering theory. Although womanism may be useful as an inclusionary strategy, the fact is that women of color are being included in an essentialized and largely mythic sense of what a woman is. Again, Walker's definition of woman, however playful and attractive the description may be, is a highly romanticized one whose characteristics, insofar as they are foundationally linked to motherhood, recapitulate all the problems of any other kind of mothering theory.

Walker's strategy aside, many other women of color have chosen to begin theorizing, not from Woman per se, but from "identity." This is a logical outcome of the fact that the category Woman is continually problematized in practice for feminist women of color as their experiences are so often and obviously excluded in white feminist definitions of woman. Identity, in contrast, is a call to reject white feminist definitions of the female identity and to assert in their place one's own multiple and relational identity of "skin, blood and heart."[76] This new focus lessens the fixed quality of identity, because the theoretical practices of women of color take place in the context of an ethnically varied group of women writing in contradistinction to a white-dominated discourse. The structural place of women of color in feminism tends not to allow the construction of a Woman without a race and ethnicity. In fact, the reason why women of color are writing their own theory is because that aspect of their identities has been left out of white feminist writings. In reality, the only people who think they can invoke Woman unproblematically are white, heterosexual women. This is, of course, a mark of unearned white skin privilege, which gives whites the luxury of not *having* to notice anyone else. As we see in the writings of women of color, this is a luxury that others do not have.

It is true, however, that defining an identity as women of color can be essentialist (as in Walker's recent work) and also risks setting up monolithic and inauthentic categories like "women of color," "third world women," "Middle Eastern women," or even "white women" as other. This too must be understood as one of the outcomes of experientialism.[77] For the experiences of "women of color" to hang together as authoritative, they have been drawn in opposition to another set of experiences—white, heterosexual, imperialist, etc.— which are not multiple, but unified and oppressive. In fact, the phenomenon of the construction of "white, Western feminists" exactly parallels the similar construction of a consolidated "male perspective" by early radical feminists (and later taken up by feminists in general). Both provide ways to talk about a common experience of oppression perpetrated by an other. In both cases, the identity of the self is defined in terms of that which it opposes.

At particular points in time, it no doubt serves a good political function to understand oppression as attached to a monolithic "other," especially when that "other" has spent most of history constructing "us" falsely as a deprecated mass. I would make this defense both of writings by early radical feminists and contemporary women of color. The problem is, however, that this ostensibly good and useful political rhetoric tends to remain within a binary us-and-them paradigm. This problem is only exacerbated by the core concepts, which have reinforced the idea that one's personal experiences conform in important ways to a universal group experience, which exists primarily *because* of the exclusionary practices of some other group, also united, albeit in their experiences of superiority and domination. The problem remains that experiences are never that unified, and experientialism will always fail to reflect a unified identity.

The notion of a universal female identity as articulated in mothering theory and natalist feminism is not benign. The widespread acceptance of mothering theory is an example of feminism on the run from the Right in the 1980s. Feminism, like other ideologies, and in some ways more so because of its reliance on experience, is susceptible to shifting ideological winds. The notion of experience, in general, has little liberatory potential, but only mirrors back to us the relations of which we are already a part. As to this point about the politics of natalist feminism, it is interesting to note the retrenchment from the abortion-on-demand position feminism once had to the current idea that abortion is a necessary evil. Note too that in the celebrated "Baby M" case, it was the natural mother, Mary Beth Whitehead, who became a feminist heroine for Gloria Steinem and Betty Friedan. All of these events are connected. The major tenet of mothering theory—that women are nurturers—sets up a new standard of "appropriate" female behavior. The idea of a maternal instinct, of "maternal thinking" once again, (as does patriarchy) risks casting women without children as selfish or pitiable. Thus, it makes sense that there is a tension between mothering theory and the old abortion-on-demand position. The tension between natalist feminism and pro-choice politics is illustrated by the early work of Adrienne Rich, who came fairly close to arguing that women have a virtually inherent desire to give birth and nurture. Mother and child, she claimed, are on a "continuum" and should not be treated as separate entities right after birth.[78] From this rather romantic view of pregnancy, Rich criticizes abortion on the grounds that it is only another avenue through which men can do violence to women. For if fetus and woman are on a continuum, violence against the fetus can be interpreted as a type of violence against women.

> Abortion is violence: a deep, desperate violence inflicted by a woman upon, first of all, herself. It is the offspring and will continue to be the accuser, of a more pervasive and prevalent violence, the violence of rapism . . ."

Rich is arguing here about how women who are raped are then forced to do even further violence to themselves by having an abortion. Still, it strikes me as an odd thing for a feminist to link abortion and rape as types of violence. The idea that mothering is a good for women has led to a new and dubious understanding of right-to-life women as well. Jean Bethke Elshtain has argued that feminists should not "castigate the family," which is "a nearly perfect structure," unless they have alternatives.[79]

> Without allowing Right-to-Life women to speak the truth as they understand it; without engaging them from a stance that respects their humanity, possibility for the creation of meaning through uncoerced dialogue . . . we will continue to treat them in distorted, presumptuous and prejudicial ways . . .

There is an attempt to build links here solely on the basis of woman-hood and shared mothering. Political allegiance becomes secondary in that membership in the class Woman is itself the politics.

There are important parallels between mothering theory and radical spiritualist feminists. Both have a romantic preoccupation with the female capacity for giving birth to and nurturing children. Although most natalist feminists explicitly reject a sentimental view of the female body and biological determinism, in holding mother-hood up as the experience that defines femininity, the mothering perspective is hard-pressed to avoid romanticizing the relationship between mother and child in its effort to argue the legitimacy and universal applicability of the values attached to "mothering."

In *Of Woman Born: Motherhood as Experience and Institution,* Rich took the view that motherhood is only an example of female experience, "not an identity for all time."[80] Rich argues that mother-hood has two aspects: One is biological, shared by all women, and gives women the capacity to nurture. The other is a "magical power invested in women by men." This latter aspect is derogatory to women because it prevents them from experiencing motherhood autonomously, i.e., without patriarchy. Rich tells us that the autonomous experience of motherhood would involve experiencing motherhood as part of female sexuality[81] and would redefine knowl-edge and power to include those facets that women are privileged to have by virtue of their mothering experience. For Rich, the "inescapable connection" between motherhood and creation is a for-midable power. Similarly, women have developed special female ways of knowing that are not perceived as knowledge by the domi-nant culture.

> The dominant male culture . . . evolved certain intellectual polari-ties which still have the power to blind our imaginations. Any deviance from a quality valued by that culture can be dismissed as negative: where "rationality" is posited as sanity, legitimate method, "real thinking," any alternative, intuitive, supersensory, or poetic knowledge is labeled "irrational."

In contrast, later mothering theory claimed that Woman's experi-ence could actually be grounded (materially or otherwise) in the experience of mothering. Ann Ferguson asserted that motherhood could be conceived of as the material basis for patriarchy, in that caretaking (mothering) is a material necessity of each human life, and socialization is a material necessity for the reproduction of the human species. Of course, even though one must certainly agree that these are necessary, Ferguson fails to demonstrate in what sense psychological and sociological needs can be construed as "material." In any case, she has generated from this assertion the concept of "sex/affective production,"[82] based on the idea that the experience of mothering is central to women since all women can become biological mothers, and most women were mothered.[83] Early work by Sandra Harding also talked about motherhood as the material basis for women's oppression: "The only aspect of women's work which evidently is universal is just this: it is women who are the primary caretakers of infants."[84]

Sara Ruddick's work represents a kind of turning point in mothering theory. She argues that the mothering experience not only explains women's oppression, but can be used to formulate a feminist theory of justice by extending the altruistic aspects of mothering to the level of a societal ethic. Thus, she sees motherhood simultaneously as a grounding for female experience and as the basis for a far-reaching prescriptive theory. She speaks of a "maternal practice," which is characterized by three demands made of mothers: the preservation, the growth, and the acceptability of children.[85] Ruddick explains differences among individual mothers by claiming that they are "governed by the interests of their respective practices." She writes that the "style, skill, commitment and integrity with which they engage in these practices differ widely from individual to individual."[86]

Ruddick shows that mothering theory is congruous with the newly emerging feminist epistemology. Without comment she asserts that women have an ambivalence to the notion of objective reality. She explains that this alleged tendency for women to reject notions of absolute truth can be explained by recourse to the practice of motherhood. She slides between treating motherhood as an archetype and a practice, and idealizing it as an integral part of female identity. It forces women to deal with a growing child, whose "open texture" is "irregular, unpredictable, often mysterious. A mother, in order to

understand her child, must assume the existence of a conscious continuing person whose acts make sense in terms of perceptions and
responses to a meaning-filled world."[87] This results in a situation
where "women *think* differently about what it *means* . . . to be a person, to be real."[88]

Ultimately, Ruddick wants to argue that maternal thinking is a
social category that could, combined with feminist consciousness,
serve as a theory of justice.[89] Yet she concludes by saying that maternal thought exists "for women in a radically different way than for
men" because women "are daughters nurtured and trained by
women."[90] Thus, maternal thinking is social to the extent that it is
not biologically necessary for women either to mother or to be mothered by women. But Ruddick resorts to biological essentialism in
arguing that women receive maternal love "with special attention to
its implications for our bodies, our passions, and our ambitions."[91] It
also begs the question by simultaneously wanting to ground feminist
values in the female and mothering, and saying that a prior knowledge of feminism is necessary in order to selectively analyze
mothering (i.e., from a "feminist perspective").

Much mothering theory represents a conservative impulse in
feminism, which chooses to accept the predominant view of women
as subjectivist, emotional creatures with weak ego boundaries.[92] It
goes on to suggest that these attributes should form the basis for
theories of justice and philosophy. Accepting and celebrating difference is precisely what mothering theory does. But it is not clear that
the difference it describes is any more than a restatement and revaluation of the patriarchal stereotypes that feminism was initially a
reaction against.

Though mothering theory is self-consciously attempting to be
materialist, it is remarkably similar to spiritualist feminism in advocating a superior feminine impulse, which it defines as intuitive,
holistic, peaceful, and earthy. Spiritualist feminists only carry this
organicism and romanticism one step further in linking women fundamentally to nature and the earth. If women think differently than
men, Susan Griffin asserts, it is logical that they should have their own
language to express their new insights. This would be beneficial, she
claims, since male language is a product of patriarchy and inherently

structures thoughts according to a male perspective. With this in mind, Griffin's works try to adopt "female words" as a new form of discourse (apparently oblivious to the fact that words do not in and of themselves equal language). In introducing her book *Women and Nature,* Griffin writes,

> In a way the book is an extended dialogue between two voices . . . one the chorus of women and nature, an emotional, animal, embodied voice, and the other a solo part, cool, professional, pretending to objectivity, carrying the weight of cultural authority. Yet, though the book is shaped by the conflict between the two voices, it sings more than it argues.[93]

Griffin is not alone in romanticizing the link between women and nature, or in calling for the abandonment of the male, including male language. Mary Daly's *Gyn-Ecology* employs what she suggests is a new feminist language. "This book," she says, "is primarily concerned with the mind/spirit/body pollution inflicted through patriarchal myth and language at all levels."[94] One of the projects of her book is to invent a new language so that women can name things from the female perspective, which is to say, to restore the *original* names to things. In doing so, she hopes to aid women in returning to the matriarchal world, which existed before patriarchal religion, to the time of the Goddess (an undeniably maternal figure), when it was accepted that everything was connected. Men have, she claims, (re)named the world from their false, unnatural perspectives. Thus, by renaming objective time (along with a host of other concepts and practices) as "male defined," Daly perceives herself as having metaphysically changed the character of time, for all intents and purposes, along feminist lines, and in doing so, she imagines that she has restored power over time to women. Like Griffin, Daly sees female thinking, and therefore feminist methodology, as intuitive. Men have a separate being from women, and women are unequivocally connected to nature: "women and our kind—the earth, the sea, the sky are the real but unacknowledged objects of attack . . ."

In 1979, Simone de Beauvoir was among those who criticized this emerging tendency toward a "feminine principle," of which mothering theory is endemic.

. . . there are a certain number of women who exalt menstruation, maternity, et cetera, and who believe that one can find a basis there for a different sort of writing. I am absolutely against all this, since, in my opinion, it means to fall once more into a masculine trap . . . there is no reason to fall into some wild narcissism and build on the basis of these givens a system which would be the culture and the life of women.[95]

From another perspective, bell hooks (sic) has criticized the trend in feminism that portrays women as ever tolerant. She has argued that the feminist stress on praising womanhood has merely inverted the stereotypes of women.[96] Similarly, hooks is critical of the romantic idea that women can teach an ethic of care. Women "affirm life whereas men are the killers, the warriors who negate life. Yet women act in nurturing roles even as they socialize young children as parents or educators to believe that might makes right . . ."

Mothering theory that employs psychology at least has an epistemological advantage over that which uses Marxism. Psychological theory comes equipped to deal with issues of gender, socialization, and their relationship to the (gendered) human body. The core concepts of feminism and psychology are also compatible in that they stress experience, personal life, and feelings. On the other hand, psychologically based theories lack a sense of politics and economics and are often ahistorical and insufficiently sensitive to ethnic, racial, and class differences. Responding to this oft leveled charge of ahistoricity in his discussion of Jacques Lacan, Louis Althusser has suggested that psychological categories such as "self" are not transhistorical, but "omni-historical."[97] That is, they do not stand outside of time but are parasitic upon it at a different level of existence. In this, Althusser says, they are similar to Marx's claim that "all history is the history of class struggle." His defense may not be definitive, but it is sufficient, I think, to cast suspicion upon the wisdom of dismissing psychological theory purely on the basis of ahistoricity. Psychological theories may provide the most compelling way to understand the phenomenon of male dominance.

While materialist feminists have attempted to historicize the category Woman, mothering theorists have returned to the idealism of radical feminists in seeking a universal female experience. To do this they have used psychological theories in sophisticated and innovative ways that appear to be more compatible with the core concepts than socialist feminist approaches. On the other hand, this would seem to indicate that the core concepts work best with transhistorical, essentialist theories that are, moreover, biased toward the white, the middle class, and the apolitical.

SEXUALITY AS UNIVERSAL FEMALE EXPERIENCE

Though there are many feminisms, there is a sense in which Catherine MacKinnon is right to say that "radical feminism is feminism."[98] Though it would be inaccurate to say that contemporary radical feminism is by itself the sum total of feminism, its importance is still difficult to overestimate. Contemporary radical feminism is different from other feminist theories insofar as it attempts to build a uniquely feminist theory that hinges on no other theories or politics. To accomplish this, contemporary radical feminists have relied on the core concepts unreconstructed. In MacKinnon's language, radical feminism is feminism "unmodified," which is among the most highly original, provocative, and politically charged bodies of work in feminism today.

Contemporary radical feminist texts also differ from those of the early radicals. This can be accounted for by noticing two significant changes in the focus of the radical feminist movement. First, contemporary radicals are no longer engaged in a dialogue with the Left at large. Rather, their primary audience is women and other feminists.[99] In this sense, feminism really does have, as Atkinson said nearly thirty years ago, "its own issues." Second, those feminists who continue to identify as part of the Marxist/Left tradition have, for the most part, chosen to be aligned, not with radical feminism, but with socialist or Marxist feminism. Thus, the two radical feminisms—both contemporary and early—share the same core concepts while constructing them in terms of different audiences and ideological commitments.

MacKinnon and Andrea Dworkin have emerged as two of the most vocal and prolific representatives of the contemporary radical feminist voice. Their particular contribution to epistemology and method has been to focus on sexuality as a component in the structure of gender inequality. In the words of MacKinnon, "sexuality is to feminism what work is to marxism; that which is most one's own, yet most taken away."[100]

MacKinnon's argument is deceptively simple: Men treat women as sex objects. Male lust and violence are closely connected—often identical. We must rely on female experience in order to change the male order. But female experience must first be filtered through a feminist method (lens), which MacKinnon argues is "consciousness raising." Although biological women are always oppressed, it is also true that the feminine and the female can be represented apart from "real" women. Thus, MacKinnon is both essentialist and postmodern in her treatment of women and the female. And she does not much care that she slips back and forth between the two modes either. This inattention to the apparatus of theoretical consistency makes her work both frustrating and remarkable. Unfortunately, MacKinnon implies that judgments made about women's experiences are to be made collectively by women themselves whose consciousnesses have been "raised" to feminist levels. But the amount of disagreement among women about MacKinnon's interpretation of the female experience makes it seem as though her plea for consciousness raising exists only to legitimate her own view is the solely acceptable feminist one. I have said that her argument is deceptively simple. Let us look at it more closely.

For MacKinnon, male power, sexuality, and objectivity are intrinsically tied together.[101] Mackinnon begins by arguing that all power is, by definition, male.[102] Female power, in fact, "is a contradiction in terms."[103] She continues by saying that "sexuality . . . is a form of power,"[104] and that heterosexuality in particular is no more than the eroticization of dominance and submission.[105] Heterosexuality, in fact, oppresses all women since sexual practices are not a matter of free choice. "If heterosexuality is the dominant gendered form of sexuality in a society where gender oppresses women through sex, sexuality and heterosexuality are essentially the same thing."[106] Women's experiences, she asserts, take place within a (gender) hierarchy in which women always exist as subordinates. Indeed, the very process of becoming a woman is the process of learning how to exist for men. "Gender socialization is the process through which women come to identify themselves as sexual beings, as beings that exist for men." Since power, sexuality, and heterosexuality are male in and of themselves, and since women are always the victims, MacKinnon concludes that gender is at work whenever women are victimized regardless of the sex of the perpetrator.[107]

This explanation of male and female is inherently linked to MacKinnon's epistemology in that, for her, objectivity is merely the epistemological manifestation of male power. "Objectivity," she writes, "is the epistemological stance of which objectification is the social process, of which male dominance is the politics, the acted out social practice."[108]

Claiming to reject both objectivity and subjectivity, MacKinnon continues to rely on a notion of women's experience in order to ground her theory of knowledge:

> . . . women's distinctive experience as women occurs within that sphere that has been socially lived as the personal—private, emotional, interiorized, particular, individuated, intimate—so that what it is to know the politics of woman's situation is to know women's personal lives . . . Thus, to feminism, the personal is epistemologically the political, and its epistemology is its politics. Feminism on this level, is the theory of women's point of view.

Indeed, this passage illustrates MacKinnon's use of all three of the core concepts: (1) women (2) know what they know from their personal experiences, which are (3) political in that they are the result of male domination.

Since objectivity is merely the name given to the male perspective, one solution to male domination is reinterpretation of the world from "women's point of view." Yet MacKinnon is careful to explain that there must be a method for interpreting female experiences, and the method she suggests is none other than the old radical feminist tool, consciousness raising. MacKinnon describes this as "the collective critical reconstitution of the meaning of women's collective social experience, as women live through it."[109] "Method," she argues elsewhere, "in this sense organizes the apprehension of truth; it determines what counts as evidence and defines what is taken as verification." Thus, the acquisition and determination of knowledge is, for MacKinnon, an essentially political activity. "Knowledge is not a copy of reality," she writes, "but a response to living in the world."

Although MacKinnon wants to argue that female experience (or a least, the feminist interpretation of it) is "truth," she also presents an explanation of female oppression that makes the idea of an authentic woman's voice problematic. For MacKinnon, women's oppression by men is so pervasive and relentless that we have come to be totally defined by the male. Much of MacKinnon's work gives the impression that there is no female voice apart from that which has been created under the yoke of male sexual demands. This leaves much doubt as to her ability to speak of female subjectivity or voice at all. For MacKinnon (and Dworkin) male power and aggression exist a priori. Although all men have access to male power, "not all men have equal access to male power, *which is theirs by default unless consciously disavowed.* A woman can also take the male point of view or exercise male power, although she remains always a woman" (emphasis mine).[110] In short, power is unequivocally male, and women can exercise it only by miming men.

It is startling when one finally realizes that MacKinnon's argument is quite literally that male sexuality defines all that a woman is: ". . . a woman is identified as a being who identifies and is identified as one whose sexuality exists for someone else who is socially male."[111] This even accounts for MacKinnon's theory of agency. Rather than worrying about a common experience, MacKinnon suggests that what we have in common is that we "are all measured by a male standard for women, a standard that is not our own."[112] Indeed, female availability to satisfy male sexual needs created the female submissiveness that we associate with traditional feminine socialization. Railing against Gilligan and feminists like her who offer "caring" as the universal "different voice" of women, MacKinnon again explains female behavior as a response to the male: "Women value care because men have valued us according to the care we give them . . ."

Let us return for a moment to discussing MacKinnon's work in terms of the core concepts and the issues they raise for feminist theory. This requires a brief review. The category Woman has always come with many attendant problems. In previous chapters, I have tried to show how the fact of women's oppression was initially "proven" through recourse to their personal experiences. The fact is, the use of experience in tandem with the category Woman implied, if not demanded, that women have some common experience of oppression, as that was in fact the whole point of the feminist turn away from objectivity. The idea of women's oppression cried out for a theory of oppression, and lacking that, the personal experiences of women had to suffice in order to prove the unity of the category.

It seems to me that given the way the theory was set up, there were two options. First, one could find some material grounding for "women's oppression" in order to explain how women everywhere are oppressed without sounding (and being) essentialist. This is the option taken up by socialist feminists. But the second option, which MacKinnon and Dworkin more closely exemplify, was to find a universal experience that could account for women's common victimization, but which did not point to a biological (and thus, immutable and asocial) cause.

The MacKinnon/Dworkin strategy has been to say explicitly that the category Woman is a social category, and then to argue further that sexual objectification unites all women in their common victimization. The MacKinnon move is to unite Woman with an essentialist understanding of "male." Thus, Woman has a social meaning that unites the category across any possible fissures because she is oppressed by men. ". . . (A)lthough a woman's specific race or class or physiology may define her among women, simply being a woman has a meaning that decisively defines all women socially . . ."[113]

Although continuing to call for an epistemology based in women's experiences, MacKinnon is very aware that the experiences of women are unlikely to conform to her and Dworkin's version of them without "consciousness raising." MacKinnon knows that experiences need interpretation. The problem is that MacKinnon believes she knows in advance what that interpretation should be. Thus, her claim to rely on experience becomes dubious. In discussing MacKinnon, Richard Rorty chooses to see her as engaging in a radical redescription of female experience that attempts to persuade us to her particular vision. Exhorting feminists to follow MacKinnon's example, he argues, (feminists) "would no longer need to raise what seem to me unanswerable questions about the accuracy of their representations of 'women's experience.' They would instead see themselves as *creating* such an experience by creating a language, a tradition, an identity . . . a pragmatist feminist will see herself as helping to create women rather than attempting to describe them more accurately."[114]

Even while this is a compelling way to reinterpret MacKinnon, when viewing her work in the context of the development of feminist theory it appears that MacKinnon does believe, contra Rorty, that the oppression of women is intrinsically wrong.

MacKinnon and Dworkin use all three core concepts but attempt to escape essentialism with the notion of the female as a social category. Traditionally, what separates an essentialist from a social category is that in the case of the latter, one can show how the category is socially produced; i.e., that it does not exist as a transhistorical entity. MacKinnon and Dworkin attempt to satisfy this requirement using the device of sexuality, but by linking this systematically to male and female kinds of sexuality, they create the impression that male sexuality is always lustful, while women's is variable. In reducing everything to sexuality, MacKinnon does not solve the essentialism problem, but shifts it onto "the male." Again, given that not all women's experiences of heterosexuality corroborate her view, MacKinnon's appeal to "consciousness raising" as a method for interpreting female experience assumes a priori what the outcome of such consciousness raising will be. Thus, her claim to rely on the female experience, however filtered through feminism, is unsupportable.

One interesting aspect of the MacKinnon/Dworkin position is that male and female are alleged to stand apart from biologically male and female people. They seem at times almost postmodern in their metaphorical use of male and female. Using none of the apparatus of discourse theory, they simply ignore the problems their analysis raises and slip back and forth between metaphorical, social, and essentialist usages of the terms "male" and "female." The advantages of doing this are that they retain a strong politics and a strong subject (which masquerades variously as female experience and the feminine voice), and evade the essentialism problem by jettisoning the notion of "experience" and simply beginning from the assumption that "man" and "woman" are social categories.

It is difficult to discuss the work of MacKinnon and Dworkin without also analyzing their important contribution to the feminist debates on pornography and sexuality. What is often overlooked in the popular press, but has not escaped the attention of most feminists, is the extent to which the MacKinnon/Dworkin position links heterosexuality, violence, and pornography. As Dworkin writes, "Any violation of woman's body can become sex for men; this is the essential truth of pornography."[115] Indeed, the bulk of Dworkin's corpus is devoted to this theme.[116] Even more problematical, their thesis, in attempting to affix blame to men and the male, proffers an exceedingly narrow vision of women's choice, voice, and freedom along with a rather authoritarian notion of the correct interpretation of her experiences. The position has been characterized as anti-sex, but it is also anti–free will and comes very close to making women out to be children, thus mirroring some of the most dangerous forms of patriarchy. Arguing against the idea of female sexual liberation, MacKinnon has written that it "does not free women; it frees male sexual aggression."[117]

MORE ON MACKINNON/DWORKIN: THE CORE CONCEPTS IN THE SEXUALITY DEBATES

For the project at hand, the most intriguing aspect of the sexuality debates is the extent to which both sides use the core concepts. Everyone takes seriously the ideas that the personal is political, women are oppressed as women, and that female experience is integral to feminist politics. Therefore, the debate is not over whether sexuality is a feminist issue; rather it has to do with whose experience of sexuality is the feminist one. However, before I go on to discuss this aspect of what has become known as the sexuality debates, it is worth noting the remarkable extent to which the sexuality debates are unself-consciously a debate among white feminists.[118] And it is not because there is a lack of scholarship by women of color. Patricia Hill Collins has written eloquently about how African-American women "form a key pillar on which contemporary pornography itself rests,"[119] and she points out that Alice Walker, Angela Davis, Audre Lorde, and Barbara Smith have all written about sexuality and the black woman. Yet, the sexuality debate has been configured around *kinds* of sexual practices and preferences, rarely, if ever, noting the racial components of the sex industry, pornography, and prostitution.

The theoretical dilemma centers around competing notions of experience, womanhood, violence, and oppression as those terms are defined by the women participating in the theoretical discussions. "Experience" plays a major role in this debate, and given that the women participating are overwhelmingly white, the stress on experience tends to make other peoples invisible. The debate serves again to illustrate the failure of the core concepts on the level of race. The omission of the racial, ethnic, and class aspects of pornography is, however, only one aspect of the way the concepts function in these debates. For the purposes of understanding the way the core concepts have worked in this context, it is more useful at the outset to look at what has been said rather than what has been omitted.

The anti-pornography movement has attempted to create a link between pornography, violence, and the male. One of the first incidents to make this link appears to have been a 1976 action by the California-based Women Against Violence Against Women (a group that formed to protect women from battering and rape). The group and its supporters forced the removal of a bulletin board advertising a Rolling Stones album bearing the caption "I'm black and blue from the Rolling Stones and I love it."[120]

This now famous event illustrates the historic connection between feminist understandings of pornography and physical violence against women.[121] Indeed, by 1979 the movement to prevent violence against women had in effect expanded its definition of violence to include pornography along with physical violence. In 1978 Women Against Violence in Pornography and the Media (WAVPM) formed in San Francisco, and in 1979 Women Against Pornography (WAP) was founded in New York City.

Almost immediately the idea that pornography was violence against women became controversial among feminists. At the same time it became one of the few feminist issues that enjoyed both serious treatment and a positive reception by the nonfeminist media. As one feminist has commented, "Porn is simply the part of women's agenda that they—politicians and others in power—can most easily buy into."[122] The combination of media hype and ambivalence within the feminist community so inflamed the debate that in 1982 a Barnard College conference (The Feminist and the Scholar IX: Towards a Politics of Sexuality) became the scene of bitter struggle between anti-pornography and anti-anti-pornography feminists.[123]

More recently this drama has continued to play in the legislative arena with the drafting of anti-pornography legislation supported by some feminists and introduced in Indianapolis; Minneapolis; Los Angeles; Washington, D.C.; and New York. The first such legislation originated with the 1983 testimonies of MacKinnon and Dworkin, who suggested that Minneapolis officials might use a civil rights approach in regulating pornography. Subsequently, they were hired to draft an amendment to Title 7 of the Minneapolis Civil Rights Ordinances of 1975.[124] Their novel approach to the perennial problem of regulating pornographic material redefines pornography, objecting to it not because it is obscene, but because it allegedly "promotes violence against women, keeps women subordinate and inhibits access to equal employment, education and opportunity."

The legislation was ultimately unsuccessful. Laws were vetoed by the mayor in Minneapolis and struck down by a federal district court judge in Indianapolis. The latter was then struck down again by the US Supreme Court on appeal on 24 February 1986. The decision, which was issued without opinion, held the proposed law unconstitutional on grounds that it violated the first amendment protection of free speech.[125] Because such legislation touched upon issues of censorship, it inevitably incurred the opposition of the ACLU as well as inspiring opposition from the Feminists Anti-Censorship Task Force (FACT), formed in 1984, and Feminists for Free Speech, formed in 1991.

Since then, similar bills have been introduced with varying success in Massachusetts, Canada, and the United States Congress. At this writing, the Pornography Victims Compensation Act of 1992 (nicknamed "The Bundy Bill"), now being debated in the United States Congress, proposes to allow victims of sex crimes to sue the producers, distributors, and sellers of obscene material and child pornography if the victims can prove that the material was a "substantial cause" of the injury.[126] Canada's unanimous ruling in February of 1992 accepted the MacKinnon view of pornography as harmful to women.[127]

Again, my concerns herein are less with the details of this kind of legislation or the restatement of old debates, and more with the intersection of this legislation and feminist theory. In particular, I am interested in the equation of heterosexuality with violence most systematically stated in the theoretical works of Dworkin and MacKinnon.

One can begin to understand the metamorphosis of pornography into violence by examining the term "violence" as it has been applied to pornography. In previous chapters I have argued that the recourse to women's personal experiences operated in conjunction with the idea that all women were oppressed as women and yielded an expanded notion of oppression. That is, one began with the idea that all women were oppressed as women and sought proof of this proposition through recourse to women's experiences of their own oppression. That idea of oppression included such things as verbal harassment so that the oppression of middle- and upper-class women could be conceptually indistinguishable from the material oppression of working-class women.

The use of "violence" as employed by the anti-pornography movement involves a conceptual leap similar to the one implied in the evolution of the idea of "oppression." In the case of violence against women, pornography, and sexuality, this ambiguity is especially evident in that the concern is not *only* with violent pornography, pornography in general, or actual violence done by men against women, but has become equally directed at modes of sexuality and representation that have been interpreted by anti-porn feminists as part of a pattern of domination.

In this view, pornography is part of a tightly interwoven fabric of patriarchal events, none of which are truly discrete or causal. This explains the negative reaction these feminists have sometimes had when asked for evidence of the link between representations of violence and violence per se.[128] The actual connection between pornography and male violence is not always at the heart of the anti-pornography efforts, and social scientific research methods appear to be used only to convince a skeptical public.

In arguing that pornography is part of a climate of violence against women, Kathleen Barry has claimed that pornographic representation is a "collective representation of violence against women" and is part of the "cultural sadism"[129] that is patriarchy. In regard to social science research, Barry has criticized the findings of the 1967 Commission on Obscenity and Pornography (which found pornography to be harmless) for trying to, "disprove what is self-evident and can be derived from common sense." The findings of the commission can be attributed to ". . . ideological bias, sexist research, masculinist values," and in the end it only "protected male vested interests."[130]

The anti-pornography view is not exclusively radical feminist. In 1980 the relatively mainstream National Organization for Women (NOW) adopted a resolution expressing its contempt for "public sex, pederasty, S and M and pornography," which it claimed were "issues of violence and not of sexual preference."[131]

What is important in all of this is the standard shifting from one that stresses experience as something to which we look in order to understand women, to another view of experience as something that feminists impute to women. The new definition of violence has called certain sexual practices into question, pointing out with blunt clarity how easily condemnations of representations can result in a negative judgment of the activities being portrayed. Subsequently, certain sexual practices have been both advanced and condemned on political grounds. The recent debate about lesbian sadomasochism (s/m) is a case in point.

In 1979 a San Francisco Bay area–group called Samois published an anthology of articles under the title, *What Color Is Your Handkerchief? A Lesbian S/M Sexuality Reader*[132]. The book immediately became controversial not only because it supported lesbian sadomasochistic sexual practices, but because it did so from a feminist perspective. This was an especially volatile position given the attention paid to representations of violence against women. Samois claims that lesbian s/m is a feminist activity because it provides a safe environment for women to act out and learn about power in sexuality. In part Samois is a reaction to the idea that there are politically correct and incorrect types of sexuality, which in turn grew out of the idea that the "personal is political." Curiously, their reaction continues to accept personal politics; they merely assert that s/m is a feminist activity from the perspective of their own experiences.

Samois argues that s/m practices are a feminist activity when they occur between women, but are destructive when they occur in heterosexual relationships. Only in all-female contexts can s/m have a cathartic effect on the women involved. Curious again, because Samois accepts the link between danger, maleness, and heterosexuality proposed by Dworkin and MacKinnon, but refutes the link between "violence" and the lesbian sexual practices in which they engage.

Importantly, critics of Samois question whether lesbians who claim to be sadomasochists are actually consenting to those activities or are, in fact, victims of "false consciousness."[133] Note that because of the centrality of the idea of experience, both the lesbian s/m advocates and those who oppose them have each had to accuse the other of inauthenticity. Both positions are conceptually problematic in that they try to derive a "truth," an authentic female identity (i.e., what is or is not going to be defined as feminist sexuality), from the subjective standard of experience.

Recall MacKinnon's solution: that female experience is a good ground for "truth" only when it is understood through a feminist method, "consciousness raising." But it is precisely in the debates centering around her very own view of pornography and sexuality that this interpretive view is shown to remain problematic. In the case of lesbian s/m activists, it is self-identified feminists who are engaging in "male" activities. Surely, the false-consciousness paradigm is much less convincing in this case. The question becomes, Which feminists are more feminist? Or, better still, What does feminism mean?

On almost any level the question of who is more feminist is an undesirable one. First, it is conceptually impossible to answer it using the standard of women's experience. There is nothing that prevents lesbian s/m groups like Samois from claiming that their experiences are authentically female and feminist, while anti-s/m people can just as easily make the same claim.

Views that rest on an imputed female experience for their legitimacy make it conceptually and practically difficult to come to terms with women who claim to have different experiences—in this case, of pornography and their own sexuality. The construction of the core concepts we see evident in the sexuality debates again necessitates either a patronizing false-consciousness argument or a conspiratorial male-identification claim to explain female experiences that deviate from a preconceived and merely asserted notion of female nature.

The culmination of this thinking can be seen in early feminist anti-pornography legislation, which attempted to make it legally impossible for a woman to consent to participation in pornographic activities. That is, it attempted to fix into law one feminist interpretation of female experience. In this legislation, the differences between men and women, the primacy of female experience, and the idea of false consciousness explored previously in a theoretical context are applied in practice.

FALSE CONSCIOUSNESS: THE LIMIT ON FEMALE CONSENT

Anti-pornography legislation of the 1980s and 1990s codifies a feminist version of false consciousness and limits female consent under the guise of feminist protectionism. One model of the proposed anti-pornography law drafted by Dworkin and MacKinnon would have made it a civil offense to coerce, intimidate or fraudulently induce anyone into performing for pornography.[134] It also claims that neither one or more of the following can be legally construed as proof of a person's consent: that she is a woman; that she is or has been a prostitute; that she has attained the age of maturity; that she is connected in any way to anyone making the pornography; that she had sex with anyone making the pornography; that she had previously posed for sexually explicit pictures; that someone else (even a relative or spouse) has given permission on the person's behalf; that the person actually consented to the act, which is then changed into pornography; that the person knew the purpose of the act was to make pornography; that the person showed no resistance; that the person signed a contract or stated their willingness to participate; that no physical force, threats, or weapons were used; that the person was paid.

Note how this way of thinking would limit female consent. The potential legal rule would have made it impossible for a woman to consent even by signing a contract and receiving money—the essence of freedom and power in liberal capitalist relationships. The implications of this are staggering for women. Imagine this approach applied to abortion or property law or other life decisions.

What this treatment of pornography says about men is interesting as well. One version of the proposed law stated that a defendant (presumably a man, because women being unable to consent to pornography would not, one would think, be liable) cannot use his ignorance of the fact that a thing was pornography as a legal defense (although damages would not have been recoverable in that instance). Therefore, although the proposed law did not recognize a woman's ability to consent (it narrowed consent for women) consent would have been broadened for men by the claim that men consent simply by acting. Even when men said that they were unaware that what they were consenting to was pornography they would still be liable.

One puzzling aspect of these laws was that, although pornography was defined as the portrayal of the sexual subordination of women, the legislation allowed that men, children and transsexuals were sometimes used in the place of women in pornography. That is, even though women were not always being portrayed, they were always the victims. If pornography is by definition about women, how can the use of "men, children or transsexuals" still be pornographic? In fact this is consistent if one dogmatically believes that gender is the primary oppression from which all others flow. It would follow from this that brutalization involving men and children occurs only to take the place of women.[135] By this logic violence is done to women even when and if it is men who are actually and materially being brutalized because injury to men from pornography is a logical impossibility. Women are by definition always the victims.

From this perspective, it becomes irrelevant whether s/m pornography portrays women dominating men or the reverse. For the purposes of this proposed law, domination is male and injures women. The law would have allowed individual women to act and consent only as in acting on behalf of women understood as a subordinated group.

The Dworkin/MacKinnon proposal incorporated the feminist idea of experience in its most subjective mode. In not defining pornography, but instead giving all women standing to sue people whom they experienced as having offended them with sexually explicit pictures or words, the proposal reflects the proposition that all women will (or should) experience certain things in given ways.

Like pro-natalist feminism, there is a lot to be said about the confluence of the feminist anti-pornography movement and the rise of the radical Right in the mainstream political arena. Indeed, other feminists have been disturbed by the links between the anti-pornography movement and the ideological right.

> I went to an anti-porn conference, because I was very confused about my own positions. At the workshops I heard some of the most reactionary politics I've ever heard about how we had to smash pornography and save the family. In fact, it was a radical right critique, much more so than a left critique.[136]

Although I too am suspicious of feminism's flirting with the Right, I would like to point out that this dilemma still casts feminism in terms of Left/Right politics. Perhaps the more important point is that when push really came to shove, our core concepts failed to help us resolve any of the really important debates within feminism. In fact, the recourse to experience, male identification, and the nature of Woman only seems to have confused things further.

4

Feminism and Epistemology

So far, I have looked at the origins of second wave feminist theory by tracing the development of three of its core concepts. I have tried to show how those concepts were conceived in the manifestos, pamphlets, and other writings of early radical feminist groups. I have also attempted to isolate some of the problems with these core concepts, and to argue that those problems have continued to dog even those feminists who were most determined to alleviate them; namely, socialist feminists. The feminist theories I have examined thus far have been unable to escape the basic essentialism, romanticism regarding female nature, and ethnocentrism of which so many theorists (most notably, poststructuralists) have complained. Since the core concepts lack a specific historical referent, they have proved remarkably elastic. This flexibility, evident in the hyphenation model itself, explains the ease with which they can be (and have had to be) grafted on to any given number of nonfeminist theories.

In particular, "experience" structures ahistoricity into feminist theory because it is itself an ahistorical notion.[1] A close reading of the sexuality debates illustrates this point by showing that even though both sides rooted their claims in the core concepts, those concepts failed to preclude, and even exacerbated, arguments about who was portraying the "true" account of women's experiences. In those debates, all sides were able to claim special insight into the nature of women, to assert a "correct" female sexuality, and to claim to define female experience. This battle of abstractions was at least partly a result of the structure of feminist theory as built around its core concepts.

What I have been doing is providing a history of ideas and making an argument with regard to those ideas. The argument I have been making is that (1) there are central feminist concepts that link all Anglo-American feminist theories, (2) those concepts have an origin in feminist politics and early discussions with the Marxist New Left, (3) the various existing feminist theories have been spun out partly as strategies to deal with problems in the core concepts, and (4) the fact that feminist theory has yet to adequately overcome these obstacles is traceable to the problematic nature of the core concepts. If feminism cannot solve the problems with the core concepts, the concepts must either be abandoned outright or fundamentally transformed.[2] Throughout this work, it is important to note that I am not simply complaining about the category Woman as several recent analyses of feminist theory have. Rather, I have been offering a structural reread-ing of some of feminism's most basic texts and controversies as a way to gain insight into the nature of the dilemmas that face feminist theory today.

Aside from providing a history of the origins of feminist ideas, and an alternative to the hyphenation model of feminist thought, I have explored in detail several ways that feminists have tried to solve problems about Woman and experience. One, materialist feminism, attempted to historicize the concepts themselves using Marxist theory as a template. Others have attempted to isolate a universal female experience (such as mothering or female sexuality) to describe and unify the category Woman.

Having posited female experience, these universalist feminist theo-rists argued further that these experiences could be used to ground feminist theories of justice, care, and social relations. Paradoxically, they sought a universal female experience to unify the category Woman by arguing that there was *a female experience,* but that it varied across time and culture. As one version of the argument goes, all mothering is done by women, though ways of mothering may differ. Arguments like this parallel earlier ones, which attempted to historicize the notion of patriarchy also by asserting its existence across history, albeit in different forms. The advantage of finding a universal female experience is that it provides some grounding for feminist critiques of "male" ways of being and organizing the world. Thus, as Gilligan's paradigmatic argument implies, female mothering leads men to think abstractly; in contrast, women think relationally. While socialist feminists have themselves admitted that their versions of high theory failed on their own terms for a variety of reasons, universalist feminist theories continue as part of a strong trend in feminism to depict the "different voice" of women. It is important to understand all of these developments in feminist theory in order to properly appreciate the nuances of feminist standpoint theory discussed in this chapter.

Standpoint theory represents a very different feminist strategy from either the socialist feminist or universalist approaches discussed in preceding chapters. In fact, standpoint theory is a kind of conceptual bridge between Anglo-American feminist theories and postmodernism, even though it is more appropriately thought of vis-à-vis its roots in the core concepts and in its affinity to Marxism. Standpoint theory overlaps with poststructuralism in that both are interested in "perspective" and interpretation,[3] though standpoint theory attempts to talk about "women" and "women's experiences" in concrete and historicized ways. Recent standpoint thinking seems to have abandoned the idea that there is a unified female identity—a single female perspective—from which various criticisms can be leveled[4] and, instead, has moved toward the idea that there are many female standpoints. The problem is, as Sandra Harding has observed, if standpoint theory does not assume some feminine universality, "then just what is feminist about standpoint theories?"[5] Thus, the trick has been to conceptualize the multiplicity of the female experience while still maintaining some notion of Woman without dissolving into mere individualism.[6] This proves to be difficult.

In this chapter I am, as always, most interested in the core concepts and their role in the development of feminist thought. With that in mind, I have several specific goals in this chapter. First, I want to

place feminist standpoint theory in the larger discussion of epistemology in general in order to understand the point of having a
feminist epistemology at all. The development of a feminized knower is significant to my inquiry regarding experience, personal
politics, and Woman. I also want to look at the ways in which the
core concepts figure in the evolution of standpoint thinking. In particular, I will talk about the way experience is used in relation to
ideas like knowledge, Woman, and truth in feminism. Third, since I
began my intellectual life as a Marxist, and still see myself as working loosely within that broad tradition, I am very interested in
analyzing the use of Marxism in standpoint theory. My claim is that
standpoint theorists use Woman and experience in attempting to
construct an epistemological basis from which to assert a truth
about the feminist analysis of female oppression. but that these concepts can provide no such foundation. In support of this, I briefly
review how concepts like experience and perspective are used in the
epistemological traditions associated with Descartes and Kant, as
well as the alternative tradition associated with Marx. I argue that
claims made by feminist standpoint thinkers are more properly
understood as a worthy (though contestable) politics than they are
as an epistemology.

FEMINIST STANDPOINT THEORY

Feminist standpoint theory is basically an epistemological argument
that tries to describe a distinctly "female" or "feminine" knowledge
through recourse to the experiences of women. Standpoint thinkers
sometimes use the metaphor of "quilting" or "weaving" to illustrate
the case that there is no single universal woman or female experience,
but rather that there are many female experiences, which when
assembled can be said to comprise a female identity.[7] Bettina
Aptheker conceptualizes these differences as a braid: "Each plait is
identifiable and useful in itself. Likewise, in the crossing of plaits we
also see how women's experiences touch each other. This way of piv-
oting the center of our thinking on women clears a space in which
differences provide meaning."

Standpoint is related to, but not the same as, the idea of perspective. Even in their early pamphlets, second wave feminists claimed to be providing a "female perspective," and standpoint thinking is the epistemological extension of this perspectivist thinking, though qualitatively different as such. Absent a universal or materialist understanding of Woman and women's experiences it has always been difficult to say exactly what this female perspective is or where it comes from. At certain points in the history of feminist theory, feminists argued that different perspectives could be layered in one's life such that the perspective of a Native American lesbian (for example) would be more privileged than simply the experiential knowledge of a lesbian, because the former has a wider variety of experiences. Thus, early perspectivism in feminism implied a norm or center (presumably the white, male, middle-class heterosexual) according to which other experiences were different and marginal. The more marginal one's experiences, the more "true" they were.[8]

Fortunately, there has been a shift away from this notion of marginality. Feminists now are less likely to speak about layering experiences to create a privileged knowledge than they are to speak about the unique identities, experiences, and perspectives gleaned from women who are poised on the border, at once inside and outside, of several oppressed groups. As Barbara Smith writes, "the meaning of blackness in this country shapes profoundly the experience of gender, just as the conditions of womanhood affect ineluctably the experience of race."[9] We now speak, therefore, of a unique identity that is more than the sum of added oppressions. Elizabeth Spelman has called this the "ampersand problem" referring to the tendency to understand oppression in terms of the layering of separate experiences such as race and gender.[10] Kimberle Crenshaw argues against "the problematic consequences of the tendency to treat race and gender as mutually exclusive categories of experience and analysis" and argues instead in favor of the "multidimensionality of Black women's experiences."[11] Black women, Crenshaw argues, have a unique identity separate from that of either black men or non-black women.

To talk in this new way about different *kinds* of women (and men) each with unique experiences and knowledges, is also to claim that there is no bird's-eye view; no one authentic perspective on reality because knowledge and reality are fragmented. Therefore, it is less important to think about whose knowledge counts more, as tends to be the case in additive analyses, than it is to piece together the various accounts of knowledge in order to create a mosaic that we can think of as real. On the epistemological level, this means that different experiences begin to be equated with different knowledges, or "ways of knowing," and suggests once again that the category Woman is not unified. It further hints that individual women may have multiple "selves."[12]

The shift in feminist thinking about race, class, and gender also speaks to an epistemological debate between those who believe in the possibility of a true account of the world and simply seek a perspective from which that truth can be attained, and those who think the very notion of truth must be reevaluated or discarded. These kinds of discussions within feminist standpoint thinking are at bottom epistemological disagreements that lead to queries such as: Is there one reality? Is there one knower? Is that one knower an individual (as classical liberal thinkers assumed), or is there a collective knower (as in the members of an oppressed group)? Can we argue that knowledge comes to us differently as members of oppressed groups? If so, can we really speak of "humanity" any longer? If knowledge is fragmented, does it makes sense to speak of truth at all?

EPISTEMOLOGY: AN OVERVIEW

In analyzing feminist theory's responses to these questions, it is useful to look at what is presupposed in the general epistemological discourse. Again, Sandra Harding has correctly observed that "once we stop thinking of modern Western epistemologies as a set of philosophical givens, we can begin to examine them instead as historical justificatory strategies—as culturally specific modes of constructing and exploiting cultural meanings in support of new kinds of knowledge claims."[13]

Of course, the attention given to knowledge claims is itself a "historical justificatory strategy," and the fact that some quarters of feminism have been so intent on developing an epistemology shows how deeply feminism is embedded in this Enlightenment project.[14] Indeed, epistemology has not always been the major focus of philosophy and theory. Several things led to its prominence.

First, the rise of science in the sixteenth century challenged faith as it was defined by the Roman Catholic Church using reason as a weapon. This moved the Western philosophical traditions from discussions about the nature of God and reality to ones about knowledge and truth. The doubt expressed in the question, "How do we know God exists?" reflects a skepticism about metaphysics that arose alongside the new empiricism of the sixteenth century. In addition to the rise of science, Seneca's earlier humanism had placed man squarely at the center of the universe, and by implication, of knowledge. Finally, Luther's bold challenge to the Roman Catholic hierarchy, articulated most clearly in his idea of a "priesthood of all believers," shifted the discussion of knowledge from "man" to "the individual." The Roman Catholic Church was not the only source of knowledge of God's will, Luther claimed; rather, all who believe in God could successfully interpret the Bible for themselves. This was simultaneously a theological and an epistemological claim in that knowledge of the word of God was, as Luther asserted, accessible to all people.

Although Luther himself backed away from the most radical aspects of his own thought, maintaining that he had intended only a relatively narrow criticism of the worldliness of the Church, his work signified an important shift. Luther's work represents a different way of thinking, not only about God, but about knowledge in general. The idea that individuals had independent claims to knowledge based on their common rationality proved to be a formidable weapon in the face of the Roman Catholic God's "one true Church" and the absolutist regimes its declarations of "divine right" supported. If the priesthood of the Roman Catholic Church was unnecessary for knowledge of God's city, maybe the feudal hierarchy was unnecessary in understanding and ruling man's.

Since all monarchs ruled because they were declared "true rulers" by the Church, ruling that had no foundation in these divine declarations of absolute truth was illegitimate. Luther's hint that truth was democratically accessible on an individual basis challenged the idea that the "true" ruler could be known at all. Thus, in defying the Church's monopoly on knowledge, Luther had also unwittingly contested the rulers whose legitimacy depended on their being declared as such according to the old notions of absolute truth. Thus, one of the tasks of sixteenth- and seventeenth-century social contract thinkers was to come up with a new theory of how to legitimize government.[15]

Changing historical events were accompanied by a revolution in philosophy. Although René Descartes began the modern discourse about knowledge by positing that the answer to the riddle of existence lay in the presence of a "knower" or "cogito," it is arguably the case that the full flowering of epistemological foundationalism can be traced to the work of Immanuel Kant. Kant, in the words of Richard Rorty, shifted the question of knowledge from one of "knowing of" to "knowing that,"[16] and reinvented the Platonic idea that claims about justice had to be grounded in truth.

Kant's insight, derived in the course of his extensive criticisms of David Hume, was that all previous debates between empiricism and idealism asked the wrong question. For Kant, the point was not as Hume had formulated it, that we cannot derive moral claims from empirical ones (i.e., "ought" from "is"); rather the question was, How is any discussion of "ought" possible at all? How can we conceptualize things about which we can (by definition) have no direct experience? This question led Kant to deduce the presence of universal categories of mind. Although we can only know things as they appear to us in their particular manifestations, universal categories must exist, otherwise how would we recognize things as representations of general categories in the first place? That is, we can recognize any given table because we hold some general notion of "table" in our minds. Or, we can recognize individual, particular women because we have some idea of what the general, universal category Woman looks like. Since we can think about universals of which we have no direct experience, Kant reasoned that one of the qualities of the mind must be its ability to order and synthesize sensual reality according to universals. Although it is true that the mind will never be able to know the *noumenal* "thing in itself," Kant asserted that the mind *is* capable of comprehending the thing as *phenomenon* (that is, the thing as it appears in the sensual world) and of synthesizing that information into something, which can then be called knowledge. It follows that the mind, Kant concluded, must come equipped with categories that enable it to make certain distinctions a priori. This is true, Kant reasoned, since knowledge cannot logically be based on the very empirical reality about which it is skeptical and seeks understanding. "Experience," Kant concluded, is the name we give to the mind acting on and interpreting the sensual world. "Although all our knowledge begins with experience, it does not follow that it all arises out of experience[17] . . . Experience teaches us that a thing is thus and so but not that it cannot be otherwise."[18] That is, experience can teach us that something exists, but tells us nothing about how things *ought* to or *can* exist. The fact that it is possible to speculate on things of which we have no direct experience suggests that experience itself cannot be the same as knowledge.

Like Anglo-American feminism, Lockeian "copy theory" and Humeian skepticism also both posit knowledge as derivative of experiences, though all of their notions of "experience" differ substantially from Kant's. After arguing that all knowledge is gleaned from empirically observable, discreet, and unconnected data, Hume was led to ponder: What is it that unites our impressions and ideas and makes us experience them as connected?[19] Unable to really answer the question and unwilling to deviate from his original hypothesis, Hume concluded that it was convention (social custom) that made coincidental experiences appear to be related to each other in a cause-and-effect sequence.[20]

In his critique of the Humeian system, Kant declared that it (and all empirical or experiential theories, presumably including ones like Locke's) were in reality not bona fide theories of *knowledge* at all, precisely because they could not explain that process of synthesis that had puzzled Hume. Knowledge, Kant held, was more than the accumulation of facts and experiences, it was the ordering and understanding of what one had observed. Thus, the actual epistemological question, Kant argued, had to address how it was possible to differentiate experiences from not experiences. If all knowledge was, as Hume had said, derived from empirically observable phenomena, one could not explain the presence of the intuitive category "not experience." That is, if all knowledge came from experience, how could one even have a category in one's mind that dealt with things one had not experienced? Kant concluded that our very ability to formulate this notion constituted a proof of the objective reality of an intuition responsible for ordering and categorizing reality. Refuting Hume, Kant wrote:

> I could not only prove the objective reality of the concept of cause with reference to objects of experience but also deduce it as an a priori concept because of the necessity of the connection it implies. That is, I could show its possibility from pure understanding without any empirical sources . . . If anything is lacking, it is the conditions for the applications of these categories, and especially that of causality, to objects. This condition is intuition, and, when it is lacking, this application for the purpose of theoretical *knowledge* of the object as noumenon is rendered impossible.[21]

In a sense, simply by knowing the meaning of the words *cause* and *effect,* one can deduce the relation between the two notions without ever having an empirical illustration. Kant is asking us to think precisely about our ability to *recognize and distinguish* a cause from an effect in the first place.

The important point for our purposes is that, in the Kantian tradition, attention to mere raw experiences is not knowledge at all. To be understood as such it needs to account for the way in which experiences are interpreted by the knowing subject. It is not true that raw experience is itself a type of knowledge. One can say that different experiences lead to different conclusions about life and so on, but this is only to speak about experience as information, which leads to knowledge. For Kant the ability to *interpret* the information of daily life is a universal feature of the human mind.

I have been discussing epistemology in order to facilitate discussion of feminist standpoint thinking as an epistemological enterprise. Kant's insight was that in order to have knowledge, the mind must act on lived reality and must be able to order it according to principles that are themselves speculative and universal rather than empirical and partial.

It should be apparent that Kant's observations about experience are relevant to any discussion of the import of feminist epistemological projects rooted in experience. However, three aspects of Kant's formulation should be troubling for feminists: (1) Kantian universalism, namely, the idea that all men (sic) think rationally, will come to similar conclusions when thinking about lived reality, and will always think in terms of universals; (2) Kantian idealism, specifically, the transhistoricity of Kant's notion of a transcendent "mind," which accounts for his inattention to embodiment; and (3) Kant's insistence that right action must be grounded in "the truth." Because Marx was also troubled by certain aspects of German idealism, his epistemological theories have proved more appealing to feminists (although I shall argue below that using Marx does not remove dilemmas with regard to truth and universality for feminists).

THE CORE CONCEPTS, EPISTEMOLOGY AND FEMINIST STANDPOINT

It is significant that feminism seeks an epistemology in order to ground its claims about justice and oppression in truth while at the same time criticizing the very concept of truth. In searching for a feminist epistemology, feminist theory transforms the questions that early radical feminists dealt with, such as the unity of women, the authority of the female voice, and the validity of the female experience, into a metatheory in the context of a discourse that has most often been, of necessity, about universals. Yet, truth about women's oppression, or about the world in general, feminist epistemologists argue, can only be gleaned from our experiences as gendered subjects—from women as knowing subjects.

Feminism remains in the Enlightenment discourse by seeking a foundation in epistemology, and thereby must accept some idea of truth as well as the subject/object discourse. Yet, feminism rejects many important elements of Enlightenment discourse—androcentric "humanism" and universalism, for example, have both been challenged by feminism. We do not "know" as Kantian neutral, rational beings, but as members of oppressed groups, and as feminized, embodied subjects. For feminists, what counts as knowledge must be grounded in experience, and "human experience differs according to the kinds of activities and social relations in which humans engage. Women's experiences systematically differ from the male experience upon which knowledge claims to have been grounded."[22] In feminism, claims about knowing are no longer taken to be universally true. Indeed, rationality itself has been largely criticized as a male paradigm, suggesting that there are different types of knowing, some of which are not rational (in the philosophical sense) at all, but intuitive and female.[23]

There are several problems with pursuing a feminist epistemology rooted in the core concepts. First, epistemology is a rationalist discourse. If feminism wants to talk about knowledge in a way that diverges from the Enlightenment understanding of it (and I think it does), an epistemological grounding does not seem to be a good place to start. As Nietzsche recognized, critiques of truth, reality, objectivity, and reason must end in the abandonment of epistemology insofar as epistemology is precisely a discourse about all of the things one is criticizing.

Second, and much more important and to the point, as Kant's discussion of experience shows, there is no way that experience can, in and of itself, be the ground for an epistemology. There is simply too much left unexplained. For one, experience does not allow for the ability to think beyond one's circumstances to some imagined liberated future: unless experience is processed by some other faculty, it is merely an account of one's lived reality. Related to this is the fact that experience is always contaminated by ideology. Liberatory critiques of that reality and those ideologies necessarily come from outside of raw experience and dominant ideologies. Finally, a purely experiential epistemology does not tell us *which* aspects of the lives of women count as epistemologically important.

A FEMINIST LENS

That women's raw experience cannot by itself be called knowledge is mentioned in passing by several feminist theorists, and though there are similarities between "woman's experience" and the idea of standpoint, they are not synonymous. For example, Nancy Hartsock writes that because of "its achieved character and its liberatory potential, I use the term 'feminist' rather than 'women's standpoint.' Like the experience of the proletariat, women's experiences and activity as a dominated group contains both negative and positive aspects. A feminist standpoint picks out and amplifies the liberatory possibilities contained in that experience."[24] Perhaps more than most other feminist theorists, Hartsock is aware of the ideological nature of experience and the essentialism of Woman and therefore suggests that a feminist standpoint is necessary to interpret women's experiences.

Similarly, Catherine MacKinnon counsels us as to the necessity of a "collective critical reconstitution of the meaning of women's collective social experience, as women live through it."[25] On the same point, Bettina Aptheker writes that we need "a different kind of philosophical space, for *an ordering of women's experience* as knowledge, for an emancipatory vision rooted in our own grounds . . . I want to *propose* a new way of seeing, a different way of thinking" (emphasis mine).[26] These underdeveloped suggestions that simply recounting women's experiences is insufficient since they also need to be *ordered,* coupled with Aptheker's admission that she is *proposing* rather then *uncovering* a new way of thinking, seem to me to be enormously provocative.

However, feminism cannot simultaneously be the lens through which experiences are interpreted, and also find its grounding in those experiences. That is, the feminist interpretive lens cannot be grounded on women's point of view. Sandra Harding has argued that "The feminist critiques of social and natural science, whether expressed by women or by men, are grounded in the universal features of women's experiences as understood from the perspective of feminism."[27] To ground feminism in women's experiences and then to look to feminism to interpret those experiences is a tautology. To the extent that feminist standpoint theory accepts this tautology, it cannot accomplish what it sets out to do.

In a later work, Harding has defended the standpoint approach: "standpoint theorists are not claiming some kind of transhistorical privilege for research that begins in women's lives. Nor, it is worth recollecting, are they arguing that women's biology, women's intuition, what women say, or women's experiences provide grounds for knowledge. What women say and what women experience do provide important clues for research designs and results, but it is the objective perspective *from women's lives* that gives legitimacy to feminist knowledge, according to standpoint theorists."[28] Thus, in *Whose Science? Whose Knowledge?*, Harding sets out to make a distinction between "women's experiences" and "women's lives," and to argue, not that knowledge comes from women's experiences, but that the questions we "start out from"[29] in order to get knowledge should come from "women's lives."[30]

This is an extremely important and useful point, but it is not an epistemological one. In fact, it begs several epistemological questions. First, it provides no clue as to what it is about women's lives that needs to be included in theoretical discussions. A feminist epistemology would have to help us determine which parts of our lives and experiences are endemic to our being female. Therefore, the epistemological question is precisely the one avoided in Harding's formulation: we need to know what it is about us *as women* that has been ignored and neglected.

Harding wants to say that women's experiences may not provide the answers to questions, but that beginning from women's lives can furnish better questions. This will enable us to escape the subjectivity of experience and to preserve some notion of objectivity. Therefore, Harding talks about looking at the objective reality of women's lives, and designing research questions from there. As I have said, this is an important notion. Where this idea becomes disappointing, however, is in its assumption that women's lives are essentially similar, and in the failure to recognize that the research agenda of looking at women's lives itself assumes a common female experience. The admonition that we begin from women's lives cannot help but suggest that there is something essential and unique about women. This is true despite disclaimers to the contrary. For example, Harding argues that "it is from the perspective of women's interests that certain situations can be seen as rape or battering which from the perspective of the interests of men and the dominant institutions were claimed to be simply normal and desirable social relations between the sexes."[31] The idea of "women's interests," which Harding invokes, still depends on Woman and still assumes a crucial similarity of women's interests.

The fact is, "women" do not have "interests" as feminists before consciousness raising. Women's interests do not exist as such before feminist consciousness raising. Women do not yet act together as a feminist subject. It could be argued that in their patriarchal construction, women do not *act* together at all. That is, *there are no universal features of women's existence* until they are named as such by feminist theory and politics. Actually, there may never be universal features of women's experience. The very idea of Woman is, at this point, still being given meaning, and, thanks to feminism, for the first time in history, women are participating in the assignation of that meaning. Dorothy Smith writes compellingly about the importance of feminist consciousness raising to feminist standpoint. Whereas early radical feminist groups used the idea of the women's perspective in the context of political organizations and consciousness raising groups, the term is now used apart from feminist practice in a discourse of high theory. Indeed, Smith worries as I do that "the theorizing of 'standpoint' within feminist discourse displaces the practical politics that the notion of 'standpoint' originally captured."[32]

Theory talk about women's interests and experiences is always essentializing, but this does not mean that there cannot be feminist descriptions of gendered lives and discussions of the ways in which feminists see gender. These descriptions should not be masked as epistemologies, however, and they certainly cannot be grounded in that which they seek to explain (i.e., the female experience). Feminism must always be invoked as avowedly political and never as organically related to women's natural interests. What we really mean by the phrase "women's interests" is the interests of women as feminists read them. The notion of women's interests is therefore always a political *goal* of feminism, but in no way can it be a grounding for it. Thus, in answer to Harding's query, "is standpoint theory really an epistemology, or only a sociology of knowledge?" I would answer: neither.[33] It is—or should be—an advocacy of female subjectivity. As an epistemology it begins from that which it seeks to explain and operates from the false assumption that its task is complete. As such, it searches in vain for an epistemology before the subject is constituted. It searches in vain for a theory of knowledge before we are quite sure who the knower is and what we, as feminists, mean by knowledge.

Despite her discussion of the importance of consciousness raising, Dorothy Smith has argued that feminist standpoint "positions inquiry but has no specific content. Those who undertake inquiry from this standpoint begin always from women's experience as it is for women. We are the authoritative speakers of our experience."[34] Even though Smith distances herself from Harding (and from standpoint theory in general),[35] she seems to support Harding's ideas about beginning inquiry from women's lives, when she says that standpoint theory "shifts the ground of knowing, the place where inquiry begins." Smith argues further that the standpoint of women is based in experience, and she goes on to say that the purpose of the alternative sociology she is engaged in creating is "to explore and unfold the relations beyond our direct experiences that shape and determine it . . . from the standpoint of women."[36]

Yet if Smith's position of inquiry is "beyond our direct experiences," how can it also be rooted in experience, and more, enable us to gain insight into the shaping of those experiences? How can such a critique be taking place from "the standpoint of women" when embodiment and gender are themselves categories of experience? In short, how can we interrogate what is *beyond* our direct experiences using our *experiences* as a basis for that investigation? Or, as Charles Lemert has asked, "is it possible both to start with women's experience and, having thus begun, to account for that experience?" Furthermore, if, as Smith acknowledges, the universe is "already ideologically structured,"[37] how can we postulate that anything, even women's experiences or the female standpoint, is beyond ideology?

The most suggestive aspect of Smith's standpoint theory comes in her idea that the female standpoint begins before experiences "have shifted upwards into the transcendent subject."[38] This, she says, locates "the knowing subject in the actual, before the differentiation between subjective and objective . . ." In Smith's words,

> The standpoint of women therefore directs us to an 'embodied' subject located in a particular actual local historical setting. Her world presents itself to her in its full particularity—the books on her shelves, the Cowichan sweaters she has bought for her son's birth-

days, the Rainforest chair she bought three years ago on sale, the portable computer she is using to write on, the eighteenth-century chair, made of long-since exhausted Caribbean mahogany, one of a set of four given her by her mother years ago—is particularized by insertion into her biography and projects as well its immediacy in the now in which she writes.[39]

From this description, it seems that Smith wants us to include everything as epistemologically important, allowing us no sieve through which to winnow out the insignificant from the significant. Smith's desire to talk about women situated in daily life is deeply rooted in early feminist notions of personal politics. But how is it possible to include absolutely everything we encounter as epistemologically important? Surely the claim is not that antique chair owners are different than owners of modern furniture, or that rock and roll listeners are epistemologically different from classical music listeners? In fact, she wants to make a claim about gendered bodies, but she has given us no reason to believe that knowledge occurs on a gendered level (or on a group level per se). In fact, if our experiences are so local, how can we even identify ourselves as members of groups in the first place?

All of this comes down to a problem of interpretation, and this problem is exacerbated by what Smith has already told us about the pervasive quality of ideology. Because of ideology, Smith wants to make the notion of "experience" more immediate and authentic. But her discussion continues to assert that knowledge is based upon experience, and this still begs the question as to how it is we are to interpret and order what we experience. If it were enough to simply reproduce what we have experienced, we would not need theories of knowledge at all. I am quite persuaded that Smith is right to say that everything we experience in life influences our choices, and that the body matters (certainly more than most of Western philosophy has thought). But I am not at all sure that all of our experiences matter in equally important ways, or that the body is always relevant to the apprehension of knowledge.

The incompleteness of "experience" alone as a category of analysis and the key role of feminist interpretation are also illustrated in the work of Patricia Hill Collins. Like Barbara Christian, Collins wants to talk about theory differently to include art, literature, and song lyrics as a way to divine the theory of African-American women who feel silenced by the current definition of theory. Collins examines the "thrown away" black women intellectuals who have been made invisible by the fact that what black women do has not been considered "intellectual" according to the dominant white male paradigm.[40] "Black women scholars may know that something is true but be unwilling or unable to legitimate our claims using Eurocentric, masculinist criteria for consistency with substantiated knowledge and criteria for methodological adequacy."

Collins makes the point that she is developing a black *women's* not a black *woman's* standpoint. Retaining the category Woman, however, Collins writes, "Women do share common experiences, but the experiences are not generally the same type as those affecting racial and ethnic groups." Collins sketches the contours of an "afrocentric feminist epistemology," which, she argues, will reflect the "Black women's standpoint" rooted in the "everyday experiences of African American women." Black women, Collins argues, do not provide a superior or truer version of reality, but an authentic, valid and important partial perspective—a "subjugated knowledge." No one is centered, Collins holds, but all groups hold distinctive standpoints. "Each group speaks from its own standpoint and shares its own partial, situated knowledge," she writes.[41]

For Collins, the experiences of black women illustrate points of contact between Afrocentric and feminist points of view.[42] But an overview of some of her examples suggests that, as with other standpoint theories, the reverse is true, and that it would be more correct to say that a politics of feminism (and in the case of Collins, Afrocentrism) informs her reading and construction of the black female experience. Like other standpoint thinkers, what is left out of Collins's analysis is the instrument with which she chooses which experiences to relate with and what to make of them. For example, in relating the lyrics of a Billie Holiday song to illustrate the theme of "self reliance and independence" in the black female experience, Collins cites the following:

> If I should take a notion, to jump into the ocean,
> If I dislike my lover and leave him for another,

If I go to church on Sunday then cabaret on Monday,
If I should get the feeling to dance upon the ceilin'
Tain't nobody's business if I do![43]

She does not cite other lyrics in this song, which include:

Cause I'd rather my man to hit me,
Than for him to jump up and quit me,
I swear I won't call no copper, if I'm beat up by my poppa,
Tain't nobody's business if I do![44]

My point is emphatically *not* that black women are not independent, but rather to call attention to Collins's (and other standpoint thinkers) methodology. The claim is that the female (or black female) experience is plainly visible if only one looks for it. But in fact, one only sees it if one looks through a certain lens. Feminist principles are not deduced from the female experience. A certain version of the female experience is created in the very act and means of looking.

THE POSSIBILITY OF A WOMEN'S STANDPOINT

In the face of criticisms of standpoint thinkers' ethnocentricism, the idea of "Woman's standpoint" has given way to "women's standpoints." The distinction is between a monolithic view of Woman and a view of women that maintains the category while embracing the differences within it. Unfortunately, this move continues to rest upon the view that there is something distinctive about the category, which holds it together even in the face of its variation. It is, in fact, the same problem socialist feminists tried to cope with in the 1970s and 1980s: how can we create a theory that reflects the reality of women, namely, that we are simultaneously the same and different?

Noting that there is opposition to the standpoint approach on just these grounds, Nell Noddings has written: "One reason for resistance is that, strictly speaking, there is no such thing as *the* standpoint of women. Women's lives and voices differ. I, for example, speak not only as a woman but as a middle class, white, mother, and academic." Noddings chooses to disregard this objection, however, concluding that although "this is an important objection, it still may be important to articulate an ethical orientation that arises in the context of women's traditional work and gives attention to women's concerns. In doing this, we must choose topics that touch as many women's lives as possible, and we must also remember to invite a broad range of perspectives to join our own."[45]

What Noddings's apology ignores is that when one looks across cultures and time, it is hard to name what we mean by "women's traditional work" and harder still to say what we mean by "women's concerns." If, as no one can deny, African-American slave women did different labor than the master's wife, what then, is the traditional work of women? Farming has at various times in history been the work of men, and at other times in other cultures it has been the work of women. In some African cultures even today, women farm and men do not.[46] Although Noddings tries to avoid it, the ethnocentrism of the notion of women's traditional work and the fact that this concept is still being used unproblematically are striking.

Neither do I understand the idea of women's concerns. For instance, while some women are concerned about their freedom of choice, others tend to be more worried about the alleged rights of fetuses. The fact that women on both sides of this debate can get pregnant in no way predisposes them to have the same thoughts about that pregnancy. Some women believe it is in women's nature to be peaceful. Others, many of whom call themselves feminists, dispute the military establishment's prohibitions against women in combat roles. For me, what all of this means is that we should not be talking about women's concerns or women's traditional work, but about *feminist* concerns and visions of new roles for men and women.

The gap between Woman and feminist should be the central issue of any discussion of feminist epistemology. Instead, with few exceptions, the necessity of a *feminist* (a) *naming* and then (b) *refiguring* female experience is only mentioned briefly and in passing by most theorists. It is undoubtedly true, as feminists and others have shown, that a change in one's perspective can lead to a fundamentally different analysis of a given set of information. What is not clear, however, is that the perspective that feminist theorists have been recounting is the result of anything having to do with a different *female* way of knowing. I am sure, on the other hand, that the new perspective on knowledge *does* have to do with the *feminist lens*, which has been mentioned, though not developed, by several thinkers. The rub is that a feminist lens cannot be grounded on female experience.

Without a feminist interpretive lens through which to see and reinvent gender, the idea of a standpoint of women will always be essentialist. As I have been arguing, this problem is impossible to escape if one begins from the category Woman. The issue is further inflamed by linking Woman to experience and remaining within an Enlightenment identity discourse in which Woman is attached to an epistemology. The argument necessary to sustain an unqualified claim that women's ways of knowing are different than men's will always devolve into some claim about a special transhistorical and transcultural identity and definition of woman.

Some feminists have wanted to argue that men and women have different life worlds and thus that their raw experiences differ systematically. They have argued that knowledge comes to us not as a universal feature of human beings, as Kant had thought, but as we exist in gendered bodies, and consequently, in gendered realities.[47] As Dorothy Smith writes, "we began with our experiences as women [however] we were always returning to ourselves and to each other as subjects *in our bodies* . . . the sexed body was always the common ground in relation to which we could find ourselves with each other *as women.*"[48]

Thus, feminists seem at various times to be making one or both of the following claims. The first one is that although the raw experiences—the data of life—may be the same for men and women, there is a systematic and gendered difference in the way that information is interpreted and acted upon. Hence, Bettina Aptheker writes, "I began then, with this idea: women have a consciousness of social reality that is distinct from that put forth by men. That is, women have a distinct way of seeing and interpreting the world . . . a way of seeing, which is common to themselves as women in that it is distinct from the way the men of their culture or group see things. All women share this *process* of distinction."[49] This appears essentialist unless it is supplemented by a second claim: that women inhabit different spaces in the world and encounter different events and circumstances, which then lead them to a distinctive female viewpoint. This latter is the claim of materialist feminist standpoint theory.

THE USE OF MARXISM IN FEMINIST STANDPOINT

So far, my analysis of standpoint has been based on a fairly tradition-al point about epistemology: that encounters with experience alone cannot provide foundations for knowledge. I have noted in passing (above) that most standpoint theorists have not taken their cues from Kant, but from Marx. It should come as no surprise that feminism should turn to Marxism in order to formulate a deessentialized epis-temology centered around women. Marx was engaged in a similar project with regard to the category "human."

It will be remembered that Kant and the German idealists essen-tialized "human" by invoking human beings as transhistorically, universally rational and transcendent beings. Though it is true that the very early Marx spoke of "man," the later Marx spoke not of humanity in general, but of classes, which were socially created vis-à-vis their positions in the production process. Through his protracted discussion of capitalism and feudalism, Marx was able to show that, as the mode of production changed, "human nature" and knowledge itself changed with them. Therefore, neither existed as transhistorical fact. Except for his brief discussions of "species being" in the *Economic and Philosophic Manuscripts,* Marx abandoned essential-izing talk about human nature in favor of a social category (class) that permitted dialectical discussions of its own material formation. By linking human history to the production process and the forma-tion of classes, Marx was able to deessentialize "man" by showing that mankind changed systematically in relation to a material process. Feminist standpoint uses Marxism to accomplish the same task with regard to Woman. Marxism is used to deessentialize Woman and recreate the category as a socio-material one. Woman, it is claimed, can be conceptualized according to a material base by not-ing the variability of women across time and cultures as they are linked to the material reality of their *daily lives.* This notion substi-tutes for earlier socialist feminists attempts to link women materially to the realm of reproduction and is meant to be analogous to Marx's linkage of the proletariat to the means of production.

Marx's epistemological claims have also been employed by standpoint feminists as a way to retain a notion of truth, by linking it to justice in a Marxian rather than Kantian way. The truth is that which is most clearly connected to real liberation for the most people. Theories of truth (such as Kant's and Hegel's) were "abstract,"[50] Marx argued, unless they could be rooted in concrete, material reality and linked to realizable freedom.[51] Therefore, a true theory of knowledge must be able to account for its own actualization in material reality as well as for its genesis in the same. Discussions of knowledge as abstract, ahistorical phenomena were no more than pointless metaphysical exercises, Marx charged. Knowledge, far from being universal and neutral as the German idealists had imagined, is always implicated in some political project. Even Hegel's theory of history was merely idealist speculation. Hegel's idea that freedom is the self-conscious unfolding of the Absolute Spirit whose goal is to recognize itself as an idea still leaves us wondering, What, then, is the Absolute Idea? Concluding that Hegel had said nothing to explain concrete reality, Marx concluded that Hegel's work, *The Logic,* is no more than "the demonstration that abstract thought is nothing in itself; that the Absolute Idea is nothing for itself; that only *Nature* is something."[52] Despite his strong critique of idealism, Marx retained, with Kant and Hegel, a belief that the telos of knowledge was universal freedom. However, it was insufficient to speak merely of the *possibility* of freedom (which the bourgeois philosophers had promised); one had to theorize and advocate its actual realization in the world.

In Marxism, the old idealist notions of "truth" and "universality" are preserved, but they are transformed in that they are grounded materially and historically. Marx accomplished this transformation by showing how the proletariat was a "universal class," which, when acting in its own self-interest as a class, could create the conditions for universal freedom. It could do this because its class position made it simultaneously the subject (creator) and object (creature) of the production process.[53] As a historically constituted class, the proletariat was epistemologically important *only* because of its place in the production process. The capitalist, in contrast, is epistemologically unimportant as the merely superfluous, exploitative appropriator of surplus value. The capitalist contributes no value. As such he (sic) lacks both the incentive and the structural position to change the world in a progressive manner. For Marx, this meant that the capitalist perspective, which masquerades as a universal one, is in reality only a partial perspective that does not move toward concrete, universal freedom. Marx writes, in advocating the link between the working class, truth, and universal justice: "All previous historical movements were movements of minorities in the interests of minorities."[54]

All of this enabled Marx to declare that the capitalist perspective is false. And it is this view that has proved immensely intriguing to feminist standpoint theorists who have wanted to argue against the alleged universal and neutral truth of the male standpoint. In sum, standpoint theorists have been piqued by Marx's revision of an essentialist category into a materialist one and by his ability to link truth to the perspective of an exploited class. As was the case with the socialist feminists from whom standpoint theory emerged, the hope was that the Marxian method could be used by analogy, substituting male for bourgeoisie and female for proletariat. That is, that the category Woman could be historicized, and further, that it could be shown that male truth is partial, while the female represents a more universal, authentic, and ultimately truer version of reality.

The analogy did not work in socialist feminism, and it does not work in standpoint theory either. First, woman has not been historicized. Marx deessentialized "human" by turning to the category proletariat. There is nothing in feminism that serves this function. Rather, man is to proletariat as woman is to . . . woman. In short, as my discussion of standpoint has shown, woman remains a nonmaterialist, essentialized category. Second, feminist theory has rejected universality in embracing the idea of experience, so it cannot claim, as Marx did on behalf of the proletariat, that women's interests (which, anyway, have not been convincingly theorized) represent universal interests, or that a female perspective of truth is any more authentic than anyone else's. This is, by the way, why standpoint is coming to look less and less like Marxism, and more and more like postmodernism. The postmodern idea of partial and multiple perspectives is far more amenable to the place at which standpoint theory has arrived than materialist theory as articulated by Marx.

One of the earliest and most impressive attempts to use Marxism to these ends was Nancy Hartsock's highly influential book *Money, Sex and Power: Towards a Feminist Historical Materialism,* published in 1983. In it, Hartsock criticized mainstream political science theories of power for being male biased and for conceptualizing power as domination. Certain theories of power, she argued, thematize community as problematic because they begin from the assumption that competition and domination are necessary.[55] Because of this, she held, these theorists cannot explain cooperative behavior.

She pointed with approval to female political theorists such as Hannah Arendt and Hanna Pitkin for advancing alternative concepts of power that assumed community as opposed to problematizing it. Hartsock termed this female understanding of power "empowerment" to distinguish it from the competition-based male theories. Hartsock was at the forefront of feminism in claiming that a "feminist theory of power" should be concerned with "energy and competence rather than dominance."[56]

A key element in Hartsock's work was her idea that differences in approaches to power varied by gender. She described male theories of power as necessarily negative. Male power virtually always involves the ability to constrain someone or something. Men think of power as the "power over," she argued. In contrast, female notions of power conceptualize it as a positive, enabling force. Thus, women think of power as the "power to" do something. "Indeed," she claimed, "one can almost argue that there is a separate and distinct women's tradition of theorizing power."

For Hartsock, this gender-based variation with regard to power also operates on the epistemological level and is connected to the different experiences—or "standpoints"—of men and women in patriarchal societies.[57] Male concepts of power and community grow from "negative, masculine forms of eros," which lie beneath "the reality of rape, sexual murder, and pornography." In contrast to what she found in male theorists, Hartsock claimed that she "was unable to discover any woman writing about power who did not stress those aspects of power related to energy, capacity and potential." Thus, for Hartsock, the gendered theories of power masked deep epistemological differences between men and women. Theories of power, she claimed, rested on epistemological assumptions that could be connected to gendered standpoints.[58] In elaborating the standpoint approach, Hartsock maintained that feminism, like Marxism, has a "perspective" theory of epistemology.[59] Since Hartsock, this notion of the female perspective, allegedly as patterned on Marxism, has played a central role in feminist standpoint epistemology.

Because it has played such a key role in feminist standpoint theory, it is important to look at the function of standpoint thinking in Marxism. While it is true that the notion of standpoint served a very important function in Marxism, it is less clear that the concept originated with Marx. Georg Lukacs used the language and thinking of proletarian standpoint as a way of enabling socialist critique on *behalf* of the working class, because the actually existing proletariat lacked class consciousness. In a passage reminiscent of Lenin's argument in *What Is to Be Done?*, Lukacs wrote that with correct dialectical thinking, "it becomes possible to infer the thoughts and feelings which men would have in a particular situation if they were *able* to assess both it and the interests arising from it . . . Now class consciousness consists in fact of the appropriate and rational reactions 'imputed' [zugerechnet] to a particular typical position in the process of production."[60] That is, standpoint thinking was necessary because the working class could not speak for itself. In fact, standpoint thinking in Marxism is the result of a problem of agency. Standpoint enabled critique from the point of view of an imagined subject, that is, from the point of view of a class that existed objectively, but which was not yet constituted as a subject.

It can be said that Lukacs's idea of imputing class consciousness to a class that did not yet have it paved the way for Stalinism. The idea of socialist realism grew from and embraced the notion of standpoint in art and art criticism. Communist art, it was decreed under Stalin, was to reflect the proletarian standpoint; a standpoint that would be imputed to it by the party, and, ultimately, by Stalin.[61] This was not one of Marxism's best moments. All of this led Theodor Adorno to criticize the very notion of standpoint. In a section of *Negative Dialectics* significantly entitled "Dialectics Not a Standpoint," Adorno wrote that the idea of standpoint assumes a static identity, which can then be adopted. As such, the very notion of standpoint is undialectical. In contrast to standpoint, Adorno explained, "dialectics is the consistent sense of nonidentity. It does not begin by taking a standpoint."[62]

The point of this brief discussion of standpoint thinking in Marxism is to look at which interpretations of Marxism have been adopted by feminism and to think about the implications of it. When we think about the history of standpoint in Marxism, the parallels between it and feminism are striking. Like the proletariat in Lukacs's time, women can be said to exist objectively as a group and, also like that proletariat, are not yet subjectively constituted. In the case of Marxism, if the proletariat had been class conscious, it would have been making its own criticisms on its own behalf in the context of a worldwide worker's movement. *A theoretical standpoint would not have been necessary.* Likewise, if women were constituted as *feminist subjects,* the need for a standpoint epistemology would disappear. (This may be what Dorothy Smith was getting at in remarking upon how standpoint tends to displace practical politics; see above.) In other words, if "woman" and "feminist" were the same thing, or at least politically the same thing, women could speak for themselves and would not have to be spoken for in elaborate academic discussions. As it is, much feminist theory speaks about women's interests not only in a monolithic way, but as though these interests could really be determined a priori in epistemological debates and abstract descriptions of women's different voices.

In both Marxism and feminism, the importance of theory is exaggerated in the absence of a large, radical movement. Feminism has a problem of agency that cannot be solved on the epistemological level. As Adorno has written, "The dismantling of systems, and of the system at large, is not an act of formal epistemology . . . We are not to philosophize about concrete things; we are to philosophize, rather, out of these things."[63] In both Marxism and feminism, standpoint theory addresses a political problem. In the case of feminism, the real issue is not to develop a feminist epistemology, but to discuss what feminism means, to try and bring more women into the movement to speak for themselves, rather than inventing an abstract female standpoint, which can then be adopted by theorists. It is the role of the feminist movement to *constitute women as feminist subjects, not only in theory, but also in practice.* Feminist *theory,* on the other hand, has an auxiliary task. As Marilyn Frye has said, feminist theory has "the power to make lives and experiences usefully intelligible"; it is a "frame for the making of meaning."[64]

The notion of standpoint has raised some discussion of "insider" and "outsider" perspectives. Again, these questions have a parallel in Marxism: if the proletariat is not yet constituted as a revolutionary agent, i.e., if there is no revolutionary agent, how can someone from inside the oppressive structure imagine a liberatory potential and a better future? Is not all thought marked with ideology and the experience of oppression? In taking the standpoint of a liberatory subject that is not yet constituted as such, must one, in effect, stand outside the dominant social relations? In her black feminist standpoint theory, Patricia Hill Collins has named an "outsider-within" position, which, she argues, provides "a distinct view of the contradictions between the dominant group's actions and ideologies."[65] Similarly, Sandra Harding has called women "valuable 'strangers' to the social order."[66] Dorothy Smith, on the other hand, has argued that it is impossible to stand outside. "A sociology from the standpoint of women insists that there is no place outside; hence it must be an insider's sociology."[67]

The whole language of insider/outsider is misplaced. It is undialectical and merely reinforces the binary trap. Though I tend to agree more with Smith that all experiential and identity-based thinking is tinged by ideology, and that no amount of thinking ourselves outside can change that, we also know from history that radical critique and change are possible. We must deduce that ideology leaves some critical space. Discussions of inside and outside are irrelevant. The question is what possibilities are immanent in this current reality, and this cannot be based on the experiences of the oppressed woman, but on the feminist revision of what woman can be. This task has heretofore been masquerading as the female standpoint.

A REREADING OF NANCY HARTSOCK

The use of standpoint as a way to solve problems of agency is problematic in both Marxism and feminism. Feminism cannot rest an epistemology on experiences that it imputes to a universal Woman and then claim that those experiences come from particular women. In making her claim about standpoint theory, Nancy Hartsock used empirical evidence to make her case about the variation in power/empower along male/female lines. But Hartsock's is a selective assortment of texts that assumes what it seeks to prove. My contention in what follows is that Hartsock is already employing some unstated idea about feminist values in selecting and interpreting texts about power and empowerment, and that she has mistaken the political distinctions she is making for epistemological ones having to do with women's values, experiences, and knowledge.

It should give us pause, for example, to recall that all of Hartsock's examples of theorists of "empowerment" were well known as communitarian theorists (Hannah Arendt, Hanna Pitkin, Dorothy Emmet), while those who espoused the so-called masculine values happened also to be mainstream market-based or liberal/individualist theorists (i.e., Harold Lasswell, Talcott Parsons, and the pluralists Robert Dahl and Nelson Polsby). What appears to Hartsock as epistemological variation by gender might actually be no more than a variation in political values—values selected to make a point about gender. Understanding Hartsock's observations this way enables us to see the different concepts of power Hartsock discusses as well as their implications for feminism apart from epistemology.

The gender-based epistemological angle necessarily links power to gendered categories, which, as I have been arguing, are necessarily essentialist and abstract. It splits the allegedly masculine impulse for domination from the female one for "energy, capacity and potential." Even if we could speak about male and female unproblematically, a question would still remain as to whether the impulses toward domination and enabling are in fact connected to males and females respectively.

Even more seriously, it is not possible to maintain the parallel structure male/female and power/empower. The power/empower dualism in its simplest form constitutes an equation that links power with domination and maleness, and empowerment with enabling and femaleness. Thus, it posits male and female as the fixed and epistemologically privileged categories that structure theories of power.

Indeed, male theories of power have changed across time. Socrates argues specifically against power as domination in his discussion with Thrasymachus in *The Republic*. The Platonic question, How can we construct a just regime? is very different from Machiavelli's that asked, How can regimes maintain power and legitimacy? Although both questions posed necessitate discussions of power, only the latter sees power as an end in itself justified by any means necessary. Whereas Plato's *Republic* begins with a discussion of the nature of justice, Jean Jacques Rousseau begins his *Social Contract* by proclaiming that he is about to show the legitimacy of the fact that "man is born free yet everywhere he is in chains." It is later revealed that the chains to which Rousseau refers are the chains of law and government. This shift from discussions of justice to discussions of legitimacy, as exemplified in the change from Plato to Rousseau, is fundamentally related to different concepts of power and its right usage. Thomas More's communitarian utopia serves as another counterexample. In short, male theories of power do not constitute a unified tradition.

The correlation of different types of power with gender is not persuasive. To prove a gender difference it would be important to show a counterintuitive relationship between theorists whose values and goals would have led us to expect one theory of power rather than one she or he in fact proffers. It would be much more persuasive, for example, were we able to show that Ayn Rand's objectivism was actually an argument for the communitarian "empowerment," or that Ghandi's notion of nonviolent civil disobedience was aimed at dominating the British. For that matter, the gender thesis would also have to show that (e.g.) Herbert Marcuse's concept of the erotic did not speak to the concerns of energy and capacity, and thus was not a theory of empowerment.

Rather than seeing knowledge as connected to political interests, feminist standpoint thinking makes epistemological links between theories and the chance gender characteristics of the people who invent them. Although we learn much from looking at the male bias in political theory, we might be better served in this instance by thinking of epistemology as a self-consciously derived theoretical tool in service of a politics. Epistemology, existing as it does merely on the level of metaphysics, must not be scrutinized to the exclusion of whatever politics it supports.

The point under contention is the ability to affix a certain concept of power to a given gender using an argument about epistemological difference as the justification. My estimation is that no particular construction of power is intrinsically linked to either gender. In fact, I am not persuaded that power, domination, or hierarchy is always and everywhere a bad thing. The whole discussion of what we as feminists think about power seems to have been short-circuited by the epistemological discussion, which has told us in advance what women with the proper consciousness ought to think about it (though, quite obviously, this outcome was not what Hartsock intended in her book).

If power and empowerment are dynamic practices, as Hartsock so correctly says, how can they be attached to a static notion of gender? Yet, for many feminists, the dissociation of power from femininity, and, in some cases, the wholesale rejection of power, is connected to a fixed and constrained notion of Woman and her experiences. Let us return for a moment to two examples from an earlier chapter regarding sexuality and mothering as universal female experiences. For anti-pornography feminists, power has been so masculinized that it is as though all other aspects of power are reducible to this one essential and immutable fact. Again, what is at fault here is the root epistemology, which sees certain behaviors as following from the male or female perspective. However, it should be a long way from saying that human sexual relationships can easily segue into power struggles to saying that power is masculine, or that all power expressed sexually is masculine-identified sexuality.

Anti-pornography feminists have set up a lust/eros dichotomy that is not unlike power/empower: lust is to power and masculinity as eros is to empowerment and femininity. Robin Morgan asserts that the "violation of an individual woman is the metaphor for man's forcing himself on whole nations (rape is the crux of war), on non-human creatures (rape is the lust behind hunting and related carnage), and on the planet itself."[68] For feminists like Morgan, the defining characteristics of male sexuality are objectification and domination. Lust, the key element in male sexuality, is power acted out sexually. All other types of domination stem from this lust.

Similarly, Gloria Steinem complains that in pornography "there is no sense of equal choice or equal power." Instead, pornography points up different types of sexuality—one, "mutually pleasurable, sexual expression between people who have enough power to be there by positive choice," the other, "pornographic: its message is violence, domination and conquest."[69] Thus, in contrast to male lust, feminine sexuality is allegedly erotic. "Making love" is not about domination, but rather about something closer to the energized expressiveness suggested in the concept of empowerment. Just as the power/empower distinction failed to stand up under close scrutiny, so the lust/eros dualism, which underpins the anti-pornography movement, disintegrates under close scrutiny.

Some feminists have begun to analyze power as a political reality rather than as an inevitable result of masculinity. As Linda Williams has argued in her brilliant analysis of the genre of hardcore pornography, the "very notion of erotica as 'good,' clean and nonexplicit representations of sexual pleasure in opposition to dirty, explicit pornographic ones is false. The erotic and the pornographic interact in hard core."[70] Indeed, Williams presents a compelling case for the possibility that pornography is far more complex in its portrayal of gender relations than most feminist critics allow. Pornography, Williams contends, poses questions about the nature of sexual pleasure, and, increasingly, those questions are specifically about female sexual pleasure. Although the perspective of pornography remains a phallic one, the results are not, Williams contends, monolithically misogynist. In the pornographic discourse, male sexual pleasure can be easily signified because it is literally visible both in erection and in the very nature of male orgasm. For Williams, female pleasure is invisible, taking place internally. This is a problem in pornography, a discourse that has sought since its inception to portray pleasure. Increasingly, pornography has been engaged in a desperate attempt to signify and come to terms with female sexual pleasure. Williams is not unaware that pornography largely portrays male fantasies, but she maintains that, over the course of the history of pornography, women have become more important in the pornographic text. In explaining what she terms the "diff'rent strokes for different folks" ethic of certain types of pornography, Williams says that it is

> indicative of a limited redefinition of sex: as a social and political interaction in which a certain amount of negotiation and give-and-take *could* take place . . . what is new . . . is quite simply a franker acknowledgment of the role of power in sexual relations than had ever been seen before. Power emerges in these films not, as anti-pornography feminists would have it, as the ultimate poison of all heterosexual relations, but as an important and inevitable component of increasingly material and fetishized forms of pleasure and of learning how to negotiate pleasure with partners.[71]

For Williams, power, when expressed sexually, is not always wielded by a man against women. Moving away from the assumption of man as predator and woman as victim allows us to analyze sexual intimacy as a political relationship. Indeed, Williams's work strongly suggests that male sexual power and, consequently, the privileged position of male sexual pleasure are being deconstructed by the female gaze(s) of women whose power and status outside of the bedroom has increased. Power is not a zero sum commodity. Just because men have it, does not necessarily mean that women do not. Neither does it mean that women should not want it. It is not at all clear that power is something we could or even should want to eradicate completely. Power/empower is inadequate to the task at hand of understanding the dynamic power-play(ing) that occurs between men and women, men and men, and women and women.

Mothering too provides a way to interrogate "empowerment." On the one hand, the power the mother wants to have vis-à-vis her children is clearly the kind described by empowerment. She wants to be able to mother well without restrictions from the state or her partner. She wants to be free from environmental dangers to her children including war and pollution. She wants to have adequate financial support to provide for them. She wants to raise them in a nurturing way that guides their minds in positive directions, but does not squash autonomy and creativity.

Yet, in aspiring to be a good mother, she also attains, and must at times employ, some amount of domination. She has power over her children through the rules she establishes for the household and for their lives. Mothering theory relies on only one kind of mother; only one aspect of mothering. The mother has authority over children in religious training, and in the types of political and social views to which they will be exposed. The mother also has sanctions to enforce her authority. Rules can be backed with force even when the rules she establishes are not really in the best interests of the child. Indeed, some mothers may establish rules with reckless disregard for the child's well-being, rules that are arbitrary ways to dominate rather than positive and helpful ways to enable the child. Sometimes mothers may harm without really meaning to do so because of their own pain and psychological disorder. Even Sara Ruddick, in a discussion about the powerlessness of the mother, is forced to admit that from the child's perspective the mother has immense power.

> A mother dealing with the daily exigencies of her own and her children's lives may not *feel* powerful. There are many external constraints on her capacity to name, feel and act. But in the daily conflict of will, at least with her children, a mother has the upper hand. Even the most powerless woman knows that she is physically powerful, stronger than her young children.[72]

Motherhood, which has become an archetypal example of empowerment and a model of justice for many in the feminist community, is in fact fundamentally connected to power that is indistinguishable from the male model.

The separation of power from values and motives and its subsequent split and reconstruction into masculine and feminine oppositions renders at least two significant points invisible. First, the distinction imagines that there is no connection between power/empower, yet upon examination, one obviously exists. Second, the dualism obscures the connection between different understandings of power and their respective value systems. Thus, the politics of power blends too fully into an epistemology of gender, which is then linked to power. Ironically, feminists who have been quick to criticize dualistic thinking on the part of nonfeminists have had recourse to it themselves in notions like power/empower. I have argued that this dichotomy is ultimately related to a male/female dualism still present in feminist theory. This dualism is a result of an epistemology that links knowledge experientially to one of two genders. These genders, in turn, claim to have empirical referents, but are in fact idealist abstractions and selective readings that deny differences of race, ethnicity, and history. The upshot is that the dualisms I have discussed as present in feminism, and at least one other which I will discuss below, are reductionist and replicate the very static visions of men and women that feminism was invented to destroy.

As a result of the emphasis on epistemology, the discussion of power becomes focused along gender-determinist lines, ignoring differences of class, ethnicity, culture, and history. However, the problem goes beyond essentialism and becomes, in fact, one of politics. Insofar as feminism has been overepistemologized, and insofar as that epistemology has been connected to a hopelessly abstract and essentialist category, *political similarities that could be cultivated to help feminists speak across difference are suppressed, while the differences that divide us as women are highlighted by one of the major foundational categories of current feminist theory.*

A remedy for some of the problem I have pointed to in feminist theory may be conceptualizing the maintenance of two genders, and subsequently of patriarchal domination, as problems of ideology and politics rather than of epistemology. Turning away from epistemology might enable us to abandon the problematic aspects of the category Woman since it is that category and the feminist problem of agency that necessitate the standpoint epistemology in the first place. In the new schema, power and politics would be linked to self-conscious ethical choices rather than being seen as the incidental results of gendered standpoints. Paradoxically, this could lead to a politics of unity around the issue of diversity.

I have analyzed Hartsock's theory of power because it has been so important to feminist theory and because it is enormously provocative, as are the ensuing discussions about power that have emerged in the feminist scholarly and activist communities. Although we have seen that, so far, this feminist standpoint is contingent on the category Woman, by making the distinction in the first place, Hartsock raised a pivotal issue about the difference between Woman and femi-nist when she opted to call the epistemological perspective she described a feminist standpoint rather than women's standpoint. This notion deserves to be developed.

This tension between woman and feminist reflects the reality of our theoretical and political enterprise. Perhaps the gap has always been more obvious to activists than to theorists. We who are primari-ly theorists have often written about women as though the category was self-evident. In our arrogance, we have often created an abstract universal Woman who is white, middle class, European, and hetero-sexual. Lately, we have evoked an ethereal Mother who is supportive, soft, and ever-present like Donna Reed rather than practical, working class, and loud like Roseanne Arnold. When Hartsock separates woman from feminist in a short passage hidden near the end of her book, she points to, but does not elaborate upon, a set of political values that are separable from Woman. Indeed, the very act of prefer-ring empowerment suggests that we as feminists have begun to denote a set of feminist values.

However, these values do not come from our natures as women, but from an as yet unarticulated politics. Why we have not been able to acknowledge these values as creations of our own politics, and instead persist in claiming that they are linked to our natures—social-ized or biological—as women is still mysterious to me. I suspect that the female/feminist separation has been rendered nearly invisible to us as we have devoted so much time to developing epistemological arguments around women's experience.

Therefore, for the Hartsock of 1983 as well as for most contempo-rary Anglo-feminist theorists, the epistemological Woman makes the political feminist possible. This continues to be true even though fem-inist scholars are increasingly aware of the highly problematic nature of the former category. We continue to use the category even with the knowledge that it assumes a single female standpoint. And absent something to take its place, we must continue to do so, as the catego-ry is, at present, foundational to feminist theory.

Although much has been said about feminist theories of power, and about experiential, gender-based epistemologies, relatively little has been said about how to describe the feminist lens through which we interpret experiences. Experiences mean little in and of themselves. The key is in how they are interpreted. Since we claim to interpret from a feminist perspective, it has become essential to understand what feminist means. bell hooks seems to agree when she notes that Woman

> radically call[s] into question the notion of a fundamentally common female experience which has been seen as the prerequisite for our coming together, for political unity. Recognition of the inter-connectedness of sex, race, and class highlights the diversity of experience, compelling redefinition of the terms for unity. If women do not share 'common oppression,' what then can serve as a basis for our coming together? Unlike many feminist comrades, I believe women and men must share a common understanding—a basic knowledge of what feminist is—if it is ever to be a powerful mass-based political movement.[73]

5

Feminism and Postmodernism

WHAT IS POSTMODERN FEMINISM?

I have argued that Woman and experience always lead to essentialist arguments, and that theories of knowledge based on women's experience are not reflections of women's lives. In my discussion of standpoint theory, I have tried to show how feminist theory's attempts to isolate and identify a subject and to base an attendant epistemology on her experience(s) or her daily life has been unsuccessful. Such theories actually tell stories about women selectively interpreted through recourse to a little examined and undertheorized feminist lens. The understanding of Woman they portray is, therefore, a normative one. Throughout this book, I have made the related claim that particular constructions of Woman and experience operate in tandem to push feminist understandings of personal politics (as well as other important concepts like liberation, violence, and power) in particular directions, and then to maintain that these directions reflect a truth about female reality.

Based on all of this, I have concluded that feminist theory is engaged in redefining Woman, not in discovering her experiences as it now claims. And although I do not thoroughly embrace postmodern thinking, the idea that feminist theory is participating in the redefinition of Woman combined with my critiques of essentialism do seem to argue for a postmodern feminism, or at least for a more postmodern one. I have pointed to an increasing overlap between recent standpoint theory and postmodern thinking. I have said that standpoint theory and poststructuralism are both interested in multiple perspectives and interpretation, and that standpoint's notion of multiple identities foreshadows feminism's attraction to postmodernism. Paradoxically, some of the things that make postmodernists move away from Anglo-American feminism are also among the reasons why the two bodies of theory are consistent in many ways. For one, Anglo-American feminism (especially post-1970s) and certain versions of postmodernism are both gynocentric theories that find liberatory potential in the feminine.

In this chapter, I will explore the relationship of the core concepts to postmodern feminism in order to evaluate the latter's usefulness in solving problems with the core concepts and in contributing to a revitalized feminist theory. In particular, I am interested in the common criticisms of the Enlightenment made by feminist and postmodern thinkers, and their mutual attempts to develop a democratized theory of knowledge and being.[1] The attempt to synthesize postmodernism with feminism represents another way of dealing with the core concepts. This case is unique, however, in that the solution involves a partial abandonment of the concepts themselves. However, the rejection of Anglo-American feminist constructions of Woman and experience has created a very interesting conversation between the two schools of feminist theory, a conversation that can even be described as a political struggle over how to conceptualize liberation and its subsequent triumph over power relations.

From this point on, the admittedly awkward term Anglo-American feminist will denote the tradition of feminism I have been discussing as formed around the core concepts. This term derives from the origins of this kind of theory as developed in the U.S. and U.K. and does not refer to the nationality or ethnicity of the theorists themselves (e.g., there can be Latina Anglo-American feminists). In turn, I will use the terms postmodernism and poststructuralism interchangeably as ways to refer to a loosely affiliated though internally diverse body of thought that has common epistemological and ontological roots in the philosophy of Nietzsche, and which has become possible as a mode of thought in this historical epoch. Particularly interesting for feminism are the radically social constructivist claims of postmodern theories and the discussions of power, especially as found in the works of Michel Foucault.

Postmodernism itself can be thought of in one of three ways: First, it is a term used to describe an epoch. Jurgen Habermas and others have used the concept of postmodernism in this way to encompass the mode of thinking that reflects the fragmented totality characteristic of late capitalism and to lament the advent of the postmodern age.[2]

Second, postmodernism can be thought of as a philosophical stance that challenges generally accepted beliefs about reality, knowledge, truth, and transcendence. Habermas uses the term this way as well, but does so as a pejorative, in contrast to Jean Francois Lyotard who uses the term to extol its virtues.[3] Some thinkers dispute the use of this definition of postmodernism altogether, preferring instead the term poststructuralism. The reasons for this have been well articulated by Andreas Huyssen who uses postmodernism in yet a third way, as connected to avant-garde movements in literature and the arts. Poststructuralism, he argues, more properly refers to theory and is wrongly viewed in the United States as the theoretical equivalent of postmodernism. In fact it is a "discourse of and about modernism."[4] Husseyn is correct to point out that postmodernism is a discourse about modernity, but in that it also tries to transform modern categories, I do not see a problem with referring to these theories as postmodern. Marx, after all, wrote mostly about capitalism, but that does not mean he is a capitalist.

Those who have been long-time feminist supporters of what I am calling postmodern thought will doubtless be put off by this wholesale treatment of postmodernism, which seems to lump together deconstruction, semiotics, and genealogy. Of such conflations, Judith Butler has chided: "It may come as a surprise to some purveyors of the Continental scene to learn that Lacanian psychoanalysis in France positions itself officially against poststructuralism, that Kristeva denounces postmodernism, that Foucaultians rarely relate to Derrideans, that

Cixous and Irigaray are fundamentally opposed . . ."[5] I am aware of these differences, and yet there is something common to these modes of thinking; something about them as a mark of the crisis of modernity and Enlightenment thought generally. And it is precisely that quality that leads me to treat postmodernism as a whole in a kind of ideal typical way, as least for the purposes of the discussion in this chapter.

In fact, Butler might also have mentioned that the women whose names we associate with French feminism (e.g., Hélène Cixous and Julia Kristeva) "at the very least do not call themselves feminists either privately or in their writing, and, at the most, posit themselves and their work hostile to, or 'beyond' feminism as a concept."[6] Likewise, according to Alice Jardin, what remains of the French equivalent of the Women's Liberation Movement (mouvement de lib- eration des femmes) eventually became synonymous with the group Psychanalyse et Politique, which "according to its own literature and public stance, is most definitely opposed to feminism . . ."[7] So, in fact, it is not even clear what it means to be a postmodern feminist. In par- ticular, it is important to ask, What is feminist about postmodern feminist theory once the core concepts are removed?

There are several possibilities. First, there is a common concern for gender and the feminine. In the case of postmodern feminism, this concern is not the idle musings of a scholar as we see in, for example, Jacques Derrida's discussion of the feminine in his *Spurs*. Rather, in both postmodern and Anglo-American feminist theory, analysis takes place from a political perspective; in short, through a feminist lens. Postmodern feminists look more to power and liberation vis-à-vis gender, and in this emphasis, they depart from the tradition estab- lished around the core concepts. What is not always clear from postmodern feminisms, however, is what female liberation will look like. The images of nonidentity that are invoked as strategies for lib- eration are often alienating, and not nearly so comforting as the peaceful community evoked in feminisms content to be grounded in a feminine principle. This does not change the fact that, in this instance as with all other hyphenated feminist theories, a feminist politics guides the use of the theory. Though it is anti-foundationalist, post- modern feminism relies on a political identity that grew out of a foundationalist feminism.

Despite ambiguity about the very idea of postmodernism and its relationship to feminism, something called postmodern feminism is currently enjoying a lively existence among feminists off the Continent. These theorists do not shy away from calling themselves feminists, but do reject many of the major categories of Anglo-American feminism. Although they eschew an essentialized use of Woman, they do, in fact (even obviously) share the Anglo-American feminist desire for women's liberation as a major raison d'être. But rather than grounding feminism in female experience, *gender* is examined as a source of *power* and *hierarchy*, which are assumed to have a differentially negative impact on women as beings who embody the "feminine." Power becomes a major category in this analysis. Epistemological questions about how to ground feminism in women's experiences, and how to define Woman, become less important than questions about how to resist power and enhance freedom.

This stress on power and freedom in some postmodern feminism is due in large part to the influence of Foucault. On the relationship between truth and power he writes, "truth isn't outside power, or lacking in power . . . Truth is a thing of this world: it is produced only by virtue of multiple forms of constraint. And it induces regular effects of power. Each society has its regime of truth, its 'general politics' of truth: that is, the types of discourse which it accepts and makes function as true; the mechanisms and instances which enable one to distinguish true and false statements . . ."[8] Truth, therefore, cannot be appealed to or relied upon as the grounds for justice or anything else, since it is itself fully implicated in power relations. By the same token, freedom, such as it is, consists in "the happy limbo of non-identity."[9] Freedom is the resistance to categorization; that is, the resistance, as far as is possible, to the totalizing aspects of power and the will to truth. The truth of what Woman is, or the truth that Woman knows, both key questions in Anglo-American feminist theory, become oppressive notions in themselves for postmodern feminists. The problem becomes how to trace the historical development of the "truth" of Woman in order to avoid it. The crucial project is to investigate the mechanisms of power that have forged the female identity in order to resist identity itself.

POSTMODERN AND ANGLO-AMERICAN FEMINISMS: SOME SIMILARITIES AND DIFFERENCES

The move toward postmodernism is a move away from the core concepts as originally constructed and a move away from epistemologically laden questions about what is. It is a move toward questions about interpretation, description, and possible new ways of being. The tension between postmodernism and the core concepts is endemic to a larger conflict between postmodernism and modernity.

Postmodernism is basically a reaction against all of the major tenets of modernist thought.[10] That is, it is a reaction against a primarily epistemological discourse that assumes a knowing and active subject seeking access to objective reality, which, at least theoretically, can be understood in its totality. Postmodernism rejects epistemological questions on the grounds that reality is multiple and historically contingent; that nothing can be understood in its totality because the whole notion of totality is a fiction. So are the idea of a unified subject defined by a single identity and the notion of a neutral, rationalist perspective.

This new postmodern feminist agenda of nonidentity, rooted neither in Woman nor experience, is exactly what is troubling to Anglo-American feminists. Postmodern feminists seem more concerned with what Woman (and the things associated with her) *means* than with what she *is*. For them, there is no woman apart from the interpretations of her. Postmodernism, in fact, seems to discuss so-called real world phenomena (such as battering or abortion) by decoding metaphors and discourses of masculinity and femininity.

Consider, for example, two methodologically different, yet equally creative and compelling accounts of the history of abortion policy. Carroll Smith-Rosenberg writes in the preface to her essay "The Body Politic": "During periods of social transformation, when social forms crack open, social dialects proliferate, blending and conflicting with one another, challenging the dominant discourses. At such times, ideological conflict fractures discourse. At such times, as well, sexuality and the physical body emerge as particularly evocative political symbols."[11] What follows is a rich discussion of the construction of femininity and masculinity in the nineteenth century and the ways in which those constructions made repressive abortion policies possible. What is of note in the context of my discussion herein is the way in which Smith-Rosenberg's *method* of discussing the history of abortion differs from that of an Anglo-American feminist. In order to understand how "our own bodies and desires are constructed and how the power that constructs the body politic is deployed," Smith-Rosenberg cautions, we need to understand that texts "constitute the locus where bodies discursive and material weave fabrics of the self."[12] Note that Smith-Rosenberg discusses abortion as part of a discourse of sexuality and discusses the body as a political symbol.

Such language can mislead modernist feminists who read words like *symbol* and *discourse* as words more appropriately applied to books and which, when applied to "real world" events like abortion, diminish the "main" or political issues. The complaint is that discourse theory deemphasizes or ignores the specific roles of women as actors and victims in abortion policies. In this regard, note that Smith-Rosenberg concentrates on the "power that constructs the body politic" rather than the actors who construct it. For Anglo-American feminists, the idea that power exists as a reified entity apart from subjects who simply participate in or resist its various discourses suggests a profound and politically debilitating powerlessness.

Contrast Smith-Rosenberg's approach with the more traditional one taken by Rosalind Petchesky, who understands the history of abortion not in terms of changing discourses of masculinity and femininity, but as manifestations of class and state power. Arguing that the idea of "right to choose" would be more appropriately understood as merely one aspect of "reproductive rights," Petchesky's book stresses the role of feminist women in the struggles for reproductive rights and the subsequent impact on them when those rights are denied. She writes, "An active and vocal feminist movement in this period was both effect and cause of a new sense of women's possibilities; it grew out of the social changes that were occurring for women, and moved, in its vision, far beyond them. It also made 'abortion on demand' a primary political goal."[13] Both Smith-Rosenberg and Petchesky present fascinating histories, each from a very different methodological perspective—Petchesky embracing the need to talk about women as major actors and participants; Smith-

Rosenberg seeing the various constructions of women as one of the effects of changing discourses of power.

The move from discussions of the *essence* of woman as related through her experience to the *interpretation* of Woman and radical *redescription* of her in terms of discourse theory can be disturbing. Luce Irigaray's evasion is typical: "The question 'what is . . . ?' is the question—the metaphysical question—to which the feminine does not allow itself to submit."[14] Anglo-American feminist critics wonder whether it is enough to redescribe; whether we should be worrying about the meaning of woman as symbolic activity when real biologically embodied women suffer in a concrete world where they feel robbed of their subjectivity. In addition, there is concern that postmodern analyses rob us of a way to conceptualize women as subjects and agents of change. Yet, for postmodernists, to discuss the interpretation *is* to discuss the real. The distinction itself wrongly assumes a reality that exists objectively apart from interpretation. Moreover, to discuss anyone as an agent of change misses an important point about the nature of discourses: they preexist the subject. We enter into already existing discourses, and though changes happen they are not always explicable in terms of radical social movements who use traditional strategies.

Because postmodernism rejects the idea of a holistic and immovable reality, new ways of seeing a thing go a long way toward constituting a "real" change. Likewise, the rejection of identity thinking on the part of postmodernism signals at the same time a dismissal of the idea that we can make radical critiques from "the female perspective." From the Anglo-American perspective, this move away from the female perspective looks profoundly apolitical. Postmodernism's aversion to subject/object discourse, it is charged, takes away any language in which to talk about "real women." In the oft quoted words of Nancy Hartsock:

> Why is it that just at the moment when so many of us who have been silenced begin to demand the right to name ourselves, to act as subjects rather than objects of history, that just then the concept of subjecthood becomes problematic? Just when we are forming our own theories of the world, uncertainty emerges about whether the world can be theorized. Just when we are talking about the changes

we want, ideas of progress and the possibility of systematically and rationally organizing human society become dubious and suspect.[15]

Thus, Hartsock and others object to the abandonment of subject/object language, at least in part, on political grounds.

An added tension is related to the tendency of some postmodern theory to be unnecessarily opaque and jargonistic, even self-indulgent. This only adds to the impression that it has even less to say about people's real lives than modernist theory, and that it is exactly the kind of inaccessible theorizing that a democratically minded movement ought to avoid.[16] Related to this problem is the idea that it is basically a Eurocentric theory used mostly by the white and middle class. This opinion persists even though some of the foremost African-American scholars of gender employ some version of postmodern theory. In defending her use of the postmodern approach, Hazel Carby has written that "Black feminist criticism has too frequently been reduced to an experiential relationship that exists between black women as critics and black women as writers who represent black women's reality. Theoretically this reliance on a common, or shared, experience is essentialist and ahistorical."[17]

Postmodernism is attractive because it allows feminists to talk about gender, oppression, freedom, and personal politics while avoiding essentialism. It also allows us to avoid questions about why women are oppressed in that it defines power relations as constant, given, and emanating from all points. The world-historical domination of the male and masculinity is explainable as a convention based on the association of women and the feminine with all that discourses of rationality consider subordinate: weakness, passivity, and irrationality itself. The coincidence of the rise of misogyny with the predominance of a discourse of rationality in the West has been well documented by feminist political theorists.[18]

Despite this enormous divide between Anglo-American and postmodern feminisms, anyone who reads either feminism or postmodern theory cannot help but notice the similarity between the two. They share, for instance, trenchant criticisms of masculinity and Enlightenment values, as well as similar critiques of the notions of reality, hierarchy, power, and truth, all of which can be used in denaturalizing concepts like gender.

Yet, important differences exist in the bases for these critiques. In the Anglo-American case, critiques of reality, truth, hierarchy, and power are accomplished by linking those notions to maleness as against an essentialized feminine. That is, power, objective truth, hierarchy, and so on are criticized because they are *male*. In contrast, similar appraisals on the parts of postmodern thinkers are part and parcel of larger critiques of the Enlightenment in general and are only secondarily about women and the feminine per se. Overall, the postmodern critique is primarily about power and only secondarily about gender. To the extent that gender hierarchy is an exercise of power, and to the extent that men have, in general, had access to the upper echelons of this hierarchy because they have been able to define themselves as embodying all that matters in the Enlightenment discourse (e.g., individuals, rational, and neutral), postmodernism is aligned with feminism. Because of their politics, postmodern feminists are likely to treat power and gender as equally important, however. Thus, we can say that postmodern feminism uses insights from postmodernism regarding power in order to talk about gender.

Postmodernists and feminists have a genuine overlapping of concerns, and though the starting points and philosophical assumptions differ dramatically, Anglo-American feminism can look very postmodern. For example, experientialism leads to conclusions that are, on the surface, quite consistent with the postmodern notion of multiplicity. For instance, if we are to believe women's experiences matter, we must become aware that these experiences differ enormously and that the experiences of women are multiple, coming as they do from manifold perspectives. In standpoint thinking, this observation is used to make an epistemological argument that grounds female knowledge in multiple experiences. Likewise, postmodernism uses the notions of perspective and multiplicity primarily to criticize theories that posit objective reality and truth, including theories with foundationalist fixed identities, ironically, including Anglo-American feminism.

Thus, postmodern feminists do not see freedom as coming from the identification with the experiences of the oppressed, but rather in resistance to identity per se. For them, it is impossible to move toward freedom if we do so by gathering political strength in identifications as members of oppressed groups. Even if we transvalue the values associated with those groups, resisting in terms of group identities that have been formed in hierarchical contexts will only reproduce those hierarchical relationships (or, at best, create new ones). Postmodernists believe that this is true regardless of the intent of the participants (subjects) in the struggle.

In contrast, Anglo-American feminism adheres to the idea that a female identity is imperative; that defining women and her interests and then revaluing the feminine will yield women's liberation. Thus, for Anglo-American feminists, the postpatriarchal way of thinking will be rooted in a reconstruction from the perspective of the female experience as is defined in the context of female identity thinking. In short, while postmodernists believe that Woman itself is (with nearly all others) a contaminated category, Anglo-American feminists look to that category as a way to ground and envision liberation. For postmodernism, the very fixity of the category Woman means that it can not allow for diversity, change, or evolution; in short, that it disallows the possibility of freedom. The critique of identity thinking and, consequently, of the category Woman is repugnant to Anglo-American feminists. As Mary Poovey writes (specifically addressing problems with deconstruction), "the challenge for those of us who are convinced both that real historical women do exist and share certain experience and that deconstruction's demystification of presence makes theoretical sense is to work out some way to think both women and woman. It is not an easy task."[19]

Postmodern and Anglo-American feminists share a common concern for difference. However, in the postmodern case, this does not derive only from the differences among women or between women and men. Rather, it refers to the multiple centers of power, meanings of words, interpretations of reality, identities, desires, and so on that exist beneath the overpowering impulse toward oneness, summarized by Nietzsche in the phrase "will to truth."[20] Philosophers, he argues, seek to prove that "reason and instinct of themselves tend toward one goal, the good, 'God.' And since Plato, all theologians and philosophers are on the same track . . . Perhaps Descartes should be excepted, as the father of rationalism . . . who conceded authority to reason alone: but reason is merely an instrument, and Descartes was superficial." In reality, philosophers are "all advocates who resent that name, and for the most part even wily spokesmen for their prejudices which they baptize 'truths.'"

Nietzsche's sentiments led Derrida to ask rhetorically and approvingly, "is not all Nietzsche's thought a critique of philosophy as an active indifference to difference . . . ?"[21] The two agree, then, that a major outcome of metaphysics has been a disastrous conflation of multiple meanings, identities, and interpretations into a mask of seamless singleness. This has meant not only the domination of the one over the many, but the domination of a *particular* one, and the rejection of all difference as inferior. Therefore, universal concepts such as reality and truth *per se* are anomalous to the postmodern project. It begins instead from the assumption of a multiple, discourse-dependent reality, which is only artificially maintained as one truth because of the relationship between power and knowledge.[22] Truth, like reality and interpretations of it, is manifold. Power, hierarchy, rationality, and truth are seen as ways to arbitrarily create a monolithic power structure that gains authority by claiming to be true and real, but which is actually no more real than the marginal discourses that are suppressed in the wake of their creation. Critics have argued that this view prohibits making any affirmative statements about anything.

Motivated by a desire to move away from an essentialized feminist theory, but hoping to avoid the feared paralysis, Donna Haraway has done much to forge an explicit link between standpoint theory and postmodernism. Her notion of "situated knowledges" and the "coyote trickster" aspire to retain some notion of subjectivity as well as an idea of the world as existing apart from one's interpretation of it. In her own words, the problem is to "have *simultaneously* an account of radical historical contingency for all knowledge claims and knowing subjects, a critical practice for recognizing our own 'semiotic technologies' for making meanings, *and* a no-nonsense commitment to faithful accounts of a 'real' world . . ."[23] Thus she argues that by acknowledging that knowledges are partial, multiple, and historically situated, we can maintain some notion of subjectivity and reality without resorting to a transhistorical, static identity politics or falling back on the "god-trick" of a neutrally accessible, objective knowledge of some allegedly seamless totality.[24] "The search for such a 'full' and total position is the search for the fetishized perfect subject of oppositional history . . . The only position from which objectivity could not possibly be practiced and honoured is the standpoint of the master, the Man, the One God, whose Eye produces, appropriates and orders all difference." Haraway envisions "feminist visualizations of the world as witty agent . . . the Coyote or Trickster, embodied in American Southwest Indian accounts, suggests our situation when we give up mastery but keep searching for fidelity, knowing all the while we will be hoodwinked." Her playful suggestion about multiple knowledges asks us to think of the world as real, though elusive, wily, and contradictory.

For Haraway, the subject, too, must be retained but reconceptualized and historicized. Asking us to imagine a being from the "post-gender world,"[25] Haraway concocts the "cyborg" as one possible version of this subject. Her cyborg is about "transgressed boundaries, potent fusions, and dangerous possibilities." The image is attractive to her precisely its tendency to resist identity thinking: "The cyborgs populating feminist science fiction make very problematic the statuses of man or woman, human, artefact, member of a race, individual entity or the body." Further, "The cyborg is a kind of disassembled and reassembled, postmodern, collective and personal self. This is the self feminists must code."

Haraway's postmodern standpoint approach is appealing in that it does not pretend to mirror women's experience or to define women's reality at all. Instead, it asks us to envision an alternative understanding of humans as perpetually unfixed and contingent. Rather than beginning with a definition of oppression, Woman, or experience, Haraway begins from the *assumption* of women's oppression and seeks a new *description* of women—a new identity of nonidentity—which might move humans away from the oppressive and static gender codes under which we currently exist. The "dangerous possibilities" of which Haraway speaks seem to hint at the possible end of gender altogether. It is not unlike Margaret Atwood's notion of "gender treachery" in *A Handmaid's Tale,* or Butler's ideas about how to cause "gender trouble." All of these notions recall the importance of shedding the master's ideas about what women are and can be, and substituting for them new concepts of the female and the human. In this desire, it is closer to early radical feminist demands that we "annihilate gender." This approach is more likely to avoid nostalgia for having such mythic female characteristics as caring, intuition, or motherhood on which to build the feminist model, and to move to a concept of free humans as unbound by gender, to an idea of humans continually choosing among as-yet-unthought combinations of practices and activities.

Ironically, a major point of overlap between Anglo-American and postmodern feminisms has to do with the idea of difference. This derives in the case of Anglo-American feminism from its construction of the category Woman. As I have argued, the core concepts of feminism have encouraged a politics that praises difference and multiplicity because *difference* bespeaks the diversity of women—the differences among us—as well as the male/female difference itself. This concept of difference has also become important insofar as it has influenced the conceptualization of oppression. The latter has evolved away from the early radical feminist tendency to speak exclusively of women's oppression. Instead feminists of late have followed insights proffered by women of color and socialist feminists who now speak of female oppression as only one of many possible oppressions created by a web of power structures including but not limited to racism, patriarchy, and capitalism.[26]

Likewise, feminists have reconceptualized notions of power to the point that it has almost become the orthodoxy in feminist theory to speak of women as being averse to power and desiring of a less hierarchical and more energetic "empowerment."[27] Finally included in this concept of power is a broader view of oppression and violence on the parts of both Anglo-American feminists and postmodernists. I have discussed examples of this in Anglo-American feminism at length in previous chapters (especially in the section on the sexuality debates). Similar explanations prevail in postmodernism. For postmodernists, oppression and violence are not restricted to describing physical events, but can be used to denote oppressive, violent applications of interpretation or onerously restrictive constructions of discourse, which occur, not at a metalevel, but in day-to-day exclusionary practices. This commonality between postmodern theory and Anglo-American feminism on the question of power has been noted by at least one feminist who attempted to "read a deconstructive political strategy through" the works of Zillah Eisenstein and Nancy Chodorow.[28] The resistance in Anglo-American feminism to power differs from the postmodern one, however, in the former's tendency to see power as solely a negative force, in contrast to postmodernists after Foucault who see power as constructive as well.[29] Power is a double-edged phenomenon. It dominates, but it also constructs our understandings of existence.

This questioning of a one true reality on the part of postmodernism has lead Anglo-American feminists to criticize it for being relativistic and nihilistic. Yet, Anglo-American feminism as built around the core concepts is equally vulnerable to this charge. As we have seen, the diversity of women as a group, combined with the Anglo-American feminist predilection to ground its theory in female experience, does in fact lead to a relativistic definition of reality. As to nihilism—a charge stemming from the view that a destruction of reality leads us to stare into the face of nothingness[30]—it is important to remember that the very concept of objective reality has already been called into question by Anglo-American feminist claims that there are many realities defined by and dependent upon one's experiences.[31] It is increasingly the case that feminists of all stripes follow Nietzsche in holding that "the epistemological subject is necessarily situated, his field of knowledge is finite; thus, no one perspective can exhaust the richness of reality . . . Nietzsche in fact defends an ontological pluralism: the essence of Being is to show itself, and to show itself according to an infinity of viewpoints."[32]

It is evident that both approaches share Nietzsche's mistrust if not outright rejection of the Enlightenment idea that truth and moral vision are connected to rationality. Reason, it is now often claimed by Anglo-American feminists, is no more than a (male/masculine) tool, which is used to dominate those defined by the power structure as nonrational.[33] However, while Anglo-American feminist critiques of reason are fundamentally connected to the core concepts (namely, assumptions about the nature of Woman), postmodern criticisms of the same explicitly invoke Nietzschian critiques of metaphysics and echo his pronounced preoccupation with language. The interest in language is a logical outcome of the shift from questions about the essence of things to questions about the socially constructed meanings of things. Language is, after all, a socially constructed set of designations and meanings that we attach to things and concepts arbitrarily in order to communicate about them. Language enables us, through a system of signs, to exchange a representation of a thing for the thing itself and to postpone or ignore questions about the actual essence of things. This explains Derrida's attraction to Nietzsche.

For postmodernists, the wills to reality and meaning are no more than signals of our own discomfort with our infinitely variable realities. For deconstructionists in particular, there are no differentiations that are not socially determined and discourse dependent. Difference and meaning are also constructed in relation to one another. In sum, nothing has a meaning apart from its precarious attachment to empirical referents, an attachment that is socially constructed.

For deconstructionists, the prototype for this meaning-making is language. Words are a principal example of something that we take to have a fixed meaning, but which is, in fact, highly contingent. The dictionary only confirms this instability by pointing to multiple meanings for each given word.[34] C-a-t means cat because d-o-g means dog, not because there is any inherent relationship between the name and the thing it signifies. The system, in this case, the language system, has coherence because of different sounds as well. C-a-t is different not only from d-o-g, but also from h-a-t and m-a-t.[35]

The relevance of this insight for social science and philosophy is the further claim that all systems have languages and form discourses that subjects enter into.[36] Roland Barthes uses Ferdinand de Saussure's example of the Highway Code to illustrate this concept.[37] As Barthes explains Saussure, we know what road signs mean because they stand in relation to each other. That is, we do not know them as single things, but as parts of a language of road signs. The code, like all discourse, can only be known because it differs internally as well as from other systems (externally). The Highway Code itself is a signifier, and each road sign in it, a signified. The language of the code is not dependent on the "real things" to which it refers for its existence. Moreover, its status as language is defined precisely by the fact that individuals cannot change it. Understood this way, the system reifies meaning; meaning stands on its own apart from acting and thinking subjects.

As this example shows, subjects learn an already existing language, which has been socially constructed in the always already existing (and again, reified) "society." *Deconstruction* is, then, a process of deciphering and denaturalizing meaning, which Joan Scott succinctly characterizes as involving the analysis of

> the operations of difference in texts, the ways in which meanings are made to work. The method consists of two related steps; the reversal and displacement of binary oppositions. This double process reveals the interdependence of seemingly dichotomous terms and their meaning relative to a particular history. It shows them to be not natural but constructed oppositions, constructed for particular purposes in particular contexts.[38]

This idea is significant for feminists trying to understand the binary oppositions of male/female, woman/man, masculine/feminine, and so on. By reversing the poles in gender and displacing or "decentering" them, we can see that each term is dependent on the fixed definition of the other. Hence, men are defined in terms of the definition of woman and vice versa. This kind of move would explain, for example, why men see their power as resting so heavily on the maintenance of women in a powerless position. Further, studying how the meanings of *man* and *woman* came to be what they are in a given circumstance exposes the definitions as socially contingent rather than natural. Still, this kind of thinking presents a problem for Anglo-American feminist theory built on Woman. If all meaning is conventional and not essential, the meaning of Woman, too, is contingent. This in turn means that any theory relying on the female experience for truth claims is merely advocating using a highly contested set of experiences as a foundation. Moreover, that female experience (if it could be shown to exist) is an experience that only exists as the opposite of the male. As gender constructions change, the experiences will change too. The female experience itself will only be valuable, if at all, to the extent that binary gender relations remain in place (e.g., if the male is powerful, the female is powerless, and so on). On this point, the tension between deconstructionists and Anglo-

American feminists exists around a question: whether to build feminism on a foundation of gendered experiences as they are currently constructed and then to revalue those experiences (as is done in "different voice" theories), or to demythologize the entire structure of gender itself.

FEMININE THINKING AND THE MOVE AWAY FROM THEORY

In some postmodern feminism, the concept of feminine thinking reemerges from a most unlikely quarter; not from Woman, but from the idea of binary opposites. Woman, as many Anglo-American feminists now describe her, appears to have much in common with the postmodern notion of femininity, despite the latter's claims against essentialism. Both the feminist concept of Woman and the postmodern "feminine" are linked to that which is pleasure seeking, nonhierarchical, tolerant of difference, and instinctual. Toril Moi summarizes Cixous' theories about binary oppositions by comprising a list as follows:

Activity/Passivity
Sun/Moon
Culture/Nature
Day/Night
Father/Mother
Head/Emotions
Intelligible/Sensitive
Logos/Pathos
Nature/History
Nature/Art
Nature/Mind
Passion/Action

As Moi observes, "These examples show that it doesn't much matter which 'couple' one chooses to highlight: the hidden male/female opposition with its inevitable positive/negative evaluation can always be traced as the underlying paradigm . . . Against any binary scheme of thought, Cixous sets multiple, heterogeneous *difference*."[39] Cixous' notion of *ecriture feminine* designates the kind of writing said to be done by women; the kind of writing where the text "works on the difference." Some French theory is even more explicit about linking the female body to feminine thinking and experiences. Like Cixous, Irigaray has talked about the feminine as linked to multiplicity and difference. For Irigaray that link is reflected in the female body itself with its multiple zones of eroticism symbolized most fully in the two lips of the vagina.[40]

Though Anglo-American and postmodern bodies of thought share a basic criticism of dualistic, hierarchical thinking and a predilection toward difference and multiplicity, they do not enter the philosophical discourse at the same level. While postmodernism is concerned first and foremost with questions about meanings, interpretation, and dualisms per se, Anglo-American feminists' concerns about binary oppositions are an outcome of a prior interest in ending women's oppression, and from the questions that arose in that effort. Thus, the two bodies of thought, however similar, begin from very different perspectives—feminist theory originating as an adjunct to a politics and postmodernism being, in many ways, primarily a theory about theory.[41] It is no exaggeration to say, however, that taking Woman as a starting point seems to have propelled Anglo-American feminism to many of the same kinds of conclusions reached in postmodern thinking.

Because of the accord that has been reached between the two bodies of thought on certain substantive critical perspectives having to do with the Enlightenment and modernity, there has been a common tendency, in some instances, to question the very enterprise of theory. This common tendency derives from at least two sources. First, both Anglo-American feminists and postmodern thinkers basically understand politics to be synonymous with power and, increasingly, see power as emanating from all points at once. For Anglo-American feminists, this is connected to the idea of personal politics (recall Shulamith Firestone's idea of the invisibility of sex-class as well as early radical feminist calls for a revolution that would even encompass thought and personal life). Theory as such is a political enterprise.

Second, they both have serious criticisms of universality. For Anglo-American feminists, the understanding of politics as power enables theories to be conceptualized as political to the extent that they are embedded in power relations. (This notion of the political nature of thought is not new to feminism or postmodernism, of course, but was explored at length by Marx in his discussions of the confluence of ideology and philosophy. The difference is that Marx saw these as connected to a material base and a class interest.) For Anglo-American feminists, Enlightenment ideas about rationality are political to the extent that they are male ideas, or ideas that serve male interests. Critiques of universalism, humanism, individualism, equality, and so on as having excluded the female experience have led some Anglo-American feminists to look instead to the particular, the gendered and specific, and to seek preferential treatment based on gendered differences rather than equal treatment based on an assumption of basic human equality. The rejection of universality is also connected to the idea of experience, since the whole point of the idea of experience in feminist theory is to force us to look at knowledge as particular and specific, as against universal and abstract. The difference versus equality issue is, of course, a major debate in feminist theory (especially feminist legal theory),[42] and I do not mean to reduce all Anglo-American feminists to the same position, but only to point out the origins of the impulse toward difference to the extent that it exists. Since Plato, theory has traditionally been understood precisely as a rationalist enterprise demanding abstract thinking and seeking universal principles. It is not really surprising that recent analyses of the maleness of this kind of thinking combines with experientialism to contribute to the notion that theory itself is suspect.

One of the most vociferous critics of the very idea of theory has been Barbara Christian, who has argued against it on the basis that it is white and male. People of color have always theorized, she declares, though their theories have been invisible when judged in terms of the hegemonic style of academic discourse: "its linguistic jargon; its emphasis on quoting its prophets; its tendency toward 'biblical' exegesis . . . its preoccupations with mechanical analyses of language, graphs, algebraic equations; its gross generalizations about culture—has silenced many of us to the extent that some of us feel we can no longer discuss our own literature . . ."[43] Christian especially objects to the fact that deconstruction and discourse theory analyze the works of people of color as the "marginalized discourses" of an "other," and worries that the tendency to "exalt theory" as an "authoritative discourse" is oppressive.

Though Sandra Harding has never written against theory per se, she does question the usefulness of the requirement that theory be internally consistent. Her view reflects the enormous impact that experientialism has had on the very idea of a feminist theory. She writes: "coherent theories in an obviously incoherent world are either silly and uninteresting or oppressive and problematic, depending upon the degree of hegemony they manage to achieve. Coherent theories in an apparently coherent world are even more dangerous, for the world is always more complex than such unfortunately hegemonous theories can grasp."[44]

Anglo-American feminist and postmodern notions of the superiority of the local and particular lead these two very different bodies of thought to converge on a profound wariness of theory as totalistic, unifying, unfree, stifling of difference, overly universal, and, thus, insufficiently attentive to local struggles.[45] In turn, suspicion is brought to bear on theory itself as an oppressive enterprise. Similarly, postmodern claims about the relationship between politics, power, and knowledge politicize theory and also call it into question. Theories that tend to categorize, to create identity, to reproduce binary oppositions, or to mitigate against the free play of difference—which is very nearly what we mean by theory—are not neutral paths to knowledge, but political practices in opposition to freedom.

Those postmodernists who question the theoretical enterprise are wont to argue that it is itself a creator of authoritarian unity. Julia Kristeva has argued, for example, that the unity of literary texts is wrought via literary theory. She writes that "the political interpretations of our century have produced two powerful and totalitarian results: fascism and Stalinism." The "intrinsic" reason for this is, she continues, "the simple desire to give meaning, to explain, to provide the answer, to interpret."[46] Kristeva's remarks illustrate the profound ambivalence with which she approaches her task as a theorist: political theory is to blame for totalitarianism. It is the same impulse that prompts Hélène Cixous to argue that theory only reproduces the fictive totality. She argues, "If we examine the history of philosophy—in

so far as philosophical discourse orders and reproduces all thought—
we perceive that: it is marked by an absolute constant, the orchestrator
of values."[47] Thus, in Kristeva's words, "it seems that one does not
interpret something outside theory but rather that theory harbors its
object within its own logic."[48]

Very few, if any, of the thinkers either in postmodern or Anglo-
American feminism have explicitly come out against theory itself.
Still, we can make two observations that imply a waning commitment to the theoretical enterprise. First, the idea that theory must be
significantly transformed so that it is not totalitarian. Second, the
idea that the subject position of the theorist is essential to understanding theory and its politics. As Judith Butler has written:

> I don't know about the term 'postmodernism,' but if there is a
> point, and a fine point, to what I perhaps better understand as post-
> structuralism, it is that power pervades the very conceptual
> apparatus that seeks to negotiate its terms, including the subject
> position of the critic; and further, that this implication of the terms
> of criticism in the field of power is *not* the advent of a nihilistic rela-
> tivism incapable of furnishing norms, but, rather, the very
> precondition of a politically engaged critique.[49]

As to the possibility of the transformation of theory, it is not clear
that a theory that moves away from universals, abstractions, and
rationality is really a theory at all. Indeed, even the various thinkers
in postmodernism rely on theoretical tools to indict the discourse of
rationality. To make remarks that are limited to the local, and which
do not follow the usual rules of rational argument (such as internal
coherence), is to create work that looks more like history or personal
narratives than theory. Theory is, in some sense, precisely a process of
relating the universal to the particular. It seems to me that if it cannot
do this, there is little point in calling it theory, or in engaging in it.

As to the second point (the subject position of the author):
although I do heartily concur that the subject position of the theorist
is vitally important since no theories are neutral, it is not clear to me
why knowing the subject position of the author matters if the text is
to be analyzed as it stands alone, apart from the author's intent in the
general milieu of a given discourse. Why does the author's intent

matter when it is itself really no more than another interpretation of the text? Unless her interpretation is privileged, or unless some very essentializing assumptions are made about the connection between her perspective and her race, class, and sexual preference, it is not clear what good it does to know these kinds of things about her before we approach a text she has written.

More important, I am not at all sure that our own self-consciousness about the nature of our theory-building protects us from creating power/knowledge regimes even when we try to resist them. Yet, postmodern theory often sounds suspiciously as though it is reflecting some more authentic reading of texts; as though difference is more authentic than oneness.

In fact, the postmodern dilemma is the same one faced by Marxist theorists of ideology. If power and ideology are all-pervasive, can our own self-consciousness about that pervasiveness really protect us from making arguments that reinforce the very hegemony we seek to criticize? Even Antonio Gramsci's idea of counterhegemony begs the question as to how such a counterhegemonous position is possible in the first place. Yet, we know—or, we hope—that criticism is possible and that changes, even radical changes, do happen. There appears to be no alternative but to resist even if one has to do so (sometimes) within the terms of debate set down by the very system one is condemning. The better idea, of course, is to subvert that system in the very reshaping and reinvention of those terms and categories of analysis. But this is no small task.

Feminist theory, whether postmodern or Anglo-American, clearly has a feminist political agenda. Anglo-American feminist claims to being more political than postmodernists are premised on the assumption that the category Woman and the idea of women's experience actually reflect some authentic connection to biologically embodied women, but, as we have seen, this is not the case. Feminisms built on the foundation of the core concepts cannot use this as a criteria for being "political." On the other hand, postmodern feminisms want to be thought of as political and politically useful, but find it more difficult to theorize about a specifically women's liberation from within the parameters of their own non-identity-based theories.

POLITICS

Beneath all of this looms the question of what it means to be political in the first place. The tradition of Anglo-American feminist theory that I have been discussing generally takes politics to denote some actual connection to women's lives, issues, movements, practices, and theory choices as political acts whether these occur as private decisions or not. The personal is political. Postmodernists would, I think, agree with this definition but would be more likely to look to interpretive discussions of gender and power as both the source and remedy for inequality. What is troublesome about the ideas of theory as political resistance to hegemonic discourses and of theory as political action is the possibility that we will come to see redescriptions of women's lives as the end of politics. It is the danger that we will imagine problems to be solved if we merely change interpretations.

More bothersome, interpretations, by their very nature, can be made from any number of perspectives, some more desirable than others. Foucault affirms the arbitrary nature of interpretation. As an illustration of the problem, in *The History of Sexuality Volume 1,* Foucault relates the 1867 story of a village vagabond arrested for obtaining "a few caresses from a little girl" in playing a game called "curdled milk."[50] This "village halfwit would give a few pennies to the little girls for favors the older ones refused him."[51] According to Foucault's interpretation, what is important about the story is the "pettiness of it all; the fact that this everyday occurrence in the life of village sexuality, these inconsequential bucolic pleasures, could become, from a certain time, the object not only of a collective intolerance but of a judicial action, a medical intervention, a careful clinical examination, and an entire theoretical elaboration."

Foucault is interested in the story because it depicts the nonidentity of peasant sexuality. The peasant's actions and the punishment they incur are illustrative of domination by the newly emerging bourgeois sexual discourse. But from an Anglo-American feminist perspective this is more likely to be a story about child molestation. The peasant is the male power figure brought to justice by the bourgeois legal system. Foucault imputes subordination to the peasant only by choosing to identify with him rather than the girl. Yet he implies that what he describes is power in the abstract. His judgment about what constitutes domination does not address the prior question of how we can recognize domination when we see it, and it fails to distinguish kinds of power. As Habermas has said, "Foucault now raises power to a basic transcendental-historicist concept of historiography as a critique of reason."[52] These issues become very significant if one is advancing a particular politics concerned with a specific type of oppression. The key question for feminists—whether postmodern or Anglo-American—is how it comes that we can advance one interpretation over another at any given time. Even in Foucault, one senses an unstated advocacy in the strength and passion of the voice behind the seemingly agnostic interpretation. Foucault might respond that there are many silences, that the problem raised by feminist concerns for the little girl in his story does not negate his observation about the peasant. But this only underscores the problems inherent in Foucault's notion of decentered power: that it is, on some level, actually unclear how to do the analysis. More importantly, it is not clear what is to be gleaned from it save for amassing more and more examples of the presence and perniciousness of power.

It turns out that postmodern and Anglo-American feminisms have more in common than it would initially appear. And they share a problem. That problem has to do with perspective and the possibility of interpretation. Though Anglo-American feminism claims to interpret from the point of view of a feminism grounded in the standpoint of women, we have seen that its attempts to do so do not—and, I would argue, *cannot*—work. Postmodern theories, on the other hand, perform deconstructive or genealogical analyses that do a good job of denaturing concepts and exposing power/knowledge systems but are handicapped when it comes to acknowledging an interpretive standpoint that is more than simply individual preference. Though the theorist herself may have an intensely political project, and the theoretical choice itself may be political, the addition of a feminist consciousness to postmodern theory does not solve this problem. Both kinds of feminism appear to call for the development of a nonessentialist feminist standpoint as a basis for critique.

6

Solutions: A Basic Outline of the Issues and Some Suggestions

An agenda for change emerges from all that has been said about the core concepts. In preparation for looking toward some possible solutions, I would like to begin this chapter by reviewing the issues I have raised so far.

The first important thing that was said in this book is simply that there *are* core concepts that exist across all Anglo-American feminisms. I have gone to great lengths to show through close textual analyses both the presence of these concepts and the fact that they carry with them many major problems. The surprising thing has been to see how much those problems persist even when the theorists self-consciously try to avoid them, as has been the case, for example, in socialist feminism.

The case of socialist feminism also illustrates how the use of Marxism has been mostly a disaster for feminist theory. The intuitive political connection between feminism and Marxism has turned out to fail as a theoretical one. This failure has not been the result of faults in Marxism, as it is becoming fashionable to assert; rather, it is traceable to the repeated misapplication and misunderstanding of Marxism, and the contradiction between the basic tenets of Marxism and feminism's core concepts.

The attempt to use Marxist economic categories by analogy, found in most early socialist feminism, misunderstands the distinction between production and reproduction. Dwelling on the idea that women who work at home were "left out" of Marx's theory because the sphere of reproduction was not considered a venue for productive labor by Marx, socialist and Marxist feminists have thought it very important to redefine women's reproductive labor as productive. But Marx's theory is about classes as they are determined vis-à-vis their position in a capitalist production process. This process is, in a very real sense, *defined* by the separation of production from reproduction and their dialectical relationship.

Similarly problematic has been the tendency of feminists to think of production and reproduction as analogous to public and private, the latter pair being wholly separate in liberal theory. In contrast, production and reproduction are fundamentally, dialectically linked in Marxism. Again, to view the two as separate misses this crucial aspect of Marx's analysis. To think that productive labor can occur in the home misunderstands the entire description of capitalism as a system of wage labor and commodity production. The economic argument needed to sustain the idea that work in the reproductive sphere is productive is very complicated. One way of making the case would have been to show that surplus value was extracted in the reproduction realm. Another would have been to use Marx's arguments about exploitation in the productive sphere and apply them analogously to women's position vis-à-vis the means of reproduction. However, neither of these could possibly work as Marx's point is precisely that capitalism is a system where surplus value is extracted at the point of production and that that extraction is exploitative.

As I have argued, the most serious problem with using Marxism, however, was the fact that the core concepts arose precisely in opposition to many of its major premises, such as the notion of an objectively visible exploitation in the entity of class, and rationality. Not surprisingly, the epistemological contradictions between Marxism's basic premises and the core concepts have been implacable. It has turned out that Marxism is just not a good theory with which to talk about issues relating specifically to gender.

When Marxism reemerged as a tool in standpoint theory, it did not fare much better than it had in socialist feminism, nor did it enhance feminist theories of knowledge. Standpoint theory's use of Marxism actually faces many of the same problems socialist and Marxist feminists have faced, albeit at the level of epistemology. One glaring problem comes in the initial assumption on the parts of standpoint theorists that Marx himself was a standpoint thinker. I have argued that this assumption is dubious, and that it is probably more accurate to say that *some Marxists* (as opposed to Marx himself) were standpoint thinkers. At that point, it becomes useful to look at the function of standpoint in Marxism.

In fact, as I have shown, standpoint in Marxism is a product of its problem of agency. Because the proletariat was constituted objectively as a class, but not subjectively as a revolutionary agent, intellectuals and critics of capitalism were advised by Lukacs to take the proletarian standpoint. Feminism faces a similar problem in that women are constituted objectively, but not all women are included in the class Woman or have been constituted subjectively as *feminist women*. That is, not all women describe their interests as women in feminist terms. This parallels the problem in Marxism.

Where Marx acknowledged that a historical materialist theory could not talk about a "universal man" and went on to create a materialist category, class, feminists have persisted in their attempts to try and think "universal Woman" and Woman as materialist category at the same time. However, it remains the case that Woman is more analogous to man as a category than it is to proletariat.

More important, in Marxism, the impulse to standpoint laid the groundwork for the Stalinist state. The idea of a female standpoint merely reproduces the most authoritarian dimensions of Marxism as rendered by Lukacs. Adorno's critique of standpoint as undialectical reminds us that the very idea of standpoint assumes a static a priori identity that, once having been defined, can simply be adopted.

Related to standpoint is the notion of feminist epistemology itself. My discussion of standpoint has, in fact, led me to interrogate the perceived need for a feminist epistemology. I have claimed that epistemological discourse entrenches feminism even further in rationalism and identity thinking, paradoxically doing so while trying to develop a theory of knowledge that rejects the same.

The most serious charge against standpoint thinking, however, is that it purports to be a theory of knowledge based on women's lives, when in fact, as I have shown, it actually uses feminism to selectively read and describe women's lives. It is, therefore, tautological: feminist principles are used to interpret women's lives, which are then claimed to be the basis for feminist principles and theory.

My point about the tautological quality of standpoint thinking is related to an important subtext of this book. Namely, feminist theorists in general have prescribed various allegedly acceptable "feminist" behaviors and then gone on to claim that those behaviors are organically linked to women's experiences. The sexuality debates illustrate the fallacy of this approach. Whenever we declare a priori what women's experiences are (even if we claim that they *really are* the female experience) and then go on to describe the experiences that are or should be associated with feminist women, we run the risk of a woman refuting us simply by saying, "I don't experience things that way." This is all the more damning if the woman claims to be a feminist.

One response to this has been to collect more and more female experiences in order to put flesh, substance, ethnicity, and color on the category Woman. This "not me" problem raised by the use of experience is perhaps less important on an individual level than it is when one gets whole *types* of people saying that feminism as described does not match their experiences, as has happened, for example, with many women of color who perceive feminism as a "white thing." Moreover, as many women of color have pointed out, even notions such as "third world women," "women of color," "Middle Eastern women," or "white women" cannot capture the experiences of all the members of those categories. Right-wing women and corporate feminists too are part of this "not me" problem; their very presence disputes the notion that we can build a feminist ethics based on already-in-place feminine values.

Remarkably, the category experience remains well entrenched in feminism to the point where the search for women's experiences has nearly eclipsed other issues in Anglo-American feminist theory. The test of good feminist theory seems to no longer be, Will this help in the liberation of women? but rather, Does this reflect the female experience? These are two very different questions. The frequency of the latter reflects the problematic theoretical agenda set by the core concepts and their intransigence in feminist theory. It must be remembered that the core concepts are no more than socially produced ideas that embody the political interests of one moment in feminism. It is emblematic of their reification that some feminists have begun to think it heretical to criticize them.

This "not me" outrage, resulting from various definitions of the female experience has been reflected, in some circles, in an overwhelming reaction to feminist critiques of pornography and certain allegedly male-identified ways of being sexual. Sadomasochism has come under close scrutiny on this note, and the subsequent charge that sadomasochism is not part of an authentically experienced range of female sexual pleasures has been furiously contested. This scenario has also been played out with regard to the idea that women are less sexually lustful than men. The view of female sexuality as having to match one or another authentically female behavior maintains, like patriarchy, an external standard of how women should behave. This kind of superimposed female identity is now reborn and revalued in some feminism. Ironically, the original reason feminists extolled the recourse to female experience was to provide feminist women with a tool to use in combating stereotypical notions of women as reflected in misogynist culture. Sometimes this resistance meant that women stopped being "nice," sexually or otherwise. Recall, for example, Joreen's "Bitch Manifesto."

The sexuality debates also reflect the feminist idea of personal politics, which has enabled us to politicize sexual choices. The idea of personal politics arises from an important critique of public/private offered by Marxists, feminists, and others. The critique has been leveled on the grounds that choices made in private may appear as outcomes of freely given consent but are actually the products of coercion. One of Marx's examples was the false freedom to sell one's labor in the capitalist market. Marx showed that this is no freedom at all when one cannot realistically opt out of participation in the economy unless one chooses not to work, i.e., to starve. In turn, feminists have made similar critiques of public/private in talking about how the sanctity of private space has often protected batterers and child abusers on grounds that "a man's home is his castle" and that women have the freedom to leave.

Another criticism has been that so-called personal choice is inevitably manipulated by ideology. For example, the vast military budget in the United States has been kept up by posing the threat of a communist menace. This threat has been ideologically constructed and maintained far beyond the reality of the situation and has been used to justify an extreme level of military spending as well as U.S. interventions all over the world.

The major advantage of personal politics has been that it offers a way to name and act on the political dimensions of personal life and to combat the fiction of unfettered personal choice. However, this critique of the public/private split has costs. For one, the idea of personal politics has an authoritarian dimension as it operates in the triad of core concepts I have been describing in this book. Sexual choices can be criticized from the point of view of feminists invoking an authentic female experience from which they allege certain practices to be a deviation. The public/private split has the advantage of protecting personal life from that kind of scrutiny from outside by recourse to its principles of personal choice and toleration. As flawed as the idea of privacy is, one unpleasant alternative is open investigation of everyone's choices about everything. This might not sound so bad until one remembers that one of the dangers in collapsing public and private has been authoritarianism at the level of the state—even to the point of fascism.

Still, there are probably more pluses than minuses to the idea of personal politics. For one, personal life is so mutilated and contaminated by hegemonic systems of power that it really does seem to be the case that power is already exercised in the personal realm. By this reasoning, the feminist notion of personal politics is only combating an already existing and pervasive system of domination at the level of everyday practice. The dangers of personal politics come mostly when statements and critiques about personal life stem from an established source of power and attempt to strengthen or maintain that power to exclude dissent. Personal politics is less dangerous when it comes from a point of view of dissent, which has no real way to enforce its viewpoint. Thus, although there is an authoritarian dimension in some feminists trying to tell other feminists what to do in bed, as long as it comes from the point of view of a dissenting social force, it is still possible to conceptualize these judgments as one side of a conversation about female sexuality.

On the other hand, if one is to believe discourse theory, this kind of conversation is also a contest about who gets to define female sexual identity. It is not, therefore, completely benign in that the power to construct an identity as an "other" is simply another *kind* of exercise of power. Thus, the idea of personal politics must always remain in a critical posture and guard against the tendency to, in criticizing, undemocratically impose unreasonable external standards, especially upon other feminists.

The mention of discourse theory brings me to another point that has been raised in this book. I have discussed postmodernism as yet another attempt to fix the core concepts—this time by abandoning them and raising alternative concepts such as power, liberation, and gender. I have pointed to a surprising overlap between feminism and postmodernism insofar as both employ notions of personal politics, difference, multiplicity, and the feminine. Likewise the two share critiques of many of the major premises of the Enlightenment as well as a growing dis-ease (in some instances) about the enterprise of theory itself. Anglo-American feminism's rejection of one truth and one reality makes it look, in some ways, very postmodern. For its part, postmodern feminism is distinct from other postmodern theory because of its feminist political identity. I have argued that this political perspective, this feminist identity, makes it distinguishable from simply postmodernism in general.

The claim of Anglo-American feminism to be more political than postmodern feminism rests on the former's alleged link to "real" women. However, as I have tried to show in this book, its categories of analysis make that claim tenuous at best. Anglo-American feminism preserves a subject that is fictive. On the other hand, although discourse and interpretation are important, as postmodernists claim, Anglo-American feminists are correct to say that politics must happen on other levels besides redescription. Although few postmodern feminists would explicitly dispute this, they sometimes behave in their theories as if they are oblivious to this point. It is easy to see how one could imagine their theories as dangerous flights from politics. It is also easy to see how one could worry that the very similar ideas of personal politics and theory as politics might supplant other kinds of activism. The postmodern problem is only nominally different than problems about political activism and subject formation faced by experiential feminisms, however, and I think we should begin to stress the important similarity between the two: namely, that both styles of theory are committed to feminism, liberation, justice, and equality.

Where do we go from here? It seems to me that in assessing Anglo-American and postmodern feminisms several questions arise: What do feminists mean by words like *politics, oppression,* and *liberation?* What does it mean to have a feminist interpretation of something? How can we avoid essentialism in feminism without killing the subject? What is the relationship between feminist theory and practice? I think we can answer these questions more fruitfully than we have in the past, but to do so, we need to turn our attention away from Woman and experience, and to be much clearer about our notions of politics. Feminist theory needs some new tools.

THE STRUCTURE OF GENDER AS IDEOLOGY AND MYTH

It is important to avoid basing a theory on women's experiences or Woman's experience if for no other reason than that it is impossible to discern those experiences authentically, and that attempting to do so has resulted in the imputing of experiences to some imagined universal Woman or group of women. That is to say, Woman and experience do not work as foundational theoretical elements.

The good news is that, unlike the early radical feminists, we do not have to prove the existence of women's oppression to some male-dominated Left which was the primary function of the core concepts. We have already proved that there are women out there who want to be self-determining and who have experienced themselves as oppressed. In fact, the long-standing existence of an active feminist movement is the living proof that many women are unhappy under patriarchy. Therefore, rather than basing our theory in the first instance on Woman or experience as a way to ground theory, why not turn our attention to the structure of gender itself? Instead of beginning from the point of view of an imagined female experience, why not begin from the point of view of human liberation from gender? Why not turn away from epistemology entirely?

To this end, I would like to explore several hypotheses:

1. Gender is a relatively autonomous, hegemonic, ideological structure that divides the world hierarchically into two mythical genders, and which reinforces itself through an elaborate system of rules and punishments enforced in all aspects of life.

In conceptualizing gender as an ideological structure, it is useful to draw on the work of Althusser. For Althusser, ideologies are structures that exist above consciousness, and which act on consciousness by means of a process that escapes us. He writes,

> In truth, ideology has very little to do with "consciousness," even supposing this term to have an unambiguous meaning. It is profoundly *unconscious* . . . Ideology is indeed a system of representations, but in the majority of cases these representations have nothing to do with "consciousness": they are usually images and occasionally concepts, but it is above all as *structures* that they impose on the vast majority of men, not via their "consciousness". They are perceived-accepted-suffered cultural objects and they act functionally on men via a process that escapes them.[1]

Ideology is furthermore, Althusser contends, always connected to an apparatus and its practices. Its very function is the constitution of subjects; indeed, "there is no ideology except by the subject and for subjects."[2] Finally, the ideological practices of the apparatus are governed by rituals in which these practices are already inscribed. That is, we are always already subjects living spontaneously in ideology and reproducing it in its own rituals and lived practices. Ideology is the lived relation between people and the world.

We can conceptualize gender as this kind of ideological structure. Gender constitutes subjects in its own image and is sustained and reproduced by rituals and practices. Gender is the mediated lived relationship between people and the world. We know the world as ideologically constructing and ideologically sustaining gendered subjects.

I have said further in my first hypothesis that the power and ideology of gender is hegemonic. As Gramsci elaborated the term, hegemony is the complete and total domination of individuals to the point at which little or no overt force is necessary to maintain control. Instead, capitulation to the dominant system appears consensual. It does not appear as domination at all, but perniciously, as common sense.[3] In the case of gender, the division and valuation of people into two types does indeed appear natural, the rituals of gender appear voluntary, and challenges to the structure of gender appear to nonfeminists merely as the nonsensical violations of the principles of common sense.

Gender, in connection with being a hegemonic ideological structure, is also a meaning-making system, or, in the terms of Roland Barthes, a myth. Barthes explains myth as a type of speech in which meaning is drained of its historical and contingent qualities and made to appear natural. For Barthes, a major power of myth is recurrence. This makes its historical contingency appear as eternal fact and also enables it to appear apolitical. In short, meanings appear not as historically and politically constituted, but as organic, appearing to have meanings in and of themselves. Decoding myth is a process of exposing meaning as socially constructed. In so doing, we are transformed from mere readers into mythologists.[4]

Gender is this kind of myth. Femininity and masculinity are terms that ascribe meaning to biologically embodied men and women. Likewise, the terms *men* and *women* have meaning only as they relate to their social constructions in accordance with the system-maintaining requirements of gender. The fact that male and female exist in a hierarchy is a function of the structure of gender and its lived practices.

However, because of the presence of other ordering systems with which gender interacts (race, for example), all men are not always dominant over all women in all things. This has been a major complicating factor in feminist analyses built on women's experience(s). There can be no theory of women's universal subordination because women are not universally subordinated. They are universally subordinate abstractly and structurally vis-à-vis their position in the gender system, but concretely, the interaction of this system with other power systems means that not all women experience gender as their primary oppression, nor do they always experience gender the same way. This is another reason why it has been futile to use women's experience as the basis for feminism. It is simply too variable and elusive.

Gender is relatively autonomous from other power structures such as capitalism and race. This means that the power and importance of gender can vary greatly. Although it has its own interests as a structure, it can, at times, be interrelated with other structures to varying degrees. Though individual feminists may be socialists, Afrocentrists, and so on, feminism must be *primarily* about gender if for no other reason than that no other political movement has named or discussed the specific, oppressive nature of gender. Feminism is the only response to the hegemonic power of the gender structure. But, as we shall see, it is likely that someone who accepts the view of gender I am suggesting will be compelled to think critically about race and capitalism as well.

Another part of my first hypothesis is that gender is a system of crime and punishment (this is not unlike Atkinson's idea that gender is a system of rules). Emile Durkheim described crime as a violation, and punishment as the expression of collective sentiments against it. In fact, the function of punishment is to sustain social cohesion by sustaining a common consciousness. The very function of punishment is "to maintain inviolate the cohesion of society by sustaining the common conscience in all its vigor . . . punishment is intended to have its effect on honest people."[5] In fact, Durkheim contended, all crimes have in common the fact that they provoke a punishment.[6] So much is this the case that Durkheim wrote, "we do not condemn it because it is a crime, but it is a crime because we condemn it."[7]

Durkheim's ideas about crime and punishment can be applied to gender. Even though gender's power is hegemonic and exercised through ritualized practices in daily life, the power of gender is also always contingent and contested. The fact that it *is* an ideological structure that mediates human's interactions with each other and the world means that its power can at times face crises. Like the society whose cohesion Durkheim hoped to describe, gender is maintained only through illusions of naturalness and consent to the principles that sustain it. For Durkheim (and Foucault as well), crime is a kind of minirevolution that shows the system *need not* be obeyed.[8] For both Durkheim and Foucault, the purpose of punishment is to show everyone else (in Durkheim's words, to show the "honest people") the consequences of transgression. Just as crime is a kind of crisis for state power, so can certain transgressive behaviors represent a kind of crisis for gender if the "crimes" are revalued through feminist (or other critical) interpretations as heroic, rebellious or otherwise transformative acts.

We can conceptualize crises of gender in terms of this model of crime and punishment. Like any power structure, gender has rules, and breaking these rules amounts to what we can call "gender crime." These gender crimes represent, in a sense, tears in the otherwise seamless and natural quality of the structure of gender. Gender crimes exact a sort of punishment. In fact, the punishments are what clue us in to their status as crimes in the first place. Gender crimes and their punishments can tell us a lot about the nature of gender itself. Let me begin by listing a few (by no means all) of the rules of gender:

- Women are sexually attracted to men and vice versa. (It follows that sexual practices connected to reproduction are considered the most "normal".)
- Women are smaller than men.
- Women are more passive than men.
- Women are not as good at thinking abstractly as men are.
- Women are more emotional than men.
- Women are physically weaker than men.
- Women are nurturing, caring, generally most fit to parent.
- Women cry, men do not.
- Women are peace loving.
- Men are aggressive.
- Women should be loyal and supportive of men.
- Women are vain and narcissistic about their appearance.
- Men do not care about their appearance.
- Women are sexually passive and care less about sex than men do.
- Men are lustful.

Note that these rules (or truisms) about gender divide the world inevitably into two genders. Note also that almost anyone in reading this list will have at least two reactions. First, that the list is an accurate depiction of stereotypes associated with gender. Second, that there are some or many things on the list which do not describe them as a particular man or woman. If they think further they might be willing to admit a third thing: to deviate too far from the list is to risk social ostracism. For instance, I had very long hair as a child. Somewhere in my twenties, I cut it very short, and have had fairly short hair ever since. Because of the rule in our European culture which says, "women have long hair," I have, at times, been called masculine. Waiters have called me "sir" (and then have been utterly embarrassed upon seeing my face more closely). My family in Pennsylvania entreats me to please "grow my hair a little longer." Why? Why does my short hair so bother them? I think it is because, in some minor way, I am breaking the rules. Let us think about a few more of the kinds of crimes and punishments attached to various gender rules.

The case of gays and lesbians. In a famous essay Adrienne Rich has spoken convincingly of "compulsory heterosexuality."[9] For my purposes, the most important point of that essay was Rich's claim that heterosexuality is a political institution that is only made to appear natural. Judith Butler makes a similar point in *Gender Trouble,* especially in her discussion of "subversive bodily acts."[10] To the extent that heterosexuality is the rule, the so-called homosexual is a gender criminal punished by ostracism and worse. Heterosexuality is a requirement of the current construction of gender since one of the main *meanings* of manhood is sexual attraction to and conquest of women, and one of the main *meanings* of woman is sexual attraction to and availability for men. However, the possibility of homosexuality shows that heterosexuality is a choice, a choice that appears in the context of the rules of gender as natural or merely common sense.

This idea about the ideological nature of heterosexuality would hold even if it were scientifically "proven" tomorrow that there is a genetic basis for homosexuality. First, it is interesting that the entire discussion of possible genetic factors in homosexuality suggests these as deviations from the "normal brain" of heterosexuals. That is, the discussion does not occur from the point of view that a genetic basis for homosexuality implies that there is also one for heterosexuality, but casts the homosexual brain as the one studied in opposition to the norm. Second, and in any case, what is significant is not whether or not homosexuality and heterosexuality *really* are based in biology. What is important is the cultural meanings attached to each. Even if we find out tomorrow that sexual preference is biologically based it would not change the fact that the rules of gender have fixed the meanings of sexual desire such that anything other than plain vanilla heterosexuality is stigmatized as a deviation, something to be hidden away in a closet. The fact that there are civil laws against what are alleged to be homosexual behaviors (oral and anal sex) and that the medical community until recently saw homosexuality as a disease only proves the extent to which the rules of gender are enforced, not merely by ideological practice, but by their translation into explicit legal and medical codes. In fact, we can say as a general rule that the further one gets from reproductive sex, the less acceptable it becomes to engage in, by the standards of the rules of gender. For example, "homosexual" practices such as oral sex are acceptable between heterosexuals who can reproduce, but less so or not at all between gays and lesbians. Oral sex is also seen as somehow racier and more illicit than simple heterosexual intercourse. Likewise, nongenital sexual practices like fetishism are almost completely unacceptable. As feminists have pointed out repeatedly, the very definition of sexual activity more often than not has to do with penetration by a penis, all the rest being sort of irrelevant and unnameable except as deviant behavior.

The case of the sex symbol. The sex symbol symbolizes sexuality as seen through the ideology of gender. Her (or, less often, his) practice as sex symbol and our practice in consuming this symbol are themselves rigorously ideological. Since, according to the rules of the structure of gender, only men can actively desire, sex symbols are most often women. As symbols of the female sex, sex symbols who commit gender crimes are subject to major ostracism. Consider the backlash against Elizabeth Taylor when she committed the crime of gaining weight, i.e., of no longer being desirable.

Even the creation of male sex symbols is often accomplished in terms of a desiring male audience. Consider the 1993 advertising campaign for Calvin Klein men's underwear in the U.S., featuring the rapper Marky Mark. The rapper, a white heterosexual, drew media attention and discussion for his coterie of gay male fans and for playing gay clubs in San Francisco. Thus, one of the few actual male sex symbols is primarily constructed as such in terms of male audience. Attractive men who at least publically have mostly female audiences—such as the late Rock Hudson—are more appropriately conceptualized as romantic symbols. They are less likely to symbolize lust the way female sex symbols do, and more likely to inspire flights of fancy about being swept away. Rock Hudson's death from AIDS and his gay lifestyle were shocking partly because his personal life so contradicted his public life as a symbol of male heterosexuality. Most Americans found his gayness shocking, as though he had done something wrong. His gender crime was manifold—not only was he a gay man, but he was masquerading as the epitome of heterosexual manhood.

The way gay men figure in the practice of gender is further evidenced by the 1993 controversy over gays in the U.S. military. It used to be said, "There's something about a man in uniform." Indeed, that something is precisely the meaning of a military uniform, which *is* masculinity—the uniform signifies the warrior, aggressively protecting the homeland. In a way, the idea of a man in a military uniform is redundant. In this sense, the idea of a gay soldier violates gender codes by seeming to negate the gendered meaning of the uniform. The gay man is, from the point of view of the ideology of gender, not a man. As a feminized man he is a gender criminal who is doubly so by donning a military uniform. By dressing himself in a major symbol of the ideologically structured heterosexual male he points to the fact that one need not be, in fact, heterosexual, or be protecting the womenfolk back home, to be a warrior. His very presence, therefore, functions to contest a major aspect of the system.

The case of women who do violence. Female violence is a major gender crime, violating as it does the rule that women must be passive, nurturing, and caring. Several recent Hollywood films are examples of the ritual practice of punishing strong women who act violently. These films also illustrate the ways in which the ideology of gender gets reinscribed in films even when they seem to present nontraditional images of women.

Thelma and Louise, a female buddy film, is the story of two unhappy women who go on an empowering adventure and end up dead. Interestingly, the *New York Times* describes it as having the "thrilling, life affirming energy for which the best road movies are remembered." The question we must ask is, In what sense is the death of these women life affirming?

The main characters are Thelma, representing the long-suffering, naively romantic, and sexual woman; and Louise (who could represent one possible future for women like Thelma), a cynical, untrusting woman who, because of past bad experiences (it is implied), has trouble relating to men.

While on a driving vacation the two stop at a roadside honky-tonk bar where Thelma, after being openly flirtatious with another patron, is sexually attacked by him. In attempting to protect Thelma, Louise shoots the man. Here's where the movie becomes puzzling. Instead of calling the police, the two go on the run, proceeding to get themselves even deeper into trouble by robbing a convenience store and shooting out the tires of a big rig belonging to a trucker who made suggestive advances to them from the road. The shooting of the tires is every woman's fantasy of how to respond to sexual harassment, and, if I may say so, the shooting of the would-be rapist is probably our collective fantasy, too. The flight of Thelma and Louise from the police ends with their decision to commit suicide by driving off the side of a mountain after leading the police on a high-speed chase. They do this rather than giving themselves up to the police—to "the man"—even though the officer in charge seems quite sympathetic to them.

Why do they run, and why do they die? Why does the *New York Times* think this is a life-affirming film? By my reading, they run because after they have shot the would-be rapist, they are already criminals, and this is a life-affirming film because the life of the gender structure remains intact.

Even though we might argue that the police will understand and that the shooting was an issue of self-defense, Louise knows better. Since Thelma was flirting, was not actually raped, and is on the run from her husband, Louise knows that, realistically, Thelma is not a believable victim. Equally important is the fact that Louise's reaction, killing the attacker, is not within the acceptable parameters of female behavior. The law says that women must fight back in order to show rape, but women cannot fight back too hard, lest they be turned from victim to villain. (This point is also exemplified in the play—later made into a film—*Extremities,* wherein a woman holds her stalker/rapist captive, terrorizing him until he is rescued by her appalled female roommates.)

Gender ideology interacts with the law of the state such that from the moment Louise shoots Thelma's attacker, the two are already outlaws in more ways than one. They have committed a "real" crime as well as a gender crime. This explains, in part, why they begin to behave like criminals. It is also true that their outlaw status liberates them (hence, another version of the "life affirming" aspect of this film). But in the end, for the crimes of power, self-sufficiency, and freedom, their lives are not affirmed, but ended. Rather than going back to face the legal consequences of their actions, and, I would argue, rather than going back to face their former unfreedom, they choose death. Another way to say this is that for the crime of fighting back aggressively and powerfully, they are killed.

This film viewed as ideological practice tells a fable about what happens to women who "go bad." The deep structure of gender is even more evident in this film since it clearly intends to portray Thelma and Louise as heroes. Instead, it ends up reflecting the power of gender by showing the clear choice faced by women acting *in the realistic context* of current gender relations. Their martyr status in the feminist community is exemplified in the popularity of a button worn for awhile among the lesbian community in San Francisco which reads, "Thelma and Louise Live."

The *Alien* series finale, *Alien 3,* is another case of powerful woman as female gender criminal. It also reflects the reinscription of gender onto female women who appear on the surface to be strongly countering stereotypically female roles. The first-order reading of the film is that it is about the struggle of workers against a corrupt and greedy mineral mining corporation clearly modeled on contemporary U.S. oil companies. But the *Alien* series is also, importantly, about gender.

The plot of the films is simple. Workers returning from a mining expedition in space encounter an intelligent, but brutal, alien race that begins life in an egg and continues as a parasite inside a (in this case, human) host until its eventual growth into a huge, buglike monster. In each of the *Alien* films, the monster kills almost everyone. In each case a woman, Ripley, is its bravest opponent.

In this series, Ripley, played by Sigourny Weaver, is positioned as a strong female savior fighting an equally strong and unsavory opponent, whom we learn in the second film also happens to be female. The evolution of Ripley's character in this film trilogy is telling.

In the first film, *Alien,* Ripley is a strong woman, but the female-centered subtext of the film trilogy is not yet primary. By the second film, *Aliens,* Ripley's hair is shortened, and nearly all of the strong characters are female: Ripley; the alien; a little girl named Newt who, through great courage, survives an alien attack on an off-world colony; and a feisty, muscular Marine named Vasquez. Even in the opening scenes, *Aliens* plays on the gender switch of attaching a traditionally male version of power to women. A very macho male Marine asks the buff Vasquez, "Has anyone ever mistaken you for a man?" "No," she replies, "how about you?"

By the end of this second film, however, Ripley is transformed into a mother, her power now stemming from a more traditionally gendered source. Motherhood is, in fact, a major symbol in this film. The ship's computer is named Mother, the alien is a mother, and, in a final scene of *Aliens,* Newt calls Ripley "Mommy." From within the text of the film, it is this transformation to motherhood that is to be Ripley's unmaking. Her power and strength, at first figured as coming from her simply as an individual, are almost unavoidably drawn so as to link them to motherhood. Ripley's power, strength, and courage become very clearly connected to her desire to protect the child, Newt. That this film invariably transforms Ripley's power to a traditionally constructed gendered power—indeed, that all power in this film is seen as either male or female—is evidence of the ritual reenactment of gender ideology. Motherhood is figured here in very traditional ways. The two females—Ripley and the alien mother—fight to protect their children, at one point literally in hand-to-hand (or hand-to-claw, as it were) combat.

The third film opens with Ripley as a bereaved and enraged mother. She has crash landed on an all-male penal colony (appropriately signifying her status as criminal and prisoner). To her horror, she finds that she has failed to protect Newt, who is now dead, having been killed by the alien, which Ripley's ship presumably has now carried onto the penal colony. After she learns of Newt's death, her hair is again shortened; this time, completely shaved. Her shaved head, prominently displayed in all advertising for this film, marks her emphatically as androgynous.

The text of this film again uses Ripley's motherhood as significant. Her feelings about Newt provide a motive for her courage and anger. But by the end of this film, she is found to have an alien growing inside her. In effect, she is pregnant with an alien. In order to kill the monster, she dives headlong in a Christ-like pose into boiling fluid. Her death is, like that of Thelma and Louise, simultaneously an act of martyrdom and punishment for the power she has enjoyed throughout these films. She is punished, too, for having been a bad mother (i.e., for Newt's death). In the end, she must kill herself and the seed of evil she carries. Women's reproductive capacities, then, are figured ambivalently in this film. Ripley is not a typical mother. She is not a mother by biological right, nor is she merely nurturing. She is powerful, fearsome, violent, arrogant, enraged, rational, and a leader. The text of the film tells us that this kind of mother will fail. By connecting Ripley's power (and, by extension, female power) to motherhood, the film shows the impossibility of female power without martyrdom. This film, too, is an enactment of the practice of gender.

Terminator 2 also features a warrior mother who has undergone a transformation from a young waitress at a Bob's Big Buns to a rampaging superwoman with the skills of a survivalist. Sarah Connor's power, too, is figured as one realized only in relationship to her being the mother of a resistance leader in some future war for control of the world. By the beginning of *Terminator 2,* Sarah has been hospitalized in an institution for the criminally insane because of her persistent ramblings about an imminent nuclear holocaust; a cyborg from the future; and her imperative need to protect her son, the future leader of the resistance. Her fantastic courage, determination, ingenuity, and sheer physical strength are shown as outcomes of her mothering of the young John Connor, which continues to present her power as gendered.

In fact in this film she is rescued, as she was in the original *Terminator,* by a male who is even more powerful and effective than she. Where in the first *Terminator,* the rescuer, Kyle Reese, was a love interest, the second rescuer is a father figure for her son. In the second instance, she is reborn as part of an ersatz nuclear family.

While hiding out with some of her paramilitary cronies, Sarah muses silently as she watches her son play with the good terminator:

> Watching John with the machine it was suddenly so clear. The terminator would never stop. It would never leave him, and it would never hurt him, never shout at him, or get drunk and hit him, or say it was too busy to spend time with him. It would always be there, and it would die to protect him. Of all the would-be fathers who came and went over the years, this thing, this machine, was the only one who measured up. In an insane world, it was the sanest choice.

As this passage shows, Sarah's image of fatherhood is highly romanticized. Although we should all be able to expect fathers who don't "get drunk and hit," it is less reasonable to expect fathers who are never busy or who will never leave. Although Sarah is describing the choice of the man/machine/father as a reasonable response given the "insane world" in which she lives, the choice of a machine father would also be the sanest choice in a world where gender structures families such that men must assume superhuman roles as protectors.

Soon after this scene, Sarah expresses similarly romantic views about motherhood. Upon meeting the man who develops the technology that will, she knows from the terminator, result in a future nuclear holocaust, she accuses him of murder. How were we supposed to know the research would lead to annihilation, the scientist asks. Sarah responds with a crazed look, "How are you supposed to know? Men like you built the hydrogen bomb. Men like you thought it up. You think you're so creative! You don't know what it's like to really create something. To create a life, to feel it growing inside you. All you know is how to create death and destruction . . ." Young John interrupts almost lightheartedly, "Mom! Mom! We need to be a little more constructive here, ok?"

Sarah's association of men with death, war, destruction, and technology, and women with peace, life, motherhood, and nature clearly splits the world into its traditional dualisms. Still, the whole thing sounds very feminist in a gynocentric kind of way. Her son's reaction, however, subverts this reading by making Sarah's words seem foolish and exaggerated. It is also true that the scientist (like the scientists in the *Alien* series) works for greedy capitalists, and Sarah's association of destructive technology with maleness glosses this corporate dimension.

The main point is that, when taken together, Sarah's two speeches reveal the strong ideological inscription of the structure of gender on this film. In spite of the fact that she is a fabulous warrior, her power as connected to motherhood does not or cannot avoid the reintroduction of a very traditional construction of mothers, fathers, families, and gender: the reforming of a nuclear family with a machinelike father-protector; the naturalistic association of motherhood with creativity and life, and men with death and destruction. John's rebuke that we "need to be a little more constructive" can be reread by feminists as an ironic statement about the need to move away from a mythical understanding of gender and toward a socially constructivist one. As feminists, we too "need to be a little more constructive."

Although Sarah provides a welcome respite from the strip, scream and whine variety of female leading roles, her power is still figured—cannot avoid being figured—as an expression of gendered practices. At least, by the way, Sarah has not been killed off for her violent behavior, but has only gone mad. However, I will be curious to see what happens to her in the inevitable *Terminator 3*.

A final example of how female power and violence occur in popular culture as a practice of gender ideology is provided by the self-consciously feminist film, *A Question of Silence*. The plot of this 1981 release from Holland deals with the murder of a male clerk in a clothing store. The opening scenes depict brief vignettes of the daily lives of three women: Ann, a waitress who endures the harassment of her boss and customers; Christine, a housewife, who suffers through the silence of her husband; and Andrea, a secretary, who, though smarter than her male superiors, is invisible to them on account of her sex.

By chance, the three find themselves in the same clothing store along with several other anonymous women. The drama begins when one of the women, Christine, is caught trying to shoplift. When she refuses to put the item back, the other women spontaneously come to her defense by blatantly putting various pieces of clothing from the store into their own bags and purses. As the clerk gets more and more frustrated and belligerent, the women erupt in a rage of kicks, blows, and punches, which result in his death.

The majority of the time in this film, however, is devoted to the subsequent relationship between these women and the female psychiatrist assigned to discern their sanity in preparation for their murder trial. In attempting to find some reason for the crime, the psychiatrist asks one of the women, "Could it have been a woman [you killed]?" "No," the murderer answers, "that is an irrelevant question." The question for the psychiatrist becomes, Why was the man killed simply because he was a man? Her epiphany comes as she tells her liberal husband that she does not believe these women are insane. He is incensed and annoyed, thus only confirming her allegience to the three women.

The film ends at the trial. The anonymous women who witnessed the murder in the shop (and who are known to be witnesses only to the murderers) sit in the spectator section of the courtroom. The psychiatrist, meanwhile, who has decided the women are not insane at all, tells the judge as much, thereby implying that there was some rational reason for their actions. The judge and the other male attorneys are outraged.

Again, like Thelma and Louise, all of the women in this film are criminals in more than one way. In A *Question of Silence,* the women are literally on trial for a murder that is simultaneously a gender crime. They have killed someone; they have killed him only because he symbolized for a moment their feelings about men; and they have also—in the words of one contemporary activist group, ACT UP (AIDS Coalition to Unleash Power)—"acted up" and "fought back." All of these are the crimes for which they are on trial.

There are several "questions of silence" in this film. First, the silence of women before the murder ever occurs, who have to endure their daily torments without comment. Second, the silence of the murderers and their coconspirator witnesses who collude in the incident. A final silence is the one that is broken at the end of the film by laughter.

This laughter occurs as spontaneously as the rage that opened the film. At one point, in answer to the judge's recriminations of them, all of the women in the courtroom respond with uproarious laughter. It is the men who are now silent and silenced. The film's final shot is of the psychiatrist on the steps of the courthouse looking up into the faces of the witnesses. She is together with them—they are all laughing women. What is the function of these laughing women?

Freud has argued that most jokes have an underlying hostile purpose. About the basic hostility of jokes, he writes:

> But the more serious substance of the joke is the problem of what determines the truth. The joke, once again, is pointing to a problem and is making use of the uncertainty of one of our commonest concepts. Is it the truth if we describe things as they are without troubling to consider how our hearer will understand what we say? Or is this only jesuitical truth, and does not genuine truth consist in taking the hearer into account and giving him a faithful picture of our knowledge? . . . What [jokes] are attacking is not a person or an institution but the certainty of our knowledge itself . . .[11]

In *A Question of Silence,* female laughter as hostility is a form of power that annihilates the judge and the lawyers as surely as the clerk in the clothing store was killed. Through their laughter, their laughter together as women, they mock the "true" definitions of sanity and insanity proposed by the judge and the male attorneys. In other words, they cast doubt on the truth of gender.

The films I have been discussing are examples of gender ideology's inscription on ritualized practices. These examples from popular culture only symbolically reflect what actually happens to people who break the rules of gender. The Hollywood films I have analyzed also point up the difficulty in portraying strong women without also portraying them in an ideologically gendered way.

It is important to note that all of these analyses were accomplished without once talking about female values, the feminine perspective, or women's experience(s). Rather, I have relied on my hypothesis about the structure of gender as a primary mediator of relationships between individuals and the world. These films do not illustrate or reflect the female experience; to the contrary, they are enactments of the ideological practice of gender or of feminist critiques thereof. The

Hollywood films reproduce and reflect the ideology itself. It is probably no accident that *A Question of Silence* as a self-consciously feminist fable is able to avoid reproducing the notion of power as figured only in terms of sexuality or motherhood. Finally, these Hollywood films can only be read as ideological expressions when interpreted from a feminist perspective. Interpreting from a *female* perspective will not work since in the context of gender ideology, expressions of the female simply reproduce the gender structure. Female is itself an ideologically structured position.

I have used the notion of crime and punishment as a way to illustrate the strength and presence of the ideological structure. We can recognize crimes against gender because they illicit punishments. Like most ideological structures, gender is both fragile and potent. Its fragility, like Durkheim's "common conscience," is a function of its mythical nature. Because it is, in some sense, not real, there must be enforceable rules to maintain it. These rules exist not so much to punish the dissenter, but to show those who *do not* dissent why they should proceed with what Marcuse called a "happy consciousness" and continue to regard the system as common sense. The meta-rule seems to be that people are not allowed to call attention to the fact that gender itself is a myth. In this context, I cautiously invoke Nietzsche's idea in *Will to Power* that crime belongs to greatness. Crimes against gender can be subversive, radical political acts if interpreted and perpetrated through feminist politics.

As a structure, gender depends on the belief that it is natural for its very presence and power as a world historical system. Since it rests on mere belief, one would think that gender is quite weak. Yet, insofar as those beliefs are reproduced in lived practices and reflected in so many tiny mirrors everywhere in our society, the opposite is true. Gender is actually quite strong. Its strength and success is marked by its very longevity and the profound skepticism one encounters upon suggesting that gender is ideological.

Gender is so strong, in fact, that, as the case of transsexualism illustrates, it is considered easier to change one's body than it is to change one's gender identity! And what is it that the transsexual imagines awaits him or her when he or she crosses over to the other side? As one of the cross-dressers in the film *Paris Is Burning* said of his hopes for the future after his operation, "I would like to be a spoiled, rich white girl." The archetype of the feminine might be studied very well by looking at the behavior of those who have themselves made a life's avocation out of imitating it—male drag queens. No, the male drag queen does not reflect what women *really* are; still, what we see reflected in male drag is, in an important sense, what Woman means in the context of the gender structure.

The drag queen of color quoted above associates whiteness with real womanhood. This only further illustrates that what Hazel Carby has shown about the nineteenth century in *Reconstructing Womanhood* can also be said about the idea of Woman today. Of the nineteenth century, Carby writes, "The ideology of true womanhood was as racialized a concept in relation to white women as it was in its exclusion of black womanhood."[12] To the extent that Woman is itself a racialized concept, as Carby has written, it *means* white woman.[13] Obviously, this does not mean that women of color are not women. It only means that the ideology of gender promotes archetypes as normative ideals, and, to the extent that we live in a racist society (which we certainly do), those archetypes will reflect that racist and classist bias. This makes an exclusionary definition of Woman in feminist theory all the more tragic, for it merely reproduces the racism of the dominant paradigm.

This is a good time for me to point out the difference between my analysis in this book and the one offered by Judith Butler in *Gender Trouble*. I am not talking about gender as a performance (what Butler calls, "performativity"). I do think there is a subject who exists apart from the practice of gender and who is consciously or not obeying gender rules. For me, gender is more than a performance which can be altered with a new act. In particular, one cannot simply subvert gender rules by inverting them. In analyzing drag, for instance, two things must be taken into account. First, the subjective moment of interpretation. That is, both the interpretation of the drag queen (her)self and of those who interpret (her). Lots of people rebel, but it doesn't always get taken up as a rebellion. I would argue that is not truly a rebellious practice unless it is recognized as such by someone. Second, the context in which the practice of drag occurs is important. In *Paris Is Burning* we saw drag occurring in terms of practices which basically reinforced the structures of gender, class and race to the extent that the drag queens defined their own practices in terms of their desires to move into dominant positions as white, rich stereotypically feminine women.

It is also important to note that though none of the things I am ironically describing as gender crimes are radical in and of themselves, there are practices which inherently sustain the gender structure. Most practices do so, in fact. This is simply because the current ideological structures of power are so overwhelming that it takes a great effort to challenge them, and a great effort to recognize someone who is challenging them as doing so. That is, truly transformative rebellion involves several interpretive moments.

If we think about what it means to be masculine and feminine and compare real people (of all colors and sexual persuasions) to those images, it is clear that no one can fulfill them completely. We are all only variations on a continuum of masculine and feminine. It should come as no surprise, then, that class, race, and ethnicity, along with size, hair color, behavior, etc., are factors in the formation of the structure of gender and its normative archetypes. This racial component of predominant images of gender is only one example of the gender structure's interaction with other existing systems of power.

This brings us to a question: How do we know when something is really about gender, as opposed to more appropriately connected to some other power system? How do we know if we are rebelling against the right thing, or enough things, or too many things? The answer is that we do not. We simply are bound to resist where we think we see gender oppression and to resist from the perspective of feminism as an oppositional ideology and practice. It is essential, therefore, that feminism not merely reproduce the old ideology, not even by reversing and transvaluing masculine and feminine. Feminism must be proactive. It must be critical and active in and of itself. As Margaret Radin has written, "feminism and pragmatism are not things; they are ways of proceeding."[14]

2. The visibility of gender as an oppressive structure has only become possible with the redescription of gender from the feminist perspective. This perspective can also be thought of as a feminist lens. It is a

self-consciously political perspective. It does not come from women's experiences; rather, it is what we use to give new meaning to human experiences. Feminist interpretations and actions are interventions into the ideology of gender, and not all women adopt this perspective. Only feminists do. The feminist subject cannot be defined a priori in theory, but only in the act of being feminist. That is, feminist subjectivity is defined in practice.

If we began from the assumption that there is nothing about women per se that necessarily leads to a uniformly gendered variance in our interpretations of lived experience, we must then ask, What is it that sometimes causes a shift in interpretive perspectives? That is, how does political consciousness about our gendered lives occur? We would then be asking a question about feminist subjects.

I think it is true that feminism cannot proceed without a subject. This is where a simply postmodern perspective fails feminism. However, needing a subject does not mean that the feminist subject can be theorized into existence. The feminist subject and the feminist lens through which she sees can only be developed in the context of political action. This is why the development of a female or feminist epistemology is quite unnecessary.

The alternative provided by Haraway's suggestion of taking a cyborg perspective is interesting, but what does it mean to take a cyborg's perspective anyway? It seems to me that there has to be a subject position for us to take in the now, and that it must derive from our own politics. It is not possible to describe the feminist subject or the female standpoint and then simply take that position. As I have argued, this simply raises the Lukacs/Adorno debate again: experiences cannot be imputed in advance to a revolutionary agent, and standpoint cannot be determined as a static identity a priori. The feminist subject must allow for internal diversity, coalition, and change, and this can only happen as we engage in activities which promote these.

I think this idea of feminism as a way to proceed should also make us worry less about whether or not deconstruction leaves us any way to reconstruct. Reconstruction takes place automatically. I cannot think of even one example of a time in history when after a revolutionary change, the world was left in limbo, unreconstructed. The question is, however, From what perspective is the reconstruction accomplished? Naturally, the hope is that it is done from the same perspective as the critique. To criticize, a subject perspective is always already in place.

The idea of "strategic essentialism" being floated in some postmodern feminist circles as a way to theorize female subjectivity is really only an admission that foundations, and moreover, foundations in Woman and personal experience, are necessary. The notion fails to tell us what is to be essentialized when; which is to say, it fails utterly. It merely states a desire to be able to talk about women again. But it is a mistake to think that we need essentialized foundations to do this. Women exist. The key is to turn them into feminist subjects, and we cannot do this solely by writing about it on our computers.

In turn, the critique of essentialism supplied by postmodernism misses the importance of the link between Woman and experience. It is not enough to say that the category Woman is a problem in itself. The problem is exacerbated when linked to experientialism because of the requirement and impossibility of universal inclusion. As I have shown, the combination of these two elements makes it impossible even to create a fictive, unitary category. The category dissolves almost immediately upon construction when confronted with the world, which inevitably contains, not only a myriad of women's experiences, but experiences that are internally multiple and shifting.

Another problem with a feminism based in female experience is the one named from the experientialist perspective as the male-identified woman. Truly, after thirty years of the women's liberation movement, it is in my mind difficult to accept anti-feminist women as victims of false consciousness. Feminism is a choice to view the world differently; a choice that such women have declined. Conceptually separating woman from feminist, as my approach advocates, clarifies the fact that the decision *not* to support feminism is a political choice rather than a result of the fact of a woman's being out of touch with her feelings as a woman. Linda Alcoff is correct in writing, "(T)he difference between feminists and antifeminists strikes me as precisely this: the affirmation or denial of our right and our ability to construct, and take responsibility for, our gendered identity, our politics and our choices."[15]

For whatever reasons, anti-feminist women do not see feminism as being in their interests. This simply means that human relations look different when viewed through a feminist lens, but not necessarily simply from the perspective of women. To argue the contrary is to say that the function of feminism is merely to bring one to consciousness of what one knew all along by virtue one's womanhood. In fact, a feminist lens demands precisely that one step beyond what one knows as a woman, because to know as a woman *means* to know from the perspective of the structure of gender. In contrast, a feminist perspective means that one has a critical distance on gender and on oneself. It means that one is reconstructing oneself in terms of a new community.

3. Feminist politics are of necessity personal politics, but the substance of this politics cannot be defined in advance or undertaken in solitude. The politics of gender must be both personal and public; it must aim to transform. Redescribing and creating new meaning in theory is not enough. The feminist lens is not, in itself, enough.

Historically, feminist politics has been defined as that which is concerned with power as it is systematically exercised by males, or in the interests of the masculine and the male. Since this power occurs and has been named at every level, the personal has had to be political. It is sound reasoning to say that personal politics are necessary because gender operates on all levels of existence.

However, gender, which is by definition an inequitable system, is also reinforced at the level of states, capitalism, and throughout the international community. This is why personal politics alone, including theoretical interventions, is an insufficient feminist tool. No amount of redescription, theory, or language changes can stop battering, promote reproductive freedom, or stop child abuse.

It is also true that not everything is always political. My choice of music, my use of a particular word processing program, my taste in clothes, my choice of sexual partner, or my sexual practices—all of these *can* be political. Any or all of these can be the *result* of political choices exercised elsewhere, the *cause* of political action, or political acts in themselves. But it is not safe to say that everything is political all the time. Things are politicized in contexts. It probably also makes sense to say that things are political because we choose to see them as such. This is especially true the further we get from defining politics as that which has to do with government.

For example, if I like the music of the band Guns 'N Roses but find it hard to listen to their music because I think their lead singer is a racist, or if I do not listen to some rap by Ice Cube on feminist grounds, I am probably acting politically. But am I acting politically if I simply do not like Guns 'N Roses or Ice Cube and am not sure why? Or, what if I like them and am oblivious to their racism and sexism?

Few would say that my patronage of women's bookstores is sufficient to make me a political person. Still, this may be a political act in the context of that act's definition as such by a larger feminist community, or in the context of my own larger political vision. Politics, personal or otherwise, is an activity necessarily connected to something outside myself. It is not only an inward-looking activity, though it always demands contemplation. The idea of feminist politics and personal politics needs to be theorized far beyond what is possible within the scope of this current project. If feminism is to be defined as a political practice rather than an organic connection to women's experiences, it is even more incumbent upon us to do more thinking about what we mean by the very provocative term *personal politics*.

Earlier in this book I discussed the feminist move of seeing theory as a political activity. I do think there is something to be said for this way of looking at theory in that theory describes, names, and makes connections from a particular point of view. If the personal is political, it follows that that point of view is implicated in politics. One might also be anti-theory on political grounds, believing that it requires universals and abstractions and finding those requirements suspect.

I think the use of personal stories, plain language, literature, and the pronoun "I" can be important political statements in scholarly and theoretical texts. Again, however, politically correct theory is not enough. There is also a need to take unpopular positions in one's university or at work, to risk one's job for one's principles, to take stands, to organize, to demonstate, to teach wisely and well, to remain connected to an active political community, and more. I know that none of these are easy.

4. The aim of feminist politics is the end of gender and the creation of new human beings who are self-determining and fully participate in the development of their own constantly evolving subjectivity. We could think of this as a feminist humanist vision.

I can almost hear the collective gasp as I write the word *humanist*. Still, I think that the logic of my analysis of the structure of gender suggests that for women to be liberated, we cannot avoid talking about men as well. I have defined gender as a hierarchical structure. This means that, by definition, women are structurally more—and differently—oppressed by gender than men are. I am not even sure that *oppression* is the right word to use when speaking about what is happening to men. There is no doubt, however, that it is time to talk about men *as men* from the feminist perspective.

There is a pragmatic logic for doing this. Given that the male and female have always existed in relation to one another, it is unlikely that we can change women without changing men. The end of gender means that gender will no longer mediate the relationships between individuals and the world. Gender will also cease to mediate our relations as people. Our biological sex will simply become one of the many facts about us as people like our hair or eye color. I envision this as an expansion of the choices that people have in life, because currently those choices are artificially restricted by gender. To be a fully self-determining person means that we need to be able to choose among the full range of human traits, without having to choose based on gender. It follows that the nature and the range of choices will change as we begin to enact the infinite possibilities of human combinations, and that those changes must necessarily include changing the male and men.

My notion of feminism as a type of humanism is really only revisioning an earlier style of feminism. Iris Young has written of the distinction between "humanism" and "gynocentrism." She writes, "Humanist feminism defines women's oppression as the inhibition and distortion of women's potential by a society that allows the self-development of men."[16] She connects this tradition with the writings of de Beauvoir and contrasts it with the kind of feminine feminism I have had occasion to discuss in these pages. Although Young may very well have accurately characterized the older tradition of human-ist feminism as a "revolt against femininity,"[17] this does not capture what I mean by feminist humanism.

The revolt I would want to plan would be against gender itself—against both masculinity and femininity as they function in various cultures and societies. In fact, I think it is pointless to revolt against one, since the two imply each other and only exist in relation to one another.

Patricia Hill Collins has also called for a feminist humanist model for black feminism. She defines this as "a process of self-conscious struggle that empowers women and men to actualize a humanist vision of community."[18] Collins quotes Fannie Lou Hamer to metaphorically sum up the values of this feminist vision nicely: "Ain' no such thing as I can hate anybody and hope to see God's face."[19]

A NEW AND IMPROVED POST-ENLIGHTENMENT HUMANISM

The category Woman lacks universality in the same way that categories based on man do. That is why feminism must entail the reconstruction of both woman and man and must be, in effect, a new version of humanism. This does not mean an end to feminism, nor even a new name for feminism. The impulse and the real need to do this restructur-ing has come from the fact of female oppression, since the structure of gender is, by definition, based on dualism and inequality.

It is simply that female subjectivity as envisioned by feminist sub-jects seems to me to require an end to male and female as we now understand those terms. This also means that by preserving the femi-nine in gynocentric feminism, we unavoidably also preserve the masculine. Even a revalued femininity reproduces the gender structure. In other words, it would do little good to refigure the female in terms of current gender arrangements. Whether we advocate revaluing femi-ninity or not, the whole notion of gender is structurally biased and the weight of it will always, as far as I can tell, reproduce inequity.

The most radical feminism would advocate, then, an end to male/female, masculine/feminism, and woman/man as we now understand those terms. I am not saying that we will no longer have male or female bodies, but simply that male and female bodies will not *mean* the same thing that they do now.

When I first began to think about the problem of gender, I was very attracted to Rubin's idea of the "sex/gender" system and thought it very important to maintain the distinction between feminine, which is of gender, and woman, which is of the body and the real. Although I think the sex/gender system is profoundly important in naming gender as distinct from the body, I now think it makes no sense to separate the two when the ideology of gender has so invaded our understanding of the body. Without feminism, it is nearly impossible to think *feminine* without also thinking female body or female sex. It is true that the structure of gender acts through and is inscribed on sexed bodies, but the whole idea of two sexes only has meaning because those meanings are required by the gender structure in the first place. We can thus speak of a nexus of sex and gender that is slightly different than the one Rubin described.

At the same time that I am saying that sex and gender are more related than Rubin's notion allows, it remains imperative not to mistake the rules of gender for the reality of people's lives. This is where Rubin's formulation remains absolutely correct. That is, people as individuals really are able to deviate from the archetypes of femininity and masculinity.

My questions are these: When such deviations from gender occur, as in what I was calling "gender crimes," or as in the infinite bleeps along the continuum of gender, are such individuals then acting as *authentic women and men* (as I think Rubin's formulation implies)? Or when they deviate from the rules of gender are they acting as authentic *human beings?* This same point can be restated in the question, Is it possible, or does it make sense, to talk about an authentic woman and man if we do not need to rely on those authentic experiences as foundational to feminism? That is, if we move away from the belief in the possibility of finding our authentic experiences as women, which we need to tap into in order to ground feminism, does it not also become possible to move away from the importance of the inevitable separation of humans into two sexes per se? The answer to this seems to be in the affirmative, in which case, in the end, we are really talking about feminist conceptions of ourselves as human beings.

If one of the main problems of feminist theory has been essentialism, how can I advocate a move toward humanism, which also has an essentialist heritage? First, feminism as I am redescribing it does not assume some transcendent, universal human to which we are returning, but posits the construction of an altogether new human, which we would construct democratically. In this sense, it would be a truly universal notion of the human; one that is not idealist, monolithic, or based on dualisms. If everyone who cares to is allowed to participate in its democratic reconstruction, I think we can avoid making ethnocentric mistakes about what it means to be human. This would mean that feminism needs to make links with other multicultural viewpoints according to some universally agreed upon values and principles for action.

In short, the new feministized human cannot be defined in abstraction. Really, it cannot be defined at all. What *can* be discussed is the political perspective from which we criticize gender and from which we go on to reconstruct ourselves. The reconstruction will not happen by moving toward some preconceived identity, but by proceeding according to an agreed upon process and set of values.

Is it not true that I am assuming Enlightenment values in this new vision of feminism? It depends on what one means by that phrase, of course, but I would say rather that they are neo-Enlightenment values. For example, I see feminism as connected to the values of freedom, equality, and universal justice. If feminism is a movement for the liberation of women, it seems to me that women (and men) must become self-determining as individuals. Historically, this has been far easier for men than for women—or, significantly, it has been easier for *some* men.

In itself a call for individual self-determination does not sound particularly feminist, since this is what most Marxist and liberal theories of justice advocate. However, it is feminist insofar as it falls to feminism to figure out exactly how gender complicates this goal of self-determination.

For example, the fact that women on the whole earn less money than men, or that women are segregated into lower paying jobs, is an example of a limitation on self-determination that would have been invisible without feminism. Given the gendered structure of the family and child rearing, the lack of universally available day care is another. The fact that reproductive rights are controlled by those who have an interest in maintaining the gender structure is another, or that abortion is not conceptualized as a reproductive right but as a separate issue, tends to reinforce gender. As the well-rehearsed argument goes, since we have no 100 percent reliable birth control, and since women are disproportionately involved in child care, a prohibition on abortion means forced child birth. This, in turn, translates into restrictions on female sexual activity (since the rational woman will know that sex can equal unwanted children), and a hindrance to women in the labor market (since the rational capitalist knows that women are the primary caretakers of children and that they can become pregnant at any time). Lack of access to abortion limits female self-determination.

The facts that most rapists are men and most victims women and that serial killers tend to be men and their victims are more often than not women both serve to increase the terrorism that exists in service of the artificial maintenance of the gender structure. First, it is well established that these crimes reflect male rage against women. As such, they are themselves outgrowths of the gender structure, which pits male against female in a hierarchy based on power and powerlessness. Second, their effect is to create a climate of fear that reinforces the idea (and the current reality) of female powerlessness and male power which has been called a "rape culture." Domestic violence and exploitative advertising function similarly.

As these examples show, every important feminist issue can be discussed in terms of the importance of self-determination and the ways in which the ideological structure of gender inhibits the same.

Feminist ideas about self-determination must include both men and women, while being aware of race and capitalism as interactive with the gender structure. People must be self-determining in a way that includes the body and differences among bodies, since, up to now, how we have treated bodily differences has been a major factor in human unfreedom. If we are to avoid humanist essentialism, we must also abandon the idea that the body can be transcended by the mind. This is simply to say that freedom can only take place in the context of the body.

WHAT DO WE MEAN BY LIBERATION?

The feminist debates about sexuality and pornography have raised the painful fact that self-determination means that some women will behave in ways that meet with feminist disapproval. However, this does not mean that we need to castigate those women as male identified. In fact, it is probably true that as gender boundaries relax women explore various modes of being that have been built either upon patriarchal conditioning as nurturers or their immediate and not always well motivated desires upon finally tasting freedom. It is important to remember that the very public right-wing women are only possible at all because gender restrictions are easing. We certainly need not seek solidarity with them or apologize for them, but we need to see them as symbols of feminist success.

Other women who appear to make bad choices might be termed "corporate feminists." Corporate feminists are those whose only concern is that they be liberated into a free market economy where there is no glass ceiling, so that they can make as much money as the men of their classes. This is a tepid feminism indeed. Still, I do think that women's self-determination and freedom from gender must be accepted as they occur along with all that they imply, and sometimes it means women will make what some of us believe to be bad choices. It is at least a partial victory if women are allowed to make choices at all. Since gender intersects other systems of power and is inscribed by their practices, we should expect that freedom for women will sometimes be interpreted as the freedom to assume a dominant role in some other hierarchy.

Importantly, the corporate feminist would probably not be at all interested in the kind of feminism I am describing in the first place. She is probably not interested in challenging gender per se, but only in challenging gender as it applies to her particular, self-interested position. Her kind of feminism is based on avarice because it is supplemented by a belief in the naturalness and justness of capitalism.

She does not see the full scope and power of gender because her feminist vision is limited. The same failure would occur in the case of formulations of female freedom that fail to take racism into account. If all white women want is to be free to dominate people of color as white men do, that *is* a type of white female freedom, but it is a kind that does not take the far-reaching implications of the gender structure into account. It is not a type of feminism infused with a humanist vision for self-determination or one that values social democracy.

It is as consistent to be a socialist and a feminist as it is to be a capitalist and a feminist. But the capitalism and the socialism when added to the feminism will create very different visions of what society should look like because their ideas about self-determination, the importance of looking at the whole person, and the relationship of the mind to the body are different.

The kind of feminism I am talking about must support freedom, but cannot stop at supporting freedom. Feminists have a tendency to charge anyone who talks about freedom of the individual with being a libertarian. This is because they do not see that freedom can be discussed along with other issues in a positive way. For feminism (as for socialism), freedom is not the only end. It is only the beginning.

All hitherto existing attempts to build a foundationalist feminism, or to link feminism, of necessity, to larger issues like socialism or peace, have rested on essentialized concepts of Woman and imputed notions of the female experience. I am suggesting that we can think of feminism in a very radical way without resorting to these tools. The idea of an ideological structure of gender from which we seek liberation, I think, solves the problems presented by the core concepts. As I have described it, it allows us to talk about the differential treatment of women and requires that we also talk about race, ethnicity, class, men, and the masculine. It also allows us to be inclusive with regard to sexual preferences. It is socially constructivist, but does not destroy the subject. It reclaims feminism as a political movement whose politics are both personal and public. I am not saying, with some critics, that we can never mention women again, but I am saying that we cannot assume her experiences, her commonality, or her organic connection to a given politics.

The ideas I have been presenting draw on several sometimes overlapping traditions. They are liberal in that they talk about freedom, the individual, and self-determination. They are humanist in their vision of commonalities among people. They are consistent with Marxism and socialism in the scope of their notions of equality and in that Marx always saw socialism as the concrete realization of the goals of the French Revolution. I have only attempted to add a feminist dimension to these. This feminist vision does not require socialism and neither does it disallow socialism; however, its requirement to deal with bodies and concrete self-determination implies economic equality. My idea is pragmatic in that it draws concepts from many traditions simply because I think they would work. It is pragmatic (and Marxist) also in arguing that subjects must be constituted in practice, and in its call to action. It is Foucaultian in talking about different intersecting systems of power, but Althusserian in its discussion of the social construction of subjects in terms of various ideological systems. Most important, it is feminist in its emphasis on gender, personal politics, and the transformation of all humankind.

SOME CONCLUDING REMARKS

In 1991 I gave a short talk on feminism and reason to a group of faculty, staff, and students at a local university. As you might imagine after having read this book, I was very critical of the essentialist impulse in feminist theory, and, in response, some of the women grew quite testy. One of them said that she thought essentialism was just some new catch phrase that legitimated ad hominem criticisms of feminism. Another asked, exasperated, why we could not be essentialist and historicist at the same time (the answer is because essentialism and historicism are opposites).

I have since met still other feminists who have expressed impatience with critiques about the categories of feminism. Do we not all *really know* what we mean by women? Are not the things that "different voice" feminine feminists say about women true with regard to most women? My point has been that we *think* we know what we mean by Woman because we slip too easily into seeing it through the lens of gender instead of through the feminist lens. Moreover, it is no surprise that things feminine feminists say about women appear true, as they conform to traditional views about women's nature.

Another fear I have heard is that if we focus on gender, men's studies will soon eclipse women's studies. Indeed, I think the likelihood of this is greater if men's studies students and faculty are left to their own devices to read books like *Iron John* instead of approaching gender through a feminist lens. The gender studies I am suggesting would still allow us to talk about women's oppression.

In fact, I am very impatient with such dismissals of the various critiques of feminist theory. Such critiques are not anti-feminist or anti-woman. I know it is bothersome and difficult to accept that some of the foundational categories of feminism may not be working as they should. I also understand that it is pleasurable to praise femininity and to revel in things that have previously been reviled. I know that hearing about the racism of feminism is tiresome to some white feminists, and I know that a depoliticized feminism fits more comfortably into the university. I also know that some of the defenses of the core concepts have nothing to do with any of the above and come rather from a genuine belief in their usefulness. This last category of feminist theorists and women's studies scholars is the audience I imagined in writing this book.

Still, there is no denying that there is an unease about criticizing these concepts. Indeed, the negative reactions I have sometimes gotten to my criticisms of the core concepts reflect their foundational status in feminism up to this point. As one person asked me recently, "But if you get rid of the idea of experience, what is left of feminism?" The answer is: a lot. Feminism is a rich tradition that has become completely obsessed with the fruitless quest for the authentic female experience. The core concepts have been fetishized, and I have attempted to demystify and evaluate them in this book. The task of constituting a feminist subject in practice, however, neither I nor anyone else can ever accomplish in the pages of a book. That task remains for us after the reading, and after the writing. Never give up.

Notes

I. INTRODUCTION

1. Jean Bethke Elshtain, *Public Man, Private Woman* (Princeton: Princeton University Press, 1981). These terms are introduced on 350, 203, and 351, respectively.

2. Alison Jaggar, *Feminist Politics and Human Nature* (Totowa, N.J.: Rowman And Allanheld, 1983); chapters 3 and 7 mention only one example of second wave liberal feminism: Betty Friedan.

3. Jaggar, 98.

4. Josephine Donovan, *Feminist Theory* (New York: Unger, 1985).

5. Ibid, ch. 7.

6. Ibid, 32 and 42.

7. Ibid, 142.

8. Rosemary Tong, *Feminist Thought: A Comprehensive Introduction* (Boulder and San Francisco: Westview, 1989).

9. Edward Said, *Orientalism* (New York: Vintage, 1979), 13.

10. All quotes from Marilyn Quayle from, "Marilyn Quayle Says the 1960's Had a Flip Side," *New York Times*, 20 August 1992.

2. INVENTING FEMINIST THEORY

1. Alice Echols, *Daring to Be Bad* (Minneapolis: University of Minnesota, 1989); Sara Evans, *Personal Politics* (New York: Vintage, 1979).

2. Jean Bethke Elshtain, *Public Man, Private Woman* (Princeton: Princeton University Press, 1981), 228.

3. Zillah Eisenstein, *The Radical Future of Liberal Feminism* (Boston: Northeastern University Press, 1981).

4. The same may be true of first wave feminism, but I am only concerned with the second wave herein.

5. Ellen Willis, "Women and the Left" in Shulamith Firestone and Anne Koedt, eds., *Notes from the Second Year* (New York: Radical Feminism, 1969), 55.

6. Ti Grace Atkinson, *Amazon Odyssey* (New York: Links Books, 1974), 97.

7. Joreen, "The Bitch Manifesto," in *Notes from the Second Year* (New York: Radical Feminism, 1969), 5–8.

8. Ibid.

9. Roxanne Dunbar, "Women's Liberation as the Basis for Social Revolution," in *Notes from the Second Year*, 53.

10. Barbara Burris, "The Fourth World Manifesto," in *Notes from the Third Year* (New York: Radical Feminism, 1971), 118.

11. Recently, I spoke at a symposium on women and reason, and a woman in the audience asked, "What is wrong with essentialism? Isn't that charge just a new way to discredit feminism? Can't we be essentialist and historical at the same time?" I wish I had answered this way: Historicism and essentialism are opposites. Concepts of God are based in essentialist understandings of the human soul. Racism is based on an essentialist view of "races" as real categories with some superior to others. It is pretty much true that essentialist arguments have been associated with the Right. As long as the debate is posed that way, then, no, we cannot be both. Marx figured out a way to historicize an essentialist concept when he used the word "human" as a social category. But even Marx stopped short of a completely social constructivist view in that he seems to have had a faith in our basic human potential as creative beings. I am not sure whether we can escape essentialism completely—postmodernism is showing that it is difficult to speak without *some* concepts of identity, even if they are multiple. As to whether charging someone with essentialism should be dismissed as

merely more feminist bashing—I think not. To posit an essence of a thing means that it cannot change. That is why basing feminism on an essentialist notion of woman is extremely risky business.

12. "The Fourth World Manifesto," 104.

13. Kate Millet, "Sexual Politics," in *Notes from the Second Year,* 111.

14. Barbara Mehrhof and Pamela Kearon, "Rape: An Act of Terror," in *Notes from the Third Year,* 79.

15. Betsy Warrior, "Man Is an Obsolete Lifeform," in the second issue of *No More Fun and Games* (February 1969).

16. Shulamith Firestone, *The Dialectic of Sex* (London: The Woman's Press, 1979) 16.

17. Ibid.

18. Hazel Carby, *Reconstructing Womanhood* (Oxford: Oxford University Press, 1987).

19. Gayle Rubin, "Woman as Nigger," in Betty Roszak and Theodore Roszak, eds., *Masculine/Feminine: Readings in Sexual Mythology and the Liberation of Women* (New York: Harper and Row, 1969), 231.

20. Among the many discussions of this phenomenon see Linda C. Powell, "Black Macho and Black Feminism," 283–293, and Luisah Teish, "Women's Spirituality: A Household Act," 331–352, in Barbara Smith, ed., *Home Girls: A Black Feminist Anthology* (New York: Kitchen Table: Woman of Color Press, 1983); and Michele Wallace, "A Black Feminist's Search for Sisterhood," in Gloria T. Hull, Patricia Bell Scott, and Barbara Smith, eds., *All the Women Are White, All the Blacks Are Men, but Some of Us Are Brave* (Old Westbury, N.Y.: The Feminist Press, 1982), 5–13.

21. "The Combahee River Collective: A Black Feminist Statement," in Zillah Eisenstein, ed., *Capitalist Patriarchy and the Case for Socialist Feminism* (New York and London: Monthly Review Press, 1979), 362. Subsequent four quotations are from the same source, 366, 364, 365, and 366, respectively.

22. Roxanne Dunbar, "Women's Liberation as the Basis for Social Revolution," in Shulamith Firestone and Anne Koedt, eds., *Notes from the Second Year* (New York: Radical Feminism, 1969).

23. Barbara Burris, "The Fourth World Manifesto," in Anne Koedt, Ellen Levine, and Anita Rapone, eds., *Radical Feminism* (New York: Quadrangle Books, 1973), 105.

24. Lisa Leghorn, "Women of the Ruling Class," in *No More Fun and*

Games (November 1969) (pages unnumbered). On the same subject see also Leah Fritz, *Dreamers and Dealers* (Boston: Beacon Press, 1979).

25. Ibid.

26. Christine Delphy, "Our Friends and Ourselves: The Hidden Foundations of Various Pseudo-Feminist Accounts," a 1977 essay reprinted in Diana Leonard, ed., *Close to Home: A Materialist Analysis of Women's Oppression* (Amherst: University of Massachusetts Press, 1984), 121.

27. See Susan Moller Okin, *Women in Western Political Thought* (Princeton: Princeton University Press, 1979), and numerous others on this topic.

28. "The Manifesto of the Redstockings," in *Notes from the Second Year*, 113.

29. *Daring to Be Bad*, 144.

30. See, for example, bell hooks, *Ain't I a Woman?* (Boston: South End Press, 1981).

31. For a contemporary example, see Dorothy E. Smith, *The Conceptual Practices of Power: A Feminist Sociology of Knowledge,* (Boston: Northeastern University Press, 1990), especially 11–31. See also Jean Grimshaw's discussion in *Philosophy and Feminist Thinking* (Minneapolis: University of Minnesota Press, 1986), especially 36–75.

32. *Amazon Odyssey*, 13.

33. "Sexual Politics," 111.

34. *Amazon Odyssey*, 13.

35. Anne Koedt, "The Myth of the Vaginal Orgasm," in *Notes from the Second Year*, 37–42.

36. *Amazon Odyssey*, 5. The next two quotations are from 7.

37. Ibid, 13.

38. Ibid, 14.

39. Ti Grace Atkinson quoted in Jill Johnston, *Lesbian Nation: The Feminist Solution* (New York: Touchstone Press, 1973), 117.

40. *Amazon Odyssey,* 62.

41. "The Feminists: A Political Organization to Annihilate Sex Roles," in Anne Koedt, Ellen Levine, and Anita Rapone, eds., *Radical Feminism* (New York: Quadrangle Books, 1973), 368–378.

42. *The Dialectic of Sex,* 121.

43. Barbara Mehroff and Pamela Kearon, "Rape: An Act of Terror," in *Notes from the Third Year,* 79–80.

44. Carol Hanish, "The Personal Is Political," in *Notes from the Second Year,* 76–78.

3. FEMINIST STRATEGIES: FROM CORE CONCEPTS TO FEMINIST THEORY

1. Shulamith Firestone, *The Dialectic of Sex* (London: The Woman's Press, 1979), 151.

2. Alice Jardin, *Gynesis: Configurations of Woman and Modernity* (Ithaca and London: Cornell University Press, 1985), 147. See related discussions throughout her book, especially chapters 1 and 7.

3. Mary Hawkesworth, "Knowers, Knowing and Known: Feminist Theory and Claims of Truth," in *Signs* vol. 14, no. 3 (1989).

4. See Joan Scott's excellent discussion of experience, and the appeal to the authority of experience, as an essentialist discourse in the discipline of history in Joan Scott, "The Evidence of Experience," *Critical Inquiry* 17 (1991): 773–797.

5. Adrienne Rich, "Disloyal to Civilization: Feminism, Racism, and Gynephobia," in *On Lies, Secrets and Silences: Selected Prose 1966–1978* (New York: W. W. Norton & Co. Inc., 1979).

6. Notable in this regard is Gerda Lerner's idea that the oppression of women is the model for all other types of subjugation. See her *Creation of Patriarchy* (New York: Oxford University Press, 1986).

7. Iris Marion Young, *Justice and the Politics of Difference,* (Princeton: Princeton University Press, 1990), 37–38. The next quotation is from 43.

8. Feminists such as Nancy Fraser and Donna Haraway who apply a postmodern approach to socialist feminism are not treated in this section. I am primarily interested in the attempt to synthesize Marxism and feminism in early socialist feminist thought.

9. Zillah Eisenstein, ed., *Capitalist Patriarchy and the Case for Socialist Feminism* (New York: Monthly Review Press, 1979), 8. See also the enormously important collection edited by Annette Kuhn and Ann Marie Wolpe, *Feminism and Materialism: Women and Modes of Production* (London and Boston: Routledge Kegan Paul, 1978).

10. Sandra Morgan, "Conceptualizing and Changing Consciousness:

Socialist Feminist Perspectives," in Karen Hansen and Ilene Philipson, eds., *Women, Class and the Feminist Imagination,* 278.

11. "Changing Consciousness," 280.

12. Michele Rosaldo argued that socialist feminists need to get more specific information about women's lives before generalizing into a grand theory. See her "Uses and Misuses of Anthropology," in *Signs* (Spring 1980).

13. Barbara Ehrenreich, "Life without Father: Reconsidering Socialist Feminist Theory," in *Women, Class and the Feminist Imagination,* 269.

14. See "The Impasse of Socialist Feminism," Barbara Haber, et al., *Socialist Review* 79, vol. 15, no. 1 (January/February 1985): 95 and 98. See also Michele Barrett, "Old Masters of the Left," in *New Statesman* 13 (July 1984).

15. Seyla Benhabib and Drucilla Cornell, eds., *Feminism as Critique: On the Politics of Gender* (Minneapolis: University of Minnesota Press, 1987), 2.

16. Of course, even this is a controversial reading of Marx. Only certain versions of Marxism set forth class as a purely objective phenomenon. The term *class consciousness* suggests that the workers must know themselves as a class. There are thus both objective and subjective aspects to class.

17. See Georg Lukacs, *The Destruction of Reason* (New York: Humanities Press, 1981).

18. Charlotte Bunch and Nancy Myron, eds., *Class and Feminism: A Collection of Essays from the Furies* (Baltimore: Diana Press, 1974), 10.

19. Rita Mae Brown, "The Last Straw," in *Class and Feminism.* The quotation that follows is from the same source, 15.

20. Barbara Ehrenreich, "What Is Socialist Feminism?" in *WIN* (Brooklyn, N.Y.: Workshop In Nonviolence Institute Inc., 3 June 1976), 5.

21. Nancy Hartsock, "Fundamental Feminism: Process and Perspective," *Quest* vol. 11, no. 2 (Fall 1975): 72. In passing I should also note that it is in homage to Hartsock that I have borrowed the phrase "fundamental feminism" for the title of this book.

22. Ibid, 70.

23. For example, see *Feminism and Materialism* (London: Routledge, Kegan Paul, 1978), 18.

24. "Fundamental Feminism," 68.

25. Lise Vogel, "The Earthly Family," *Radical America* vol. 7, nos. 4 and 5 (1973): 20.

26. Ibid, 28–29.

27. "What Is Socialist Feminism?," 5.

28. Eli Zaretsky, *Capitalism, the Family and Personal Life* (New York: Pluto, 1976), 82. The following quotation is from 83.

29. Ibid, 83. The following quote is from 137.

30. Juliet Mitchell, "Women: The Longest Revolution," a 1966 article originally published in *New Left Review,* reprinted in Karen V. Hansen and Ilene J. Philipson, eds., *Women, Class and the Feminist Imagination* (Philadelphia: Temple University Press, 1990). See also Mitchell, *Psychoanalysis and Feminism* (New York: Vintage, 1974), and Mitchell, *Woman's Estate* (New York: Vintage, 1973). Interestingly, Shulamith Firestone thought she was doing the same thing as Mitchell—i.e., synthesizing Marx and feminism. They also shared an interest in employing Freud in the service of feminism. Indeed, Mitchell's critique seems to have been intended partly to differentiate herself from Firestone. See especially *Women's Estate,* 89.

31. *Women's Estate,* 51.

32. Ibid, 21.

33. Ibid, 94–96.

34. Ibid. 13.

35. Ibid, 38.

36. Ibid, 60.

37. Ibid, 64.

38. Ibid, 101–108.

39. See Zillah Eisenstein's introduction in *Capitalist Patriarchy.*

40. Michele Barrett, *Women's Oppression Today: Problems in Marxist Feminist Analysis* (London: Verso, 1980), 10–19.

41. *Capitalist Patriarchy,* 25.

42. Heidi Hartmann, "The Unhappy Marriage of Marxism and Feminism: Towards a More Progressive Union," in Lydia Sargent, ed., *Women and Revolution: A Discussion of the Unhappy Marriage of Marxism and Feminism* (Boston: South End Press, 1981) 4–8; Maria Dalla Costa, "Women and the Subversion of Community," in *Radical America* vol. 6, no. 1 (January/February 1972); Paddy Quick, "The

Class Nature of Women's Oppression," in *The Review of Radical Political Economics* vol. 9, no. 3 (1977): 42–53; Maxine Molyneux, "Beyond the Domestic Labor Debate," in *New Left Review* (Spring 1985); Lydia Sargent, ed., *Women and Revolution* (Boston: South End Press, 1981).

43. *Capitalist Patriarchy*, 61.

44. Nancy Hartsock, "Feminist Theory and the Development of Revolutionary Strategy," in *Capitalist Patriarchy*, 71.

45. Alison Jaggar, *Feminist Politics and Human Nature* (Totowa, N.J.: Rowman and Allanheld, 1983), 134.

46. *Capitalist Patriarchy*, p. 7; Hartmann also argues that the Marxist method can be used without the economics in "Unhappy Marriage," 10.

47. *Feminist Politics and Human Nature*, 135.

48. Louis Althusser, "Ideology and the Ideological State Apparatuses," in *Lenin and Philosophy* (London: Monthly Review Press, 1971), 128–129 and 132.

49. For examples of feminist theorists who make the best case that domestic labor is labor in the Marxist sense see Dalla Costa's "Women and the Subversion of Community," 79. She argues that housewives produce use value and surplus value by contributing to the exchange value of labor power. She goes on to argue that the family is the pillar of capitalism and not just part of the superstructure, 81–82. She continues on 84 that housework is a precapitalist form of labor and women must move into the work force to organize for liberation.

50. Karl Marx, *The Grundrisse: Introduction to the Critique of Political Economy* (New York: Vintage Publications, 1973), 94. The following quotation is from the same page.

51. Ibid, 96. The following quotation is from 89.

52. Sheila Rowbotham, *Woman's Consciousness, Man's World* (London: Pelican, 1973), 117.

53. Gayle Rubin, "The Traffic in Women: Notes on the Political Economy of Sex," in Rayna Reiter, et al., ed., *Towards an Anthropology of Women* (New York: Monthly Review Press, 1975), 168.

54. *Capitalist Patriarchy*, 31–32.

55. See, for example, Gloria Joseph, "The Incompatible Menage at Trois: Marxism, Feminism and Racism," in *Women and Revolution*.

56. "The Impasse of Socialist Feminism," 107.

57. *Women's Oppression Today.*

58. I would say that most of the literature developing around an "ethic of care," which was inspired by Carol Gilligan's distinction between an "ethic of justice" and an "ethic of care," could easily be subjected to the same kinds of criticisms I make of mothering theory in this section.

59. Carol Gilligan, *A Different Voice* (Cambridge: Harvard, 1982), 71.

60. Ibid, 44. The following three quotations are from 100, 5, and 5, respectively.

61. See *A Different Voice,* 13, 105–106, 130–131, 148, 155, 157–160, 170, etc., etc., etc.

62. Judy Auerbach, Linda Blum, Vicki Smith, Christine Williams, "Commentary on Gilligan's *In a Different Voice,*" *Feminist Studies* vol. 11, no. 1 (Spring 1985): 155. The following quotation is from 158.

63. Ibid, 160. It should also be pointed out that the analysis may be assuming a patriarchal family that no longer exists. See Zillah Eisenstein, "The Sexual Politics of the New Right: Understanding the Crisis of Liberalism for the 1980's," in Nannerl O. Keohane, Michele Rosaldo, and Barbara Gelpi, eds., *Feminist Theory: A Critique of Ideology* (Chicago: University of Chicago Press, 1981), 77–98. She points out that the patriarchal family is dead and single-parent, woman-headed families are as common as traditional ones.

64. Nancy Chodorow, *The Reproduction of Mothering: Psychoanalysis and the Sociology of Gender* (Berkeley: University of California Press, 1978), 3 and 7.

65. Roger Gotlieb, "Mothering and the Reproduction of Power: Chodorow, Dinnerstein and Social Theory," in *Socialist Review* vol. 14, no. 77: no. 5 (September/October 1984).

66. Ibid.

67. "Commentary on Gilligan," 155.

68. Dorothy Dinnerstein, *The Mermaid and the Minotaur* (New York: Harper and Row, 1983), 203 and 205.

69. Ibid, 205.

70. Ibid, 210.

71. Ibid, 213.

72. Ibid, 213–219.

73. Ibid, 234.

74. Alice Walker, *In Search of Our Mothers' Gardens,* (New York and

London: Harcourt, Brace, Jovanovich, 1983), xi.

75. Alice Walker, "One Child of One's Own," in *In Search of Our Mothers' Gardens*, 378.

76. The phrase comes from Minnie Bruce Pratt, "Identity: Skin, Blood, Heart," Elly Bulkien, Minnie Bruce Pratt, and Barbara Smith, eds., *Yours in Struggle: Three Feminist Perspectives on Anti-Semitism and Racism* (New York: Long Haul Press, 1984), 11–63.

77. For related discussions see Kathleen B. Jones, "Authority and Representation: Sisterhood Is Complicated," paper delivered in Jing Lyman Lecture Series, Stanford University, Institute for Research on Women and Gender, 29 January 1992; Marnia Lazreg, "Feminism and Difference: The Perils of Writing as a Woman on Women in Algeria," *Feminist Studies* vol. 14, no. 4 (September 1988): 81–107; and Biddy Martin and Chandra Talpade Mohanty, "Feminist Politics: What's Home Got to Do with It?" in Teresa de Lauretis, ed., *Feminist Studies, Critical Studies* (Bloomington: Indiana University Press, 1986), 191–213.

78. Adrienne Rich, *Of Woman Born: Motherhood as Experience and Institution* (New York: Norton, 1976), 180. The following quotation is from 269.

79. Jean Bethke Elshtain, *Public Man, Private Woman* (Princeton, N.J.: Princeton University Press, 1981), 322. The following quotation is from 312.

80. *Of Woman Born*, 37. The following quotation is from the same page.

81. Ibid, 264–265. The following quotations are from 72 and 62, respectively.

82. Ann Ferguson, "On Conceiving Motherhood and Sexuality: A Feminist Materialist Approach," in Joyce Trebilcot, ed., *Mothering: Essays in Feminist Theory* (Totowa, N.J.: Rowman and Allanheld, 1984), 154.

83. Ibid.

84. Sandra Harding, "What Is the Real Material Base of Patriarchy and Capital?" in Lydia Sargent, ed., *Women and Revolution* (Boston: South End Press, 1981).

85. Sara Ruddick, "Maternal Thinking," in Trebilcot, 215.

86. Ibid, 216.

87. Ibid, 219.

88. Ibid, 224.

89. Ibid, 225–226.

90. Ibid, 225.

91. Ibid.

92. Nancy Chodorow, *The Reproduction of Mothering: Psychoanalysis and the Sociology of Gender* (Berkeley: University of California Press, 1978) claims to show how this is reproduced socially, but she is often ambiguous on the inherent traits of women. See Janet Sayers, *Biological Politics: Feminist and Anti-Feminist Perspectives* (London and New York: Methuen, 1982), 158, who criticizes Chodorow for assuming that child care differences are based upon differences between men and women.

93. Susan Griffin, *Woman and Nature: The Roaring Inside Her* (New York: Harper and Row, 1980).

94. Mary Daly, *GynEcology: The Metaethics of Radical Feminism* (Boston: Beacon Press, 1978), 9. The following quotation is from 28.

95. Jessica Benjamin and Lilly Rivlin, "The de Beauvoir Challenge: A Crisis in Feminist Politics," *Ms* (January 1980): 50.

96. bell hooks, *Feminist Theory: From Margin to Center* (Boston: South End Press, 1984), 67. The following quotation is from 86.

97. "Ideology and the Ideological State Apparatus."

98. Catherine MacKinnon, *Toward a Feminist Theory of the State* (Cambridge: Harvard University Press, 1989), 117.

99. For a good discussion of so-called "cultural feminism" and the Left today see Ellen Willis, "Radical Feminism and Feminist Radicalism," in Sohnya Sayres, Anders Tephanson, Stanley Aronowitz, Fred Jameson, eds., *The 60's: Without Apology* (Minneapolis: University of Minnesota Press, 1984).

100. *Toward a Feminist Theory of the State*, 3.

101. For a good discussion of the generally bleak picture of male and heterosexual sexualities in the antipornography movement see Kate Ellis, "I'm Black and Blue from the Rolling Stones and I'm Not Sure How I Feel about It: Pornography and the Feminist Imagination," in Karen Hansen and Ilene J. Philipson, eds., *Women, Class and the Feminist Imagination* (Philadelphia: Temple Press, 1990), 431–451; see especially 443–444.

102. *Toward a Feminist Theory of the State*, 94 (and many places elsewhere).

103. Catherine MacKinnon, *Feminism Unmodified: Discourses on Life and Law* (Cambridge: Harvard University Press, 1987), 53.

104. Ibid.

105. *Toward a Feminist Theory of the State,* 178–179.

106. *Feminism Unmodified,* 60. The following quotation is from 242–243.

107. *Toward a Feminist Theory of the State,* 178–179.

108. *Feminism Unmodified,* 50. See also 54–55. The following quotation is from 247.

109. *Toward a Feminist Theory of the State,* 83. The following quotations are from 239 and 98, respectively.

110. *Feminism Unmodified,* 52.

111. *Toward a Feminist Theory of the State,* 118.

112. *Feminism Unmodified,* 76. The following quotation is from 39.

113. *Feminism Unmodified,* 90.

114. Richard Rorty, "Feminism and Pragmatism," in *The Michigan Quarterly Review* vol. 30 (Spring 1991): 238. Although Rorty has claimed publically that MacKinnon is his favorite feminist theorist, I wonder whether he is persuaded by the substance of her claims, or merely suspects that he is appropriating her to try and persuade feminists to adopt the pragmatic method.

115. Andrea Dworkin, *Intercourse* (New York: The Free Press, 1987), 138.

116. See also Andrea Dworkin, *Pornography: Men Possessing Women* (New York: E. P. Dutton, 1989) and *Woman Hating: A Radical Look at Sexuality* (New York: E. P. Dutton, 1974).

117. *Feminism Unmodified,* 99.

118. For a discussion of the sexuality debates that does take race into account, see "The Subject of Struggle: Feminism and Sexuality," in Gloria Joseph and Jill Lewis, *Common Differences: Conflicts in Black and White Feminist Perspectives* (Boston: South End Press, 1981), 231–273.

119. Patricia Hill Collins, *Black Feminist Thought: Knowledge, Consciousness and the Politics of Empowerment* (New York and London: Routledge, 1992), 168. See related discussion 163–180.

120. "New FACT Group Battles Censorship Laws," in *New Directions for Women* vol. 14., no. 1 (January/February 1985): 1.

121. For a more thorough account see Miriam Hirsch, *Women and Violence* (New York: Van Nostrand Reinhold Co., 1981).

122. Lisa Steele, "A Capital Idea: Gendering in the Mass Media," in Varda Burstyn, ed., *Women Against Censorship* (Vancouver: Douglas and

McIntyre, 1985), 60. See also Ellen Willis, "Feminism and Moralism," in Anne Snitow, et al., eds., *Powers of Desire* (New York: Monthly Review Press, 1985).

123. "New FACT Group," 1.

124. Mary Kay Blakely, "Is One Woman's Sexuality Another Woman's Pornography? The Question Behind a Major Legal Battle," *Ms* (April 1985): 40–47.

125. See "Pornography Foes Lose New Weapon in Supreme Court," *The New York Times,* 26 February 1986.

126. MacKinnon and Dworkin have dissociated themselves from this act because of its reference to "obscenity." However, the right-wing context in which this type of legislation has arisen and the zeal with which the Right has embraced this new way to attack pornography are both striking and dangerous.

127. *Butler v. Her Majesty the Queen.* For related information regarding this history see Blair Kamin, "Victim's Rights, First Amendment Clash in Porn Bill," *Pittsburgh Press,* 8 March 1992; John Elson, "Passions over Pornography," *Time Magazine,* 30 March 1992; Tamar Lewin, "Canada Court Says Pornography Harms Women," *New York Times,* 28 February 1992; Tamar Lewin, "Anti-Pornography Proposal Reemerges," *New York Times,* 15 March 1992; and Senate 1521, The Pornography Victim's Compensation Act, 102nd Congress, second session, 1991–92.

128. Neil Malmuth and Edward Donnerstein, *Pornography and Sexual Aggression* (Orlando, FL.: Academic Press, 1984), is often cited as providing evidence of a link between pornography and violence, even though they have only shown a short-term correlation.

129. Kathleen Barry, "Beyond Pornography: From Defensive Politics to Creating a Vision," in Laura Lederer, ed., *Take Back the Night* (New York: William Morrow and Co., 1980), 307.

130. Ibid., 311.

131. Dierdre English, Amber Hollibaugh, and Gayle Rubin, "Talking Sex: A Conversation on Sexuality and Feminism," *Socialist Review* 58, vol. 11, no. 4: 61.

132. See also their 1981 publication, Samois, *Coming to Power* (Boston: Alyson Press, 1981).

133. Jeanette Nichols, Darlene Pagano, and Margaret Rossof, "Is Sadomasochism Feminist? A Critique of the Samois Position," in

Robin Ruth Linden, Darlene Pagano, Diana E.H. Russell, Susan Leigh Star, eds., *Against Sadomasochism* (Palo Alto: Frog in the Wall Press, 1982), 137–138.

134. The following discussion relies on a model of the Dworkin/MacKinnon legislation which appeared in Mary Kay Blakely, "Is One Woman's Sexuality Another Woman's Pornography? The Question Behind a Major Legal Battle," *Ms* (April 1985): 37–75, especially 46–47.

135. Susan Brownmiller uses this reasoning throughout her illuminating *Against Our Will* (New York: Simon and Schuster, 1975).

136. "Talking Sex: A Conversation on Sexuality and Feminism," 51. For related discussion see Varda Burstyn, "Political Precedents and Moral Crusades," in Burstyn, ed., *Women Against Censorship*.

4. FEMINISM AND EPISTEMOLOGY

1. For a related discussion see Joan Scott, "The Evidence of Experience," *Critical Inquiry* 17: 773–797, 1991.

2. Another option is that the problems to which I am pointing be ignored. This has actually been suggested to me over the years. Several well known feminist theorists have told me variously that "essentialism is old news," or that "we all know what 'Woman' means in our day-to-day conversations," or that "I am sick of talking about certain women being left out (of mothering type feminist theory). The fact is, most women are mothers." I am not persuaded by any of these assertions. The problems with feminist theory are deep, structural, and significant.

3. It is from the vantage point of the problems faced by standpoint thinkers that the turn toward postmodernism becomes very understandable. The idea of perspective, as opposed to standpoint, is not an epistemological argument, but a claim about the variability and importance of interpretation. But this discussion is for a later chapter.

4. For an excellent discussion of the links between feminist epistemologies and arguments about female nature see Mary Hawkesworth, "Knowers, Knowing and Known: Feminist Theory and Claims of Truth," in *Signs* vol. 14, no. 3 (1989).

5. Sandra Harding, *Whose Science? Whose Knowledge? Thinking from Women's Lives* (Ithaca: Cornell University Press, 1991), 175. To avoid this problem, Harding proposes to ground claims about women's lives in the differences "within women" as well as between men and women. The similarities that hold women together, however, still remain

unspecified and presumably essentialist. See also 180.

6. If there is not one female experience and "female" must always be qualified by another variable like "working class" or "black," then at some point one must ask what "women's oppression" really means. For a related discussion about the category Woman in first wave feminist thought, see Denise Riley, *Am I That Name?*, (Minneapolis: University of Minnesota Press, 1988).

7. Bettina Aptheker, *Tapestries of Life: Women's Work, Women's Consciousness and the Meaning of Daily Experience* (Amherst: University of Massachusetts Press, 1989), 68. The following quotation is from 28.

8. In discussing this point, Patricia Hill Collins has said, "One implication of standpoint approaches is that the more subordinated the group, the purer the vision of the oppressed group. This is an outcome of the origins of standpoint approaches in Marxist social theory . . ." There has been a tendency to blame the ills of standpoint on Marxism. I hope that my discussion of Marx in this chapter makes clear that Marx advocated no such privileging of marginality. The problem Hill Collins points to has to do with the core concepts of feminism. Patricia Hill Collins, *Black Feminist Thought: Knowledge, Consciousness and the Politics of Empowerment* (New York and London: Routledge, 1990), 207.

9. Barbara Smith, "Toward a Black Feminist Criticism," *Conditions Two* 1 (October 1977): 47.

10. Elizabeth V. Spelman, *Inessential Woman: Problems of Exclusion in Feminist Theory* (Boston: Beacon Press, 1989).

11. Kimberle Crenshaw, "A Black Feminist Critique of Antidiscrimination Law and Politics," David Kairys, ed., *The Politics of Law* (New York: Pantheon, 1990), 195.

12. The notion of multiple identities foreshadows and illustrates feminism's attraction to postmodernism.

13. Sandra Harding, *The Science Questions in Feminism* (Ithaca: Cornell University Press, 1986), 141.

14. Kirstie McClure has made the related point that the modern project is evident even in the ways in which we define feminist authority and feminist theory. See her "The Issue of Foundations: Scientized Politics, Politicized Science, and Feminist Critical Practice," in Judith Butler and Joan Scott, eds., *Feminists Theorize the Political* (New York and London: Routledge, 1992).

15. Basically, their idea was that since no truth could be known absolutely and a priori, a legitimate ruler was one to whom the governed consented by way of a social contract.

16. Richard Rorty, *Philosophy and the Mirror of Nature* (Princeton: Princeton University Press, 1979), 147.

17. Immanuel Kant, "The Critique of Pure Reason," in Carl Friedrich, ed., *The Philosophy of Kant* (New York City: Random House/Modern Library, 1949), 24.

18. "Critique of Pure Reason," 25–26.

19. David Hume, "An Enquiry Concerning Human Understanding," in Walter Kaufmann, ed., *Philosophic Classics: Vol. 2 Bacon to Kant* (Englewood Cliffs, N.J.: Prentice Hall, 1968), 296–297.

20. Immanuel Kant, *A Critique of Practical Reason* (Indianapolis: Bobbs-Merrill, 1956), 54.

21. *A Critique of Practical Reason*, 55–56.

22. Sandra Harding and Merrill Hintikka, eds., *Discovering Reality* (Boston: Reidel, 1983), x.

23. See for examples Sara Ruddick, *Maternal Thinking* (Boston: Beacon Press, 1989); Adrienne Rich, "Disloyal to Civilization"; and Bettina Aptheker's brief mention of this notion in *Tapestries of Life*, 58.

24. Nancy Hartsock, *Money, Sex and Power*, 232.

25. *Toward a Feminist Theory of the State*, 83. See also my discussion of her epistemological views in chapter 3 of this volume.

26. *Tapestries of Life*, 15.

27. Sandra Harding, *The Science Question in Feminism* (Ithaca: Cornell University Press, 1986), 26.

28. Sandra Harding, *Whose Science? Whose Knowledge?* (Ithaca: Cornell University Press, 1991), 167.

29. *Whose Science? Whose Knowledge?*, 124.

30. Harding's discussion of the confluence of the descriptions of blacks and women in African American vis-à-vis feminist theories of knowledge is absolutely fascinating. For this observation and analysis alone, her book should be essential reading.

31. *Whose Science? Whose Knowledge?*, 126.

32. Dorothy Smith, "Sociology from Women's Experience: A Reaffirmation," *Sociological Theory* 10:1 (Spring 1992): 89. Smith does not seem to be saying with MacKinnon, however, that conscious-

ness raising is necessary for interpreting the female experience. However, consciousness raising, too, is problematic, as I have indicated in a previous chapter. Therefore, I think, despite the name, that this activity should not be conceptualized as a raising of consciousness to a new level of truth and reality, but as a collective reinterpretation of life in gendered existence. Smith's point, however, is about the importance of female embodiment to feminist consciousness raising.

33. *Whose Science? Whose Knowledge?*, 164.

34. Dorothy Smith, *The Conceptual Practices of Power* (Boston: Northeastern University Press, 1990), 28.

35. "If I could think of a term other than 'standpoint,' I'd gladly shift, especially now that I've been caged in Harding's (1986) creation of the category of 'standpoint theorists' and subjected to the violence of mis-interpretation, replicated many times in journals and reviews, by those who speak of Hartsock and Smith but have read only Harding's version of us . . .": Dorothy Smith, "Sociology from Women's Experience," 91. Author's note: I have read Smith's version.

36. *Conceptual Practices of Power*, 27.

37. Ibid, 57.

38. "Sociology from Women's Experience," 89. The following quotation is from 93.

39. Dorothy Smith, *The Everyday World as Problematic: A Feminist Sociology* (Boston: Northeastern University Press, 1987), 108.

40. Patricia Hill Collins, *Black Feminist Thought: Knowledge, Consciousness and the Politics of Empowerment* (New York and London: Routledge, 1990), 5. The following quotations are from 204, 27, and 206–207, respectively.

41. *Black Feminist Thought*, 236.

42. Ibid, 24, 207, and 225.

43. Ibid, 110.

44. Billie Holiday, "T'aint Nobody's Business," from the Original Decca Masters, MCA Records, Universal City, CA, 1986. See also, Bessie Smith: The Collection, CBS Records, Columbia Jazz Masterpieces, Columbia Records, New York City, 1989. Thanks to Stan Rosen for use of his record collection.

45. Nell Noddings, "Ethics from the Standpoint of Women," in Deborah Rhode, ed., *Theoretical Perspectives on Sexual Difference,* (New Haven: Yale University Press, 1990) 161. Nodding goes on to make a

persuasive case that all ethics has always been a gendered activity. See also Noddings's larger work, *Caring: A Feminine Approach to Ethics and Moral Education* (Berkeley and Los Angeles, University of California Press, 1984).

46. Indeed, American government aid packages have often faltered on the assumption of what women's traditional work is. By going into third world countries and training men as farmers on the assumption that it is men's work, ethnocentric aid packages have displaced thousands of women workers throughout the world. See Esther Boserup, *Women's Role in Economic Development* (New York: St. Martins, 1970) and Barbara Rogers, *The Domestication of Women: Disc in Developing Societies* (New York: Tavistock, 1980).

47. Noddings and others have made the point that the so-called objectivity of these thinkers was in reality a male perspective; often explicitly so. See Nell Noddings, "Ethics from the Standpoint of Women."

48. Dorothy Smith, "Sociology from Women's Experience: A Reaffirmation," *Sociological Theory* vol. 10, no. 1 (Spring 1992): 89.

49. Tapestries of Life, 12.

50. Marx took the term "abstract" from Hegel, who used it to mean "one-sided." Since Marx believed reality to be many faceted, being comprised of active and passive sides, Marx used the term "abstract" to refer disparagingly to ideas or actions that were "partial," or rooted only in one half of reality. See Karl Marx, "The Theses on Feuerbach," in Robert Tucker, ed., *The Marx-Engels Reader* (New York: Norton, 1978).

51. As is well known, Marx was also responding to Hegel's idealist dialectics. However, Hegel is sufficiently far afield from feminist theory that we need not discuss that aspect of Marxism here. For a good discussion of Marx's critique of Hegel see Seyla Benhabib, *Critique, Norm and Utopia: A Study in the Foundations of Critical Theory* (New York: Columbia University Press, 1986).

52. Karl Marx, *The Economic and Philosophic Manuscripts of 1844*, Dirk Struik, ed., (New York City: International Publishers, 1964), 189.

53. Marx says the proletariat is a class in and for itself. Therefore, by becoming both subject and object, the constitution of the proletariat is the end of the subject/object dualism assumed in Kantian epistemology and solved in an idealist fashion in the Hegelian system.

54. Karl Marx, "The Manifesto of the Communist Party," in *The Marx/Engels Reader*, 482.

55. Nancy Hartsock, *Money, Sex and Power* (Boston: Longman, 1983), 74.

56. Ibid, 224. The following quotation is from 151.

57. Ibid, 117 and 151. The following quotations are from 210.

58. Ibid, 92.

59. Ibid, 115–144.

60. Georg Lukacs, *History and Class Consciousness,* trans. Rodney Livingstone (Boston: MIT Press, 1968), 51.

61. For a discussion of the dangers of the standpoint in Marxism and its connection to Leninism and Stalinism see Martin Jay, *Marxism and Totality: The Adventures of a Concept from Lukacs to Habermas* (Berkeley and Los Angeles: University of California Press, 1984), 112–127.

62. Theodor Adorno, *Negative Dialectics* (New York: Continuum, 1973), 5.

63. Ibid, 33.

64. Marilyn Frye, "The Possibility of Feminist Theory," in *Theoretical Perspectives on Sexual Difference,* 183.

65. *Black Feminist Thought,* 11. See also "Transforming the Inner Circle: Dorothy Smith's Challenge to Sociological Theory," in *Sociological Theory* vol. 10, no. 1 (Spring 1992): 78.

66. *Whose Science? Whose Knowledge?,* 124.

67. Dorothy Smith, "Sociology from Women's Experience: A Reaffirmation," *Sociological Theory* vol. 10, no. 1 (Spring 1992): 94.

68. Robin Morgan, "Theory and Practice: Pornography and Rape," in Laura Lederer, ed., *Take Back the Night: Women on Pornography* (New York: William Morrow, 1980), 140.

69. Gloria Steinem, "Erotica and Pornography: A Clear and Present Difference" in *Take Back the Night,* 37.

70. Linda Williams, *Hard Core: Power, Pleasure and the Frenzy of the Visible* (Berkeley and Los Angeles: University of California Press, 1989), 277.

71. Hard Core, 172.

72. Sara Ruddick, *Maternal Thinking: Towards a Politics of Peace* (Boston: Beacon, 1989), 35.

73. bell hooks, *Talking Back: Thinking Feminist, Thinking Black* (Boston: South End Press, 1989), 22–23.

5. FEMINISM AND POSTMODERNISM

1. Sandra Harding has a similar, extremely interesting and important discussion regarding the confluence of feminist and African-American thinking. See her *Whose Science? Whose Knowledge? Thinking from Women's Lives* (Ithaca: Cornell University Press, 1991), 191–248.

2. See especially Jürgen Habermas, *Philosophical Discourse on Modernity,* trans. Frederick Lawrence, (Cambridge: MIT Press, 1987).

3. Jean Francois Lyotard, *The Postmodern Condition,* trans. by Geoff Bennington and Brian Massumi, with forward by Frederic Jameson (Minneapolis: University of Minnesota Press, 1988).

4. Andreas Huyssen, "Mapping the Postmodern," in Linda Nicholson, ed., *Feminism/Postmodernism* (New York and London: Routledge, 1990), 259. Huyssen deemphasizes the important fact that the appellation "poststructuralism" has also to do with theories that were influenced by the structuralism of thinkers like Louis Althusser, Claude Levi-Strauss and Ferdinand Saussure.

5. Judith Butler, "Contingent Foundations: Feminism and the Question of Postmodernism," in Judith Butler and Joan Scott, eds., *Feminists Theorize the Political* (New York and London: Routledge, 1992), 4.

6. Alice Jardin, *Gynesis* (Ithaca: Cornell University Press, 1985), 20. For examples of early French "feminism," see Hélène Cixous, "Sorties," in E. Marks and I. de Courtivron, eds., *New French Feminisms* (New York: Schocken, 1981); Luce Irigaray, "The Sex Which Is Not One," trans. Gilligan Gill (Ithaca: Cornell University Press, 1985) and *Speculum of the Other Woman,* trans. Gillian Gill (Ithaca: Cornell University Press, 1985); also Julia Kristeva, *Powers of Horror: An Essay on Abjection,* trans. Leon Roudiez (New York: Columbia University Press, 1982).

7. *Gynesis,* 20.

8. Paul Rabinow, *The Foucault Reader* (New York: Pantheon, 1984), 73.

9. Michel Foucault, *Herculine Barbin: Being the Recently Discovered Memoirs of a Nineteenth Century French Hermaphrodite* (New York: Pantheon, 1980), xiii.

10. My use of the term modernism may be confusing. I use the term to refer to post-Renaissance Enlightenment-based thinking. For clarification see David Harvey, *The Condition of Postmodernity* (Cambridge and Oxford: Basil Blackwell, 1989); discussion begins on 12.

11. Carroll Smith-Rosenberg, "The Body Politic," in Elizabeth Week, ed.,

Coming to Terms: Feminism, Theory, Politics (New York and London: Routledge, 1989), 103.

12. "The Body Politic," 102.

13. Rosalind Petchesky, *Abortion and Woman's Choice: The State, Sexuality and Reproductive Freedom* (Boston: Northeastern University Press, 1984), 115.

14. Luce Irigaray, *This Sex Which Is Not One* (Ithaca: Cornell University Press, 1985), 122.

15. Nancy Hartsock, "Foucault on Power: A Theory for Women?" in Linda Nicholson, ed., *Feminism/Postmodernism* (New York and London: Routledge, 1990), 163–64.

16. For example, I am thinking of almost every, but not every, piece in Alice Jardin and Paul Smith, ed., *Men in Feminism* (New York and London: Routledge, 1987) and many in Elizabeth Weed, ed., *Coming to Terms* (New York and London: Routledge, 1989). The essays in question are unbearably tedious and self-consciously deep and dramatic (not unlike the worst French films and the worst work presented at the Modern Language Association).

17. Hazel Carby, *Reconstructing Womanhood* (New York: Oxford University Press, 1987), 16.

18. Excellent examples include Wendy Brown, *Manhood and Politics: A Feminist Reading in Political Theory* (Totowa, N.J.: Roman Littlefield, 1988); Christine Di Stefano, *Configurations of Masculinity: A Feminist Perspective on Modern Political Theory* (Ithaca: Cornell University Press, 1991); Susan Okin, *Justice, Gender and the Family* (New York: Basic Books, 1989) and *Women in Western Political Thought* (Princeton: Princeton University Press, 1979); Carole Pateman, *Sexual Contract* (Palo Alto: Stanford University Press, 1988); Mary Lyndon Shanley and Carole Pateman, *Feminist Interpretations of Political Theory* (State College: Pennsylvania State University Press, 1991).

19. Mary Poovey, "Feminism and Deconstruction," in *Feminist Studies* vol. 14, no. 1 (Spring 1988): 52–53.

20. Friedrich Nietzsche, *Beyond Good and Evil: Prelude to a Philosophy of the Future,* trans. with commentary by Walter Kaufman (New York: Vintage, 1966), 9. The following quotations are from 104 and 12–13, respectively.

21. Jacques Derrida, "Difference," in *Margins of Philosophy,* trans. Alan Bass (Chicago: University of Chicago Press, 1972), 17.

22. Michel Foucault, *Power/Knowledge: Selected Interviews and Other Writings, 1972–1977* (New York: Pantheon, 1980).

23. Donna J. Haraway, "Situated Knowledges," in Donna J. Haraway, *Simians, Cyborgs and Women: The Reinvention of Nature* (New York: Routledge, 1991), 187.

24. "Situated Knowledges," 189. The following quotations are from 193 and 199, respectively.

25. Donna J. Haraway, "A Cyborg Manifesto," in Donna J. Haraway, *Simians, Cyborgs and Women,* 150. The following quotations are from 154, 178, and 163, respectively.

26. See Zillah Eisenstein, *Capitalist Patriarchy and the Case for Socialist Feminism* (New York: Monthly Review Press, 1979) and bell hooks, *Talking Back.*

27. Nancy Hartsock, *Money, Sex and Power.*

28. Leslie Rabine Wahl, "A Feminist Politics of Non-Identity," *Feminist Studies* vol. 14, no. 1 (Spring, 1988): 22.

29. See Jana Sawicki, *Disciplining Foucault* (New York and London: Routledge, 1991), for an important discussion of power in Foucault and his relevance to feminist theory.

30. The problem of nihilism has been discussed by and in terms of thinkers such Fredrich Nietzsche, Jean Paul Sartre, Albert Camus, Martin Heidegger, and others. It is basically the idea that the removal of absolutes and universals as a way to understand "being" forces us to turn to its opposite, "nothingness."

The problem can itself, however, only be understood as such from a philosophical perspective that links justice (and all meaningful things) to a knowable, single truth. This thinking is most notable in the Kantian tradition I discussed earlier in my chapter on feminism and epistemology. From this perspective, since truth is linked to justice, a disdain for the very notion of truth must mean that distinctions between justice and injustice are impossible. (Or, to apply this to the Sartrian variation, to admit that life has no meaning means that we might as well die.) This delinking of perennial concepts from truth and organic essences is the basis for the charge of nihilism.

On the other hand, if truth claims are situated in a multiple and contested reality as postmodernists claim, it does no good to allege that justice needs to be connected to one truth. There can be many possible justices, which are not organically just in some Platonic sense, but which are (merely?) socially constructed as just. The trick for them is, who does the constructing and what are the effects? Postmodernists claim that we are faced with a choice: lie to ourselves and pretend that justice is not an arbitrary definition in order to solve all problems by recourse to this "noble lie," or admit to the social nature of justice (and all other essentialist ideas) in order to actively participate in their reconstruction.

31. See, for example, the essays in Sandra Harding and Merrill Hintikka, eds., *Discovering Reality* (Boston: Reidel, 1983).

32. Jean Granier, "Perspectivism and Interpretation," in David B. Allison, ed., *The New Nietzsche: Contemporary Styles of Interpretation* (Cambridge,: MIT Press, 1985), 190–191.

33. Genevieve Lloyd, *Man of Reason* (Minneapolis: University of Minnesota Press, 1984).

34. For excellent and understandable discussions of deconstruction see Toril Moi, *Sexual/Textual Politics* (London and New York: Routledge, 1985); Michael Ryan, *Marxism and Deconstruction* (Baltimore and London: Johns Hopkins University Press, 1982); and Raman Selden, *A Reader's Guide to Contemporary Literary Theory* (Louisville: University of Kentucky Press, 1985).

35. These examples are from *A Reader's Guide*, 72.

36. Roland Barthes, "Where to Begin?" in Barthes, *New Critical Essays,* trans. Richard Howard, (New York: Hill and Wang, 1980), 79.

37. Fashion is also a favorite example. See Roland Barthes, *Elements of Semiology*, trans. Annette Lavers and Colin Smith (New York: Hill and Wang, 1967).

38. Joan Scott, "Deconstructing Equality Versus Difference," in Marianne Hirsch and Evelyn Fox Keller, eds., *Conflicts in Feminism* (New York and London: Routledge, 1990), 137.

39. Toril Moi, *Sexual/Textual Politics* (London and New York: Routledge, 1985), 104–105. The following quotation is from 108.

40. *This Sex Which Is Not One.*

41. The history of many of the figures whom we would associate with postmodernism does suggest, however, that there is often a connection between postmodern thinking and political movements both on the Left and the Right. See Peter Dews, *Logics of Disintegration: Post-Structuralist Thought and the Claims of Critical Theory* (London and New York: Verso, 1987); Arthur Hirsh, *The French Left: A History*

and Overview (Montreal: Black Rose Books, 1982); David Lehman, *Signs of the Times: Deconstruction and the Fall of Paul de Man* (New York: Poseidon Press, 1991); and Richard Wolin, *The Heidegger Controversy: A Critical Reader* (New York: Columbia University Press, 1991).

42. See, for examples, Martha Minow, *Making All the Difference: Inclusion, Exclusion and American Law* (Ithaca: Cornell University Press, 1990) and Deborah Rhode, ed., *Theoretical Perspectives on Sexual Difference* (New Haven: Yale University Press, 1990).

43. Barbara Christian, "The Race for Theory," *Feminist Studies* vol. 14, no. 1 (Spring 1988): 68. The following quoted phrases are from 67–79.

44. Sandra Harding, *The Science Question in Feminism* (Ithaca: Cornell University Press, 1986), 164.

45. This same debate about theory is occurring in pragmatist and New Historicist circles; in both cases, the arguments are also due to the new phobia about universals. See Steven Knapp and Walter Benn Michaels, "Against Theory," in *Critical Inquiry* 8 (1982), 723–742, and a related piece by Stanley Fish, "Consequences," in *Doing What Comes Naturally* (Durham and London: Duke University Press, 1989), 315–342. Finally, recall Richard Rorty's preference for literature as an explanatory apparatus vis-à-vis theory, "Heidegger, Kundera and Dickens," in Rorty, *Essays on Heidegger and Others: Philosophical Papers Volume 2* (Cambridge: Cambridge University Press, 1991), 66–85.

46. Julia Kristeva, *Powers of Horror: An Essay on Abjection* (New York: Columbia University Press, 1982), 78.

47. Hélène Cixous, "Sorties," in Elizabeth Marks and Isabelle de Courtivron, eds., *New French Feminisms* (New York: Schocken Books, 1981), 91.

48. *Powers of Horror*, 79.

49. Judith Butler, "Contingent Foundations: Feminism and the Question of Postmodernism," in Judith Butler and Joan Scott, eds., *Feminists Theorize the Political* (New York and London: Routledge, 1992), 6.

50. Michel Foucault, *History of Sexuality Volume 1: An Introduction* (New York: Pantheon Books, 1978), 31. I first used this example in my paper "Feminist Theory in Contemporary Theoretical Perspective," presented at the 1988 meetings of the American Political Science Association in Washington, D.C., 31 August–4 September 1988, and subsequently used it again in "What's at Stake? Postmodernism as a

New Direction for Feminist Theory," Working Paper Series, Program for the Study of Women and Men in Society, University of Southern California, 1991–92.

51. Ibid, 32. The following quotation is from 31.

52. Jurgen Habermas, *The Philosophical Discourses on Modernity* trans. Frederick Lawrence (Cambridge: Massachusetts Institute of Technology Press, 1987), 254.

6. SOLUTIONS: A BASIC OUTLINE OF THE ISSUES AND SOME SUGGESTIONS

1. Louis Althusser, *For Marx,* trans. Ben Brewster (London: Verso, 1979), 233.

2. Louis Althusser, "Ideology and Ideological State Apparatuses: Notes towards an Investigation," *Lenin and Philosophy* (London: Monthly Review Press, 1971), 170.

3. Antonio Gramsci, "State and Civil Society," in Quintin Hoare and Geoffrey Nowell Smith, eds. and trans., *Prison Notebooks* (New York: International Publishers, 1971).

4. Roland Barthes, "Myth Today," in *Mythologies,* trans. Annette Lavers (New York: Noonday Press, 1972), 109–159.

5. Emile Durkheim, *Durkheim and the Law,* Steven Lukes and Andrew Scull, eds., (London: Basil Blackwell, 1983), 69.

6. *Durkheim and the Law,* 39.

7. *Durkheim and the Law,* 48.

8. Michel Foucault, *Discipline and Punish: The Birth of the Prison* (New York: Vintage, 1979).

9. Adrienne Rich, "Compulsory Heterosexuality and Lesbian Existence," *The Signs Reader,* Elizabeth Abel and Emily K. Abel, eds., (Chicago and London: University of Chicago Press, 1983), 139–169.

10. Judith Butler, *Gender Trouble: Feminism and the Subversion of Identity* (New York and London: Routledge, 1990), 79–142.

11. Sigmund Freud, *Jokes and Their Relation to the Unconscious,* James Strachey, ed. and trans. (New York: Norton, 1960), 115.

12. Hazel Carby, *Reconstructing Womanhood* (New York: Oxford University Press, 1987), 55.

13. *Reconstructing Womanhood,* 34.

14. Margaret Jane Radin, "The Pragmatist and the Feminist," *Southern California Law Review* vol. 63, no. 6 (September 1990): 1706.

15. Linda Alcoff, "Cultural Feminism versus Post-Structuralism: The Identity Crisis in Feminist Theory," *Signs* vol. 13, no. 3: 432.

16. Iris Young, "Humanism, Gynocentrism and Feminist Politics," *Throwing Like a Girl and Other Essays in Feminist Philosophy and Social Theory* (Indianapolis: Indiana University Press, 1990), 73.

17. Ibid, 74.

18. Patricia Hill Collins, *Black Feminist Thought* (New York and London: Routledge, 1990), 39. See also full discussion 37–40.

19. Ibid, 39.

Index

Abortion, 68–69, 133–34
ACLU, 82
ACT UP, 174
Adorno, Theodor, 114– 15, 179
Against Our Will (Brownmiller),
    206n
Agency, in Marxism, 114, 155
AIDS, 167
Alcoff, Linda, 180–81
Alien, 169–71
Althusser, Louis, 73, 161–62, 190
Amazon Odyssey (Atkinson), 21
Am I That Name? (Riley), 207n
Androgyny, 22–23
Anglo-American feminism, 127–28;
    and core concepts of feminism,
    153–60; and postmodernism,
    132–144
Anti-pornography legislation,
    82–83, 86, 205n
Aptheker, Bettina, 92, 101
Arendt, Hannah, 113, 117

Arnold, Roseanne, 124
Atkinson, Ti-Grace, 6, 11–12, 21,
    74; on gender as system of rules,
    163; on John Rawls, 34–35; on
    sexuality, 36–37
Atwood, Margaret, 139
Auerbach, Judy, 62

Baby M case, 68
Barrett, Michele, 58
Barry, Kathleen, 84
Barthes, Roland, 142–43, 162
Benhabib, Seyla, 47
Beyond Good and Evil (Nietzsche),
    137–38
Biological Politics (Sayers), 203n
"Bitch Manifesto" (Joreen), 21–22,
    30, 157
Black Feminist Thought (Collins),
    207n
Black Panthers, 18
Black Power movement, 27, 28

Blakely, Mary Kay, 206n
Blum, Linda, 62
Body, female, 145, 185, 187–88
"Body Politic, The" (Smith-
    Rosenberg), 132–33
Brown, Rita Mae, 48
Brownmiller, Susan, 206n
Bunch, Charlotte, 47–48
"Bundy Bill," the, 82
Burris, Barbara, 22, 23
Butler, Judith, 129–30, 139, 148,
    165, 177

Camus, Albert, 214n
Canada, 1992 anti-pornography leg-
    islation in, 82–83
Carby, Hazel, 26, 135, 177
Chekhov, Anton, 61
Cherry Orchard, The (Chekhov), 61
Childbearing, 35; as a control mech-
    anism, 187
Chodorow, Nancy, 62–63, 64, 141,
    203n
Christian, Barbara, 105, 146
Civil Rights Act of 1964, Title VII,
    18
Cixous, Hélène, 130, 144–45,
    147–48
Collins, Patricia Hill, 80–81,
    105–107, 116, 184, 207n
"Combahee River Collective: A
    Black Feminist Statement," 27–28
Combat, women and, 108
Coming to Terms (Weed), 213n
Commission on Obscenity and
    Pornography, 1967, 84
Communist menace, as ideological
    construct, 158
Conference on The Feminist and the
    Scholar IX, 82
Consciousness raising, 37–38, 75–76
Conservative impulses in feminism,
    71
Core concepts of feminism, 6, 12;

and Anglo-American feminism,
    153–60; and early feminist theory,
    17–39; and epistemology, 99–127,
    207n; as fetishized, 191; and
    mothering, 59–74; and new vi-
    sions of feminism, 153–91; racism
    of, 66; and revisionist strategies,
    41–88; and sexuality, 77–88; and
    socialist feminism, 45–59
Cornell, Drucilla, 47
"Corporate feminists," 188–89
Costa, Dalla, 200n
Crenshaw, Kimberle, 93
Crime, punishment, and gender,
    163–65
Critiques of feminism, 190–91
Cultural feminism, 2, 203n

Dahl, Robert, 117
Daly, Mary, 72
Davis, Angela, 81
Day care, 187
de Beauvoir, Simone, 25, 72–73
Deconstruction, 143–44, 147
Derrida, Jacques, 130, 138, 142
de Saussure, Ferdinand, 142–43
Descartes, René, 92, 96
Dews, Peter, 215n
Dialectic of Sex, The (Firestone), 25
"Dialectics Not a Standpoint"
    (Adorno), 115
Dinnerstein, Dorothy, 63–64
Discourse theory, 159
Doing What Comes Naturally
    (Fish), 216n
Douglass College, 9
Drag as a gender crime, 177–78
Durkheim, Emile, 163–64
Dworkin, Andrea, 74–75, 77,
    78–80, 205n

*Economic and Philosophic
    Manuscripts* (Marx), 110
Ehrenreich, Barbara, 46, 48

Eisenstein, Zillah, 19, 52, 141, 201n
Ellis, Kate, 203n
Elshtain, Jean Bethke, 1–2, 19,
    68–69
Emmet, Dorothy, 117
"Empowerment/power duality,"
    117–25, 140–41
English, Dierdre, 58
Enlightenment, the: and the enter-
    prise of theory, 159; and ideas of
    knowledge, 95–96, 100; and iden-
    tity discourse, 109; values of, 135,
    141; values of in new visions of
    feminism, 185–87
Epistemology: of feminism, 13, 15,
    155–56; and gender, 42; history
    of, 94–99, 208n; and Marxism,
    110–117; and modernism, 212n;
    and politics, 122–25; and sexuali-
    ty, 76; and standpoint theory,
    97–125, 155–56, 206n
Equal Pay Act of 1963, 18
Erikson, Erik, 61
Erotica/pornography distinction,
    120–21
Essentialization in feminism, 6, 10,
    15, 23–28, 45, 79, 127, 190,
    194n, 206n
Ethics, as gendered activity, 210n
"Experience" in feminist theory, 4,
    19, 29–39, 156–57; and gender,
    41–42; and Marxism, 47, 50–51;
    and mothering, 59–74; and new
    visions of feminism, 190–91; and
    postmodernism, 127–51; and sex-
    uality, 76–77, 80–81; and
    standpoint theory, 100–107
Extremities, 169

False consciousness, 31–39
False freedom, 157–58
Family, the, 49, 88, 187, 200n, 201n
Farming as gendered work, 108
Female nationalism, 14

Female violence in films, 167–74
Feminine Mystique (Friedan), 18
"Feminine," the: and thinking,
    144–51; and values, 72–73,
    156–57
Feminism: Anglo-American, 41, 91,
    127–28, 132–44, 146, 153; and
    class, 52–59; core concepts of, 6,
    12, 17–39, 41–88, 99–128,
    153–91; "corporate," 188–89; cri-
    tiques of, 190–91, 206n; early, 4;
    and epistemology, 41–44, 89–125,
    155–56; and existentialism, 1–3;
    fundamental, 4–6; and gender,
    153–91; gynocentric, 10, 72, 183;
    and liberalism, 1–3, 18–19,
    188–89; and liberation, 188–91;
    and Marxism, 1–3, 9, 13, 46–59,
    155–57; and mothering theory,
    59–74, 122–24, 201n, 206n; neo-
    humanist, 14; new directions for,
    14, 153–91; and postmodernism,
    127–51; and psychoanalysis, 1–3,
    63–64, 128–29; and race, 26–28,
    42–43, 64–67, 85–86, 105–107,
    135, 188; and race/class, 42–43,
    125, 188–91; and radicalism, 2–3,
    17–22, 28–39; and sexuality,
    74–88; socialist, 45–59
Feminist lens, 75, 109, 181–83, 191
Feminists Anti-Censorship Task
    Force, 82
Feminists for Free Speech, 82
Feminist subject, the, 14, 42–43,
    134–35, 139, 155, 178–81, 191
Feminists, The, 17, 36
Feminists Theorize the Political
    (Butler and Scott), 207n
Feminist theory, history of, 17–39
Feminist Thought (Tong), 3
Ferguson, Ann, 70
Fetishism, 166
Firestone, Shulamith, 6, 25, 29, 37,
    41, 145, 199n

Fish, Stanley, 216n
Foucault, Michel: and Marxism, 7;
  on power, 129, 131, 141, 150–51,
  190, 216n
"Fourth World Manifesto, The"
  (Burris), 22, 23
Fraser, Nancy, 197n
French Revolution, 190
Freud, Sigmund, 63, 199n
Friedan, Betty, 18, 68
Frye, Marilyn, 116
Fuller, Margaret, 2
Future of an Illusion (Freud), 63

Gays and lesbians and gender,
  165–66
Gender: and experience, 41–42; and
  gays/lesbians, 165–66; as ideologi-
  cal structure, 14, 23, 28–39,
  161–78; liberation from, 161–65,
  180–91; and Marxism, 56–59; as
  an oppressive structure, 178–81;
  and postmodernism, 130–51; and
  race, 162–63, 166–68; and sexual-
  ity, 74–88; and standpoint theory,
  89–125
"Gender crime," 163–65
Gender Trouble (Butler), 165, 177
Ghandi, 118
Gilligan, Carol, 60–63, 77, 91, 201n
Gilman, Charlotte Perkins, 2
Goddess, the, 72
GOP Convention of 1992, 10
Gramsci, Antonio, 149, 162
Griffin, Susan, 71–72
Guns 'N Roses, 182
Gyn-Ecology (Daly), 72
Gynocentrism, 183

Habermas, Jurgen, 129, 151
Hamer, Fannie Lou, 184
Handmaid's Tale, A (Atwood), 139
Hanish, Carol, 37–38
Haraway, Donna, 138–39, 179,

197n
Harding, Sandra, 91, 94, 101–104,
  116, 147, 206–207n, 208n, 209n,
  212n
Hartsock, Nancy, 49, 52, 101, 113–
  14, 117–25, 134–35, 198n, 209n
Hegel, G. W. F., 111, 210n
Hegemony of gender, 162
Heidegger, Martin, 214n
Heterosexuality, 75–76, 83–84,
  165–66
Historicism, 45, 73, 90, 194n
History of Sexuality, The, Volume
  One (Foucault), 150–51
Holiday, Billie, 106–107
hooks, bell, 73, 125
Hudson, Rock, 167
Hull, Gloria T., 27
Humanism, 7, 14–15, 146, 183, 190
Hume, David, 96
Huyssen, Andreas, 129, 212n

Ice Cube, 182
Idealism, German, 99, 110, 111
Identity theory, 13
Indianapolis, anti-pornography leg-
  islation in, 82
Individual self-determination,
  186–87
In Search of Our Mothers' Gardens
  (Walker), 64–65
Insider/outsider perspectives, 116–17
Interpretation, 59–60, 98, 149
Irigaray, Luce, 134, 145
Iron John (Bly), 191

Jaggar, Alison, 2
Jardin, Alice, 41–42, 130, 213n
Jay, Martin, 211n
Joreen, 21–22, 30, 157
Justice, feminist theory of, 70–71

Kant, Immanuel, 92, 96–100, 109
Kennedy Commission on the Status

of Women, 18
Klein, Calvin, 167
Knapp, Steven, 216n
Knowledge: Kant on, 96–99; and
  postmodernism, 138–39; and
  standpoint theory, 100–127;
  women's, 42–43, 76–77
Knowledge claims, 94–95
Koedt, Anne, 35
Kohlberg, Lawrence, 60, 61
Kristeva, Julia, 130, 147

Lacan, Jacques, 73
Language, as male, 71–72
Lasswell, Harold, 117
Lemert, Charles, 104
Lenin, 7, 114
Lerner, Gerda, 43
Lesbianism, 19, 42–43, 165–66
Lesbian sado-masochism, 84–85
Liberation, 188–91
Locke, John, 3
Logic, The (Hegel), 111
Logics of Disintegration (Dews),
  215n
Lorde, Audre, 81
Lukacs, Georg, 114, 115, 155, 179
Lust/eros dualism, 120
Luther, Martin, 95–96
Lyotard, Jean Francois, 129

McClure, Kirstie, 207n
Machiavelli, 118
MacKinnon, Catherine, 74–88, 101,
  204n, 205n, 208–209n
Male identification, 32–33
"Maleness" as an essentializing con-
  struct, 135–36, 146
Marcuse, Herbert, 118, 176
"Marginality," 93, 207n
Marky Mark, 167
Marxism, 6–7, 9; and the creation of
  feminism, 28, 45–59; and essen-
  tialism, 45–59; in feminist

standpoint theory, 110–17, 207n;
  in feminist theory, 13, 91, 186,
  190, 197n; and gender, 154–55;
  as misapplied in feminism, 153;
  and mothering theory, 73–74; and
  new visions of feminism, 186,
  190; and postmodernism, 149;
  and Stalinism, 114–115
Marxism and Totality (Jay), 211n
Marx, Karl, 25, 53–54, 74, 92, 99,
  110–17, 129, 154–55, 157, 186,
  190, 194n, 198n, 199n, 210n
Marxist Left, 4, 46–59, 74
Marxist-Leninism, 47
Masters and Johnson, 35
Maternal instinct, 68
"Men" as a category, 37, 41–42, 45,
  77–78, 81, 162–63
Men in Feminism (Jardin and
  Smith), 213n
Men's studies, 191
Michaels, Walter Benn, 216n
Millet, Kate, 23, 34
Minneapolis Civil Rights
  Ordinances of 1975, 82
Misogyny, 1; and rationality, 135,
  141, 146
Mitchell, Juliet, 46, 49, 50–51, 199n
Moi, Toril, 144–45
Money, Sex and Power (Hartsock),
  113–114
More, Thomas, 118
Morgan, Robin, 119–120
"Mothering": as a core concept of
  feminism, 13, 59–74; and power,
  122–124, 201n, 206n
"Myth of the Vaginal Orgasm"
  (Koedt), 35

Naming, as a feminist activity,
  108–109, 134–35
National Organization for Women,
  18, 84
National Women's Studies

Association, 9, 12
Nature as female, 71–72
Nature, human, female and male, 23–28
Negative Dialectics (Adorno), 114–115
New Historicists, 216n
New Left, the, 2, 17–18, 20, 28
New York Radical Women, 17
New York Times, 168
Nietzsche, Friedrich, 100, 137–38, 141–42, 176, 214n
Nihilism, 141, 214–15n
Noddings, Nell, 107–108, 210n

"Objectivity," as a gendered construct, 70, 75–76
Of Woman Born (Rich), 69
Oppression, 30–32, 47–48, 56, 77; gender as, 160, 178–81

Paris Is Burning, 177–78
Parsons, Talcott, 117
Patriarchy, the, 39, 57–58, 157, 161
"Personal politics" in feminist theory, 4, 14, 19, 33–39, 76, 158–60, 188–91
Perspectivism, 93
Petchesky, Rosalind, 133–34
Pitkin, Hanna, 113, 117
Plato, 118
Politics: and epistemology, 122–25; new approaches to, 188–91; theory as, 160
Polsby, Nelson, 117
Poovey, Mary, 137
Pornography, 80–88; 119–22
Pornography and Sexual Aggression (Malmuth and Donnerstein), 205n
Pornography Victims Compensation Act of 1992, 82–83
Postmodernism, 6–7; and feminism, 13, 75, 127–51
Poststructuralism, 129–30, 212n

Power and gender: in the personal realm, 158–59; in postmodernism, 131, 135–37, 140; in standpoint theory, 113–14, 117– 25
Power/knowledge systems, 151
Pratt, Minnie Bruce, 202n
Privacy, idea of, 158
Psychanalyse et Politique, 130
Psychology, and mothering theory, 60–61, 73–74

Quayle, Marilyn, 10
Question of Silence, A, 173–76

Racism, 43, 64, 81, 189, 191, 194–95n
Radical Future of Liberal Feminism, The (Eisenstein), 19
Radical Right and the anti-pornography movement, 88
Radin, Margaret, 178
Rand, Ayn, 118
Rape culture, 119–20, 187–88
Rawls, John, 34–35
Reconstructing Womanhood (Carby), 177
Redescription: 159; of gender, 178–81
Redstockings, The, 17, 31
Reed, Donna, 124
Representation: of sexuality, 80–88; of violence by women, 168–74
Reproduction and production, 52–54, 154–55, 187, 200n
Reproduction of Mothering, The (Chodorow), 203n
Republic, The (Plato), 118
Revisionist strategies of feminism, 13, 41–88
Rich, Adrienne, 43–44, 64, 68–69, 165
Riley, Denise, 207n
Rolling Stones, the, 81
Roman Catholic Church, 95–96

Rorty, Richard, 78, 96, 204n, 216n
Rosaldo, Michele, 198n
Rousseau, Jean Jacques, 118
Rubin, Gayle, 26, 56, 58, 184–85
Ruddick, Sara, 70–71, 122
Rutgers University, 9

S & M, 84–85
Said, Edward, 7
Samois collective, 84–85
Sartre, Jean Paul, 214n
Sayers, Janet, 203n
Scott, Joan, 143
Scott, Patricia Bell, 27
"Second Wave" feminist theory,
    41–88
Seneca, 95
Sex symbol, the, 166–67
"Sexuality": as a core concept of
    feminism, 13, 35–39, 74–88; defi-
    nitions of, 166; and power,
    75–80; and race, 80–81; and radi-
    cal feminism, 74–77; as a standard
    of behavior, 157; and standpoint
    theory, 119–122
"Sexual Politics" (Millet), 23
Smith, Barbara, 27, 81, 93
Smith, Dorothy, 103–105, 109, 115,
    116, 208–209n, 209n
Smith, Vicki, 62
Smith-Rosenberg, Carroll, 132–33
Social constructionism, 7
Social Contract (Rousseau), 118
Socialism, 7, 45–59
Socialist feminism, 45–59, 140, 153
Socialist realism, 114– 15
Socrates, 118
Soviet Union, 7
Spelman, Elizabeth, 93
Spurs (Derrida), 130
Stalinism, 114– 15
Standpoint theory, 13; and episte-
    mology, 91–125; and
    ethnocentrism, 100–107; and

Marxism, 207n; and postmod-
    ernism, 138–39
Steinem, Gloria, 68, 120
"Strategic essentialism," 180
Surplus value, extracted in the realm
    of reproduction, 154–55

Taylor, Elizabeth, 166
Terminator 2, 171–73
Terrorism, rape as, 187
Thelma and Louise, 168–69
Theory: as a political construct,
    145–47; as politics, 160; as a
    product of the Enlightenment, 159
Thrasymachus, 118
Tong, Rosemary, 3
Traditional work, women's, 93,
    210n
Transhistorical theories of feminism,
    73–74

Universality, critiqued, 145–46
USC, conference on Women and
    Reason, 11–12
US military budget, 158
US military, gays in, 167
US Supreme Court, 82

Vaginal orgasm, 35–36
Violence: against women, 187; com-
    mitted by women in films,
    167–76; idea of in anti-pornogra-
    phy, 83–85, 205n
Vision, feminist-humanist, 183–91
Vogel, Lise, 49, 58

Walker, Alice, 64–66, 81
Warrior, Betsy, 23–24
Weather Underground, 18
Weaver, Sigourny, 170
Weed, Elizabeth, 213n
What Color Is Your Handkerchief?
    (Samois), 84–85
What Is to Be Done? (Lenin), 114

Whitehead, Mary Beth, 68
White Power groups, 43
Whose Science? Whose Knowledge?
  (Harding), 102, 206–207n
Williams, Christine, 62
Williams, Linda, 120– 21
Willis, Ellen, 203n
Will to Power (Nietzsche), 176
WITCH, 17
Wittig, Monique, 2
"Woman as Nigger" (Rubin), 26
"Woman" in feminist theory: as
  essentializing term, 6, 10, 19,
  23–28, 29, 37, 39, 46, 49, 59, 76,
  88, 101, 109, 123–25, 127–28,
  132, 162, 185, 194–95n
Womanism, 64–66

Women Against Pornography, 81
Women Against Violence Against
  Women, 81
Women Against Violence in
  Pornography and the Media, 81
Women and Reason conference, 11
Women of color: and "experience,"
  156–57; and feminist theory, 5;
  and "mothering," 64–67; and new
  visions of feminism, 189–90; and
  oppression, 140; texts by, 3
Women's Liberation Movement, 4,
  20, 26–27, 130

Young, Iris Marion, 44, 183–84

Zaretsky, Eli, 50, 53